# Praise for *Rescued*

"*Rescued* is a riveting book about amazing people who truly make a huge difference to countless animals with whom we share our homes and our planet. Its personal stories about unsung and selfless heroes who work behind the scenes clearly illustrate the deep passions that bind us to a wide variety of animals."

— Marc Bekoff, professor of biology at the University of Colorado,
author of *Animal Passions and Beastly Virtues,*
and editor of the *Encyclopedia of Animal Behavior*

"Through firsthand accounts of the sweeping tragedy of Hurricane Katrina, this indispensable primer on disaster response and support networks melts away the notion that a cat or dog is anything less than a family member."

— Jonathan Balcombe, author of
*Pleasurable Kingdom: Animals and the Nature of Feeling Good*

"Hurricane Katrina taught us that public policy must be revised to reflect the love between people and their nonhuman family members. *Rescued* is a finely written, touching, and important book that will warm the hearts of all readers whose animals are an indispensable part of the family."

— Karen Dawn, founder of the animal advocacy media watch
DawnWatch.com

"The Andersons have placed animals center stage and taught us their value. This must-read, riveting account helps us understand that Hurricane Katrina caused the evolution of both the human and animal spirit."

— Barbara J. Gislason, chair,
American Bar Association TIPS Animal Law Committee

"*Rescued* is a wonderful tribute to all the individuals, organizations, and government entities that give their all to save and protect animals every single day. It should be required reading for anyone considering entering the world of animal welfare or animal rescue."

— Susana Della Maddalena, executive director, PetSmart Charities

"American Humane applauds the Andersons' tireless efforts to pay homage to the hundreds of individuals from scores of animal welfare groups who gave so much to rescue the animal victims of Hurricane Katrina."

— Marie Belew Wheatley, president and CEO,
American Humane Association

# RESCUED

## Other books by Allen and Linda Anderson

*Angel Animals: Exploring Our Spiritual Connection with Animals*

*Angel Cats: Divine Messengers of Comfort*

*Angel Dogs: Divine Messengers of Love*

*Angel Horses: Divine Messengers of Hope*

*God's Messengers: What Animals Teach Us about the Divine*

*Rainbows & Bridges: An Animal Companion Memorial Kit*

# RESCUED

## Saving Animals from Disaster

Life-changing Stories and Practical Suggestions

# Allen & Linda Anderson

Foreword by John Ensign, U.S. Senator

NEW WORLD LIBRARY
NOVATO, CALIFORNIA

New World Library
14 Pamaron Way
Novato, California 94949

The material in this book is intended for education. No expressed or implied guarantee as to the effects of the use of the recommendations can be given nor liability taken.

Photo credits appear in captions and on pages 321–22.

Text design and typography by Tona Pearce Myers

Library of Congress Cataloging-in-Publication Data
Anderson, Allen,
Rescued : saving animals from disaster / by Allen and Linda Anderson.
     p.   cm.
Includes bibliographical references and index.
ISBN-13: 978-1-57731-544-5 (pbk. : alk. paper)
   1. Animal rescue—Louisiana—New Orleans. 2. Disaster relief—Louisiana—New Orleans. 3. Hurricane Katrina, 2005. 4. Pets—Louisiana—New Orleans. 5. Pet owners—Louisiana—New Orleans. 6. Animal rescue—United States. 7. Disaster relief—United States. I. Anderson, Linda C. II. Title.
HV4765.L8A63 2006
976.3'35044—dc22                                 2006012050

First printing, September 2006
ISBN-10: 1-57731-544-8
ISBN-13: 978-1-57731-544-5
Printed in Canada on acid-free, partially recycled paper

g  Member of the Green Press Initiative (www.greenpressinitiative.org)

Distributed by Publishers Group West

10  9  8  7  6  5  4  3  2  1

# Contents

# Foreword

Hurricane Katrina was one of the worst human tragedies in American history and brought unforgettable images of destruction and despair. Once the people whose homes and lives had been ravaged began to cope with the storm's immediate aftermath, another crisis emerged: the plight of the tens of thousands of pets who were left to fend for themselves and the desperate owners who returned, at great risk to themselves, to search for them. It is important to tell their stories so we can learn from both the successes and disappointments of that unforgettable ordeal.

John Ensign, DVM
United States Senator, Nevada
March 17, 2006

# Acknowledgments

We give our sincere appreciation to Georgia Hughes, the New World Library editorial director, who has worked on this book with patience and tons of encouragement. Thank you, Alexander Slagg, who had the brilliant idea for this book.

We are grateful to the diligent copyeditor Priscilla Stuckey, art director Mary Ann Casler, type designer Tona Pearce Myers, managing editor Kristen Cashman, our enthusiastic publicity manager Monique Muhlenkamp, the wise marketing director and associate publisher Munro Magruder, the wonderful visionary Marc Allen, and to all the staff at New World Library.

A hearty and sincere thank-you to Harold Klemp and to Joan Klemp for inspiring us on our journey of giving service by writing books about the animal-human spiritual bond.

We thank all the animal rescue volunteers and staff of organizations who talked to us about the wonderful work they do to save animals. Your interviews, generosity, and wisdom made this book possible. To the people who survived Hurricane Katrina and shared your reunion stories and courage with us we are especially grateful.

Our gratitude to Matt McCullough and Catherine O'Mara, who facilitated our request to Senator John Ensign for the inspiring foreword he wrote for this book.

Our special appreciation to the people who have endorsed the book.

Some people were so invaluable that parts of this book could not have been written without them. Thank you to Barbara J. Gislason, chair for the TIPS American Bar Association's Animal Law Committee and Animal Disaster Relief Network.

We especially appreciate Amelia Kinkade for introducing us to Rue McLanahan, and also to Tammy Masters and Lorie Zerweck for sharing their Hollywood connections to animal-loving celebrities. And thanks, Claudie Courdavault, for translating Brigitte Bardot's letters from French to English.

To our friends, who supported us and went through long periods of time without hearing from us but welcomed us back after we emerged from the long winter of 2006, thank you.

We also extend our heartfelt gratitude to Stephanie Kip Rostan of the Levine-Greenberg Literary Agency, our dynamic literary agent with the heart of a poet.

Our families instilled a love of animals in us from an early age. We feel a special appreciation for Allen's mother, Bobbie Anderson, and Linda's mother and father, Darrell and Gertrude Jackson. To our son and daughter, Mun Anderson and Susan Anderson, you're the best.

A special thank-you to Darby Davis, editor of *Awareness Magazine*, for publishing our column Pet Corner all these years and to Kathy DeSantis and Sally Rosenthal for writing consistently beautiful book reviews. Lessandra MacHamer, you have always been in our corner, and we love you for it.

And thanks to our animal editors: Taylor, Speedy, Cuddles, and Sunshine. Without you, we wouldn't know what animals think.

# Introduction

Days after the levees in New Orleans broke, Chris Cutter, communications director for International Fund for Animal Welfare, worked on a boat that maneuvered through toxic water. No one, human or animal, would have wanted to spend a minute more than necessary in it. Chris recalls, "We saw a dog swimming in the muck." Chris's boat steered toward the dog. Instead of allowing the rescuers to help him into the vehicle, the dog turned around and swam away from the boat. That's when they heard barking coming from inside a house.

The rescuers steered to follow the dog. He led them to the back of his house where a female dog, "his girlfriend," as Chris calls her, was trapped inside. Only after the rescuers freed the female dog did this big shaggy husky allow the rescuers to haul him into the boat.

As the boat moved away one of the rescuers petted him, saying, "You're such a good boy." Her hand jerked suddenly off the dog's head, as if she had touched a sizzling stove. "My hand is burning," she told Chris.

"The dog could have saved himself," Chris says. "Instead, he swam off so we would find his girlfriend. When you're dealing with things like that, it's hard not to think that there's a validity in what you are doing. That there is something bigger going on."

Indeed, something bigger was going on. The hurricanes of 2005 — three ferocious storms named Katrina, Rita, and Wilma — precipitated the most comprehensive animal rescue effort in history. Millions of animals were stranded in ravaged cities and farmlands. They survived with the help of thousands of people who risked their lives to save them.

Animal rescue work is not a clandestine activity, even though until Katrina the call to save animals had remained a barely audible rumble below the surface of mainstream American life. Animal rescue work has often been considered the passion of individuals who, observers suspect, relate better to animals than they do to people. Before Katrina the average person going to work, raising a family, and grappling with daily life challenges rarely thought about the volunteers and charitable organizations that focus their time and attention on the plight and welfare of animals.

Lack of awareness about the need for animal rescue began to change after the devastating storms hit in August 2005. Network news broadcasts, national talk shows, and other shapers of the country's sensibilities started showing images of suffering four-legged creatures. Their wide eyes and bedraggled bodies pleaded from the ruins of Louisiana and Mississippi. The world awakened to the fact that animals were the forgotten, voiceless victims of this tragedy.

People who had lost everything expressed anguish over being forced to leave their animal family members behind. Photos and accounts of beloved pets being snatched from the arms of human survivors or left alone on rooftops tugged at our collective consciousness.

Immediately after Hurricane Katrina, representatives of animal rescue organizations, their names and missions previously unknown to most Americans, were interviewed by national media outlets and their volunteers documented on film. Animal rescue was finally recognized as a vital aspect of survival on this planet, on which oceans and winds sometimes wipe out entire sections of continents.

## Purposes of This Book

Hurricane Katrina opened the window into a world that is usually invisible to American society. *Rescued: Saving Animals from Disaster* explores animal rescue and brings it back onto the world's radar screen. The purpose of this book is to show why it is essential in a disaster to save the animals and to make animal rescue a priority. It also demonstrates that rescuing animals saves the lives of humans.

In *Rescued* we ask questions for you to consider: What place does animal rescue occupy in a society that spends more than $39 billion on pets, with almost $7 billion of that amount spent on accessories for pampering dogs and cats? How has viewing animals as members of the family changed disaster and emergency response requirements? What changes are needed to ensure that animal rescue is never again an afterthought in national planning for the next disasters?

Animal rescue has grown in importance in today's world for five major reasons. First, more than 60 percent of American homes include pets. Millions of animals, many more than in previous eras, depend on humans for their survival.

Second, as became evident after Hurricane Katrina, people refuse to leave a disaster site without their pets, and if separated they try to find the animals, endangering themselves and others. Organized and highly publicized animal rescue alleviates their anxiety and keeps everyone safer.

Third, charitable organizations, which collected millions in donations for Hurricane Katrina, have prioritized emergency disaster response as part of their mission. They are training thousands of volunteers to save animals in future disasters. You and your community leaders need to know how to work with these volunteers and organizations effectively to prevent chaos and promote relief from disasters.

Fourth, since disasters caused by both nature and humans are on the rise, including household accidents and chemical spills that affect entire neighborhoods, it is likely that sometime in your life you will have to evacuate quickly with your pets. Having a personal understanding of how to rescue animals will help you to prepare to save the lives of your family pets.

Fifth, animal rescue is essential to a society that is becoming more humane. As a culture we are evolving toward a deeper respect for all life and an unparalleled appreciation for the value of human-animal families.

To illustrate how genuinely important your fellow Americans view animal rescue, consider the response when people found out we were writing this book. In our efforts to learn how animal rescue is transforming America, we conducted hundreds of interviews with individuals and animal organizations' staff and volunteers. When we put out the call asking for interviews, we received more than a thousand responses.

## Animal Rescue Is a Love Story

In this book you will find love stories. After Hurricane Katrina people and animals fought through chaos and every imaginable obstacle to be

Animal rescue workers in
hazardous conditions.

together again. They demonstrated the strength of a love between species that has existed for thousands of years. It is the love that drives people from every occupation and socioeconomic level to put aside daily life responsibilities and comforts so they can help animals.

One of the greatest ironies in the animal rescue efforts of 2005 is the fact that the people who feel the most distress at seeing animals suffer chose to experience that suffering firsthand. Animal lovers set out for the Gulf Coast, anticipating that they would find animals in dire straits. They intended to comfort people who were in agony over the loss of animal family members. Time and again, volunteers would be reminded that this could happen to them, in their hometowns, to their pets.

Thousands of animal lovers packed their suitcases, made plane reservations, rented cars and SUVs, tied boats to pickup trucks, arranged time off work, secured babysitting for their pets and children, gathered medical supplies, withdrew cash from their bank accounts, and raised the balance on their credit cards. They tried to reassure nervous spouses and friends while visiting doctors to get inoculated against hepatitis and tetanus. They ignored the alarms going off in their own heads and the voices of those who warned of risks and dangers ahead.

Volunteers and organizations from all over the country entered the fray. They improved the situation in most ways and contributed to disorganization in other ways. They worked with and against state, local, and federal authorities and prearranged protocols. They saw the best and the worst in human nature and sometimes in themselves.

*Rescued* introduces gutsy heroes dealing with situations as harrowing as any crime or adventure drama. These heroes didn't leap tall buildings with a single bound. Instead they crawled beneath teetering houses and gently coaxed frightened animals to come to them. Ordinary people, not Olympic athletes, scrambled over barbed-wire fences and fended off mold, rot, mosquitoes, snakes, and alligators. Their lives changed forever by fulfilling a commitment to rescue animals. Meeting them in this book will renew your belief in people's ability to show courage and kindness.

## Why Animal Rescue Is Important
## Long after Hurricane Katrina

*Rescued* explains why, how, and where you can prepare for evacuation and train for saving animals — your own and those of other people. No matter how prepared individuals or communities may be, some will always be too sick or ill-equipped to leave quickly. When disasters strike unexpectedly, vacationers will be out of town, pets will be boarded or in veterinary clinics, workers will be too far away to get back to their homes. This is why trained animal rescuers and preapproved plans will always be crucial elements in any community's disaster response. In the future, temporary shelters for animals will become as standard as designated shelters for humans.

In addition to showing large-scale disaster rescue, this book portrays the changing world of daily animal protection and welfare, which proceeds with little fanfare in American communities across the nation. Animal shelters and sanctuaries represent the closest contact most people have with animals in distress. We offer you an overview of the past, present, and future of housing, medicating, fostering, adopting, and protecting animals, as well as preventing their population.

If you have ever wondered why you should donate to an animal rescue organization, this book will show you how your charitable-giving dollars are spent.

If you performed animal rescue for the Gulf Coast disaster or any other place where animals and people were separated, you will find your devotion and service fully appreciated in this book. You may want to give this book to people who didn't understand why you traveled to places that local citizens had fled. To those who asked why you couldn't put animal rescue out of your mind when you came home, this book offers insights. The rewarding, fulfilling, and frustrating aspects of volunteerism are recurring themes in *Rescued*. The book presents motivation and inspiration for people who want to bridge the gap between loving their pets and giving selfless service to *all* life.

*Rescued* is filled with astonishing connections between people and animals. You will witness lives previously separated by continents threaded together into a patchwork quilt of kindness, generosity, loyalty, courage, and love.

What do animal organizations and volunteers do? Why do they do it? What jobs and careers are available in animal rescue? What does it feel like to save the life of an animal? Why do the celebrities we interviewed — Tippi Hedren, Rue McLanahan, Joe Mantegna, Molly Sims, Dee Wallace, Brigitte Bardot — and the mainstream media support animal rescue? We explore these questions, and many more, in this book.

We were honored that Senator John Ensign, from Nevada, wrote the foreword for this book. Senator Ensign received his Doctor of Veterinary Medicine degree from Colorado State University in 1985 and practiced veterinary medicine in Las Vegas at his own animal hospital. Since being elected to the Senate in 2000, he was awarded the 2004 Jacob K. Javits Award for his efforts and action on behalf of Americans with disabilities and the 2005 Educational Pioneer Award for his vision and contributions to the disadvantaged student population of Nevada.

In addition to his service to people, Senator Ensign champions the protection of domesticated animals, exotic animals, wildlife, and the environment. The Humane Society of the United States has cited his ongoing work to advance animal protection legislation at the national level by naming him Legislator of the Year for 2005. In 2004 the Humane Society named Senator Ensign "top lawmaker" for his commitment to the humane treatment of animals. His dedication to animal welfare led him to visit the Gulf Coast after Hurricane Kat-

*Dave Pauli (HSUS), U.S. Senator John Ensign, and Laura Maloney (LA/SPCA) at LSU Emergency Center.*

rina and to talk with and listen to volunteers, organizational leaders, and people who were separated from their pets. He returned to Washington with a long to-do list of ways he and government resources could support the rescue efforts. You'll see later in this book that Senator Ensign kept his promises.

As much as we wanted to bring to light every aspect of animal rescue, we had to focus on rescuing domestic pets and farm or ranch animals in the United States. Although we weren't able to include chapters on the important work of wildlife, marine, and international rescue operations, the resource section includes helpful information about these aspects.

An old saying in ancient religious traditions is that soul equals soul. One life is not more precious than another; all life deserves respect. Animal rescue shows that despite our shortcomings, humans are growing wiser and kinder. Animal rescue opens people's hearts and minds to the need to preserve the gifts of sharing life with animal friends. As Antoine de Saint-Exupéry wrote in *The Little Prince*, "Many have forgotten this truth, but you must not forget it. You remain responsible, forever, for what you have tamed."[1] This book is for the Earth, on which animals multiplied long before humans gained dominion over them and accepted responsibility for their lives.

# PART ONE

# RESCUING MEMBERS OF THE FAMILY

*Photos on previous page, left to right:*

Chris Robinson's Sugar/Jazz.

Richard Crook, Grassroots
Animal Rescue, saves a dog on
the second floor of a house.

HSUS volunteer and ARNO
cofounder Jane Garrison's first
rescue in New Orleans.

# CHAPTER ONE

# The Changing Relationship between People and Animals

Only in the past hundred years have animals become full-fledged, indoor-dwelling members of American families. Prior to this change in domestic life, most pet lovers had a casual relationship with their yard dogs or neighborhood cats. In bygone times, animals would no more be allowed inside the house than chickens could lay eggs on the dining room table.

Animals and humans forming socially and emotionally interdependent family units has had a profound impact on disaster preparedness and rescue operations. Hurricane Katrina indisputably proved that people today will risk their lives to keep from abandoning their pets. Whether decision makers like it, think it is a nuisance, or are pleased that the obvious has finally been recognized, today this is true: *Animals are members of the family*. Now every aspect of American society must deal with it. No longer is it permissible to separate people from the animals who share their homes, sleep in their beds, and have become their cherished friends.

Dr. Melissa Hunt, associate director of clinical training in the department of psychology of the University of Pennsylvania, studied the psychological impact of being forced to abandon a pet during the evacuations following Hurricane Katrina. She recruited survivors of the hurricane for the study. Half of them had lost their pets during the storms and flooding, and half had not gone through pet loss. Dr. Hunt told us that people who lost their pets experienced significantly more acute stress during evacuation and were significantly more depressed, showing more symptoms of post-traumatic stress disorder than survivors who safely evacuated with their pets. Based on her study, Dr. Hunt concludes, "You were just as likely to be depressed if you lost your pet as if you lost your home." The results of Dr. Hunt's study suggest that failure to implement effective companion animal evacuation policies carries a high cost in terms of the human survivors' mental health.

*A grateful family thanks rescuers.*

Our society has made animals dependent on the kindness and generosity of humans. In return, animals serve as conduits for people to fulfill their primal need for connection to nature. The animals in a home may be a person's only and deepest source of unconditional love. Millions of people need this kind of love — love without judgment, artifice, or stinginess — in a universe of emotional and spiritual isolation. Animals bridge the gap between our hearts and minds. As became apparent after Hurricane Katrina and other disasters, many people will die rather than lose a relationship for which there is no human substitute.

## Animals Are Essential to the Good Life

Even though animals play large roles in mythology, folklore, and religious practices of cultures around the globe, until recently they were not members of the American family. Only in the past century did dogs transform from working, herding, hunting, mostly outdoor protectors into car-riding, blanket-stealing, birthday party recipients. Among the wealthier classes of society, cats have always enjoyed hearth-occupying status. But in most rural and working-class American households, cats had to graduate from being exterminators who rid the property of mice and lived in the barn to being cuddly creatures with their own brightly decorated food and water bowls in the kitchen. Horses no longer earn their keep by pulling plows. Today they provide city dwellers with companionable rides through the countryside. Horses are more likely to be gentled, not broken; stabled, not tethered. Rather than leading the charge in battle on bloody fields, horses are dominant in the growing area of animal-assisted therapy, where they give rides to at-risk or disabled children and adults.

Respect for the profound connection between humans and animals has blossomed in this country since World War II. Within the past fifty years researchers have shown that people benefit in measurable ways from interactions with animals. Respected scientific journals publish studies proving that animals offer healthy rewards to their human guardians, such as lowered blood pressure, extended life span, and stress relief. National news segments show dogs detecting cancer cells better than sophisticated medical testing. University of Missouri–Columbia researchers report that walking the family dog daily promotes fourteen pounds of weight loss in a year — more weight than most people lose by participating in weight-loss programs.[1] At the beginning of the twenty-first century, the message has become clear: animals are good for your health.

As a nation, we have started expressing gratitude for the presence of animals and mourning their absence. Robert K. Anderson, cofounder and director of CENSHARE, an organization at the University of Minnesota dedicated to illuminating the benefits of human-animal connection, writes, "Today it is socially acceptable to grieve the loss of a pet, to carry pet pictures in your wallet or purse, to celebrate your pet's birthday with a party, to have pet medical insurance, and to buy special food. The newest trend is to buy special clothes for pets."[2]

Hundreds of churches around the country celebrate the "blessing of the animals" on the feast of Saint Francis of Assisi, patron saint of animals and ecology. Annually their sanctuaries fill with dogs, cats, chickens, fish, bunnies, and gerbils alongside human worshippers.

With an estimated 65 million dogs and 77.6 million cats inhabiting American homes, and expenditures of $39 billion per year on pet food, toys and other products, and veterinary care, ours has become a pet-obsessed nation. Americans spend $5 billion annually on presents for their pets. They take vacations with animal companions. They buy them fashionable clothes, relaxation and exercise at day spas, and stays at hotels that cater to canine and catly comforts. Animals receive advanced medical treatment from veterinarians who specialize in orthopedics and oncology. Alternative and holistic vets treat them with acupuncture and herbs.

At the risk of being labeled anthropomorphic, researchers study and publish scholarly papers on pet personality and animal emotions. And, as if to punctuate the belief in animal personality and emotion, in 2005 millions of people made a blockbuster hit out of the wildlife love story *March of the Penguins*. We have definitely come a long way, baby!

Jeannine Moga, clinical counselor at the University of Minnesota Veterinary Medical Center, calls this trend a win–win situation for everyone. She says, "The American lifestyle has become transient over time. This means that social networks and family systems are much more spread out, even splintered. For the many Americans who choose to share their lives with animals, those animals have also become family members and very important sources of social and emotional support." The increasing numbers of Americans who embrace pets as family have precipitated drastic changes in how the country views the merciful act of animal rescue. How can you look into the loving eyes of a companion with whom you share your home and turn away from your friend's species in an hour of greatest need?

## Animal Rescue Gets Noticed

Almost a century and a half after the American Society for the Prevention of Cruelty to Animals (ASPCA) and the American Humane Association (AHA) came into being, animal rescuers continue the good fight. With thousands of shelters and sanctuaries all over the country, virtually every community includes individuals or organizations devoted to protecting the welfare of animals. Yet if you ask your friends and neighbors the name of the closest animal shelter, where it is located, how big it is, and how it operates, you will probably get only blank looks and shoulder shrugs. Most people assume there is a humane society or SPCA somewhere in their community. Some may have used its services for adopting a pet or ridding themselves of an unwanted or stray animal, but most probably don't know much about it or even that it's there.

In spite of Americans' professed love affair with pets, the work of local, state, and national animal protection organizations flies under the radar of mainstream society. Except for a small number of caring people who hold fund-raisers and donate time and money regularly, animal shelters and welfare organizations operate in relative obscurity. No big-name celebrities host or perform at nationally televised fund-raisers for animal charities. Until recently, animal welfare and rescue weren't significant to America's vision of itself as a compassionate and caring nation.

Much of this lack of attention to animal rescue changed after Hurricane Katrina. Staff members of animal welfare organizations worked around the clock, and thousands of volunteers joined them. Schoolchildren gathered dog and cat food for Katrina animals. Manufacturers and suppliers donated crates, leashes, collars, and their parking lots for makeshift emergency triaging and sheltering.

As happened in Minnesota with Animal Humane Society and Animal Ark, media covered the stories of animal shelters from around the country answering calls for help from the stricken Gulf Coast. Photographers took pictures of staff and volunteers loading supplies onto trucks or minivans with animal shelter signage prominently displayed on their vehicles. Television newscasters profiled shelter personnel, who dressed in T-shirts with the names of their organizations displayed prominently for the camera. Accompanied by reporters and videographers, shelter workers formed caravans and drove thousands of miles to places that most of them had seen only on MapQuest.

People watching television were horrified to see dogs stranded on rooftops and cats cowering under houses. Because of the boon in media exposure, local and national animal shelters and organizations received an outpouring of donations. The Humane Society of the United States (HSUS) collected the largest amount of money in its history. Folks who barely knew there was an animal shelter in their community looked up its phone number and stopped in to make tax-deductible donations. Unused to an influx of visitors, animal shelter staff and volunteers gave tours of their facilities and offered up languishing animals for adoption.

Later, when local animal shelter staff and volunteers came back with "Katrina dogs and cats," the organizations held well-publicized adoption fairs. Unlike the animals that get surrendered every day, most of the cleaned-up and medicated hurricane and flood-survivor animals found themselves in good homes, some living in better conditions than they had ever known.

Another transformation occurred after local animal shelter staff and volunteers returned from the Gulf Coast. They were either invited to take or insisted upon taking a seat at the table when their community and the nation did disaster and emergency planning. Now, they wanted to make sure that if there were ever a disaster where they lived, the animals and people who love them would be safely evacuated, sheltered, and reunited if separation occurred.

## Saving Animals Is Connected to Saving Humans

After Hurricane Katrina, community emergency planners all over the country began to understand that saving the lives of animals is necessary for the survival of humans. On an economic level, it costs a lot more to have to go back into a danger zone and retrieve stranded animals. On an emotional level, as noted above in the empirical data from Dr. Melissa Hunt's study, the depression that survivors suffer over separation from a pet is equal to other disaster-related losses they experience. Freelance writer and animal rescuer Barb Prindle of Minneapolis expressed to us why she believes animal rescue also has moral, ethical, and spiritual significance: "You are looking at the face of innocence when you look at a dog or a cat. They did nothing to create the situation. They did not create global warming or poor rescue plans. It is heartbreaking beyond my ability to ignore it. When you ignore innocent, helpless need, you are doing damage to your own soul, in my opinion."

For animals, a disaster is any situation that results in loss of the home or the humans that animals rely on for their health and welfare. Every day humans create disasters for animals through neglect, abuse, abandonment, and disruption of natural habitats. Preventing disaster for animals requires widespread support for organizations that protect animals' lives. And, in the case of human-created disasters, preventing disaster requires that we change our destructive behaviors. Both aspects of saving animals from disaster — prevention and making changes in attitudes and practices — are concepts whose time has come.

## CHAPTER TWO

# Who Rescues the Animals?

Thousands of Americans traveled to the hurricane-ravaged areas to help people and pets reunite and to aid in saving the lives of animals. Who are these people who devote their time, talents, and money to rescuing animals? What motivates them to leave the safety and comfort of their homes, whether after a national tragedy or to regularly volunteer at animal shelters? Why does your neighbor, your co-worker, your fellow parishioner, your relative, your friend, or your spouse have such an unrelenting desire and need to save animals from disaster? While researching this book, we had the opportunity to talk with hundreds of people who save animals. We asked them why they often put themselves in harm's way to make animals safer and to help them find good homes.

Who rescues animals? The following snapshots may surprise you.

## Beyond the Stereotypes

The stereotype of the animal rescuer, like some we saw in the media after the hurricanes, is one of a person who wears hip-high wader boots and a face mask to keep from breathing in toxic chemicals. If she is a woman, she pulls her hair back into a ponytail and covers it with a baseball cap, looking like a determined macho chick on a mission. But, as we found out, not all animal rescuers match this stereotype.

Andrea Kozil works at the Portland, Oregon, administrative office of Defense of Animals–Africa. Andrea went to New Orleans to volunteer and was placed in charge of running Barn 5 at the temporary shelter that the HSUS had set up at the Lamar-Dixon Expo Center. It was the intense week of September 7, right after the levees broke in New Orleans. Inexperienced in shelter operations, Andrea struggled with having responsibility for hundreds of animals and not nearly enough resources to do the job.

One day Andrea noticed a woman wearing clean sweatpants and a fancy T-shirt. In the one-hundred-degree heat and stifling humidity, sweat trickled down the woman's face and streaked her makeup. Andrea watched as the woman walked a rambunctious, powerful German shepherd. In an attempt to control him, the woman held the dog's leash in a way that caused his front legs to lift off the ground.

Andrea rushed out of the barn to correct what she viewed as the mishandling of an already stressed-out animal. "That dog has four legs," Andrea scolded. "He needs to have all of them on the ground."

The woman snapped back, "I know what the hell I'm doing. I've been doing it for years."

"This," Andrea recalled for us months after it happened, "was me at my worst and her at her worst."

When the woman returned the dog to the shelter, she had a hard time getting him back into his cage. Afterward, Andrea says, "The woman tapped my shoulder. Then she said, 'This is pretty rough, isn't it?' We both cried and hugged each other as we each apologized. We had been stretched as far as could be. 'This is rough' had said it all. I thanked her for being there. She went on with her work. And so did I."

A couple days later Andrea noticed a fancy car pull up into the parking lot outside her barn. The same woman had returned to walk dogs again. Andrea noticed that the woman's fingernails were manicured. Her hair was coiffed. She wore a fashionable sun visor. Andrea says, "If I had not met her previously, there is no way I would have believed that this woman was going into Lamar-Dixon. After that, I watched as the same woman came back, over and over, to walk the dogs. She amazed me. I wouldn't have expected her to be there. But she was on the front line every day. She lived in the area and cared about animals. This really touched me."

Would you imagine a pregnant marketing manager hoisting fifty-pound crates off a conveyor belt at the Seattle airport? Angela Badie did just that when she helped Barb Peterson's project, Delta Angels, fly hundreds of dogs and cats to animal shelters where they would be fostered, adopted, or reunited with their hurricane-afflicted humans.

Anita Wollison, founder of No Animal Left Behind, has a master's degree in counseling. After the hurricane she didn't go to the Gulf Coast. Instead, she spent sixteen- and eighteen-hour days helping to coordinate animal rescues and organize other volunteers from all over the country as part of the No Animal Left Behind organization that she founded. They used the Internet to help track down rescued pets and facilitate reuniting them with their owners.

Ron Silver is a film producer from Nebraska who writes, shoots, directs, and distributes his own documentaries. In New Orleans he rescued animals and shot videos of the houses where he and his team found them. Later, when other volunteers tried to match people with missing pets, Ron's videos ensured that the right animal would return to the right person.

Along with those who regularly rescue animals — veterinarians, veterinary technicians, animal shelter workers, animal control officers — people from all walks of life every day place themselves on the giving and preserving end of the human-animal relationship. Office cubicle dwellers, homemakers, executive assistants, teachers, nurses, social workers, lawyers, socialites, and information technology personnel clean cages at animal shelters, organize fund-raisers, foster animals in their homes, comb the Internet to bring people and animals together. And when the animals needed them most, they went to the hurricane-ravaged areas to rescue them.

In other words, as Andrea Kozil discovered, you would be wrong to pick any one type of person as more likely than others to rescue animals. Chris Cutter of the International Fund for Animal Welfare (IFAW) says, "It was kind of funny in New Orleans. People asked us to break into their houses and find their animals. So there would be this real tough, kind of intimidating guy kicking in people's doors. Then he'd be down on all fours going, "Here, kitty, kitty, kitty."

## What Were Rescuers Like as Children?

We asked many of those we interviewed how they got into animal rescue and if they had been doing it all their lives. We found that if you had shared a neighborhood playground with any of these folks, you might have guessed that they would grow up to do something meaningful for animals.

Barb Peterson, who arranged all those Delta rescue flights, told us that she grew up in Kona, Hawaii, on the Big Island. She lived on a Kona coffee and macadamia nut farm with rabbits, chickens, cats, and dogs. As a child, she always felt that the loss of one of her pets was like losing a best friend. This depth of feeling for animals gave her the empathy to understand how important it is for people to find their pets after they have been separated from them.

Jane Blythe worked at an animal rescue site in New Orleans that she described as a "tarp and stick site in a parking lot with no electricity, no running water." In the early eighties Jane was one of a small group of dedicated animal lovers who started an animal shelter in their Rhode Island city, a venture that for Jane followed naturally from her childhood upbringing, in which her parents always took in stray animals and gave them a loving home. "All my toddler pictures show me feeding birds and squirrels in the park, alongside my parents," she says.

"While I was in college, somebody brought a baby duck to the dormitory where I lived. After it was heard quacking, the student had to give it up. I brought the little duckling home. He imprinted immediately upon my mother. Whenever she washed dishes, the duck would sit on her feet. After several months of living with my mother, he grew so large that we brought him to the duck pond in the local park to release him. We checked often, and he did very well there."

Some animal rescuers began their lives as horse lovers. Hilary Wood, founder of Front Range Equine Rescue, says about her childhood, "I read every horse book as a kid. I read *Black Beauty* and other horse books over and over again. About the time I first got my horse, Dancer, the one who inspired me to do horse rescue, I asked for *Black Beauty* as a Christmas present. I'd loved it so much as a kid. One of my sisters found a hard copy, and when I read it again, I started to cry. After I moved Dancer out of the terrible conditions where I had found him to another stable, one girl who boarded there said, 'Dancer is like your own Black Beauty.' She got it. I was starting to get it too. At that point I didn't know there was such a thing as horse rescue. But I pulled three more horses out of that awful facility."

Ed Powers, director of shelter outreach and business development for Petfinder.com, an Internet organization that facilitated thousands of reunions after Hurricane Katrina, says about his childhood, "I did not have a lot of pets. My mom and dad limited them because I had three brothers and a sister. We had a couple of dogs while I was growing up, but my sister and one of my brothers were allergic to animals, as was I, so it became a health issue. I was willing to put up with allergy testing and vaccinations. When the allergist would ask what I did for a living, I stopped admitting that I worked at the Animal Rescue League of Boston. My dorm mates and friends used to tease me that I was the only person they knew who was allergic to his college major."

Amanda St. John, founder of MuttShack Animal Rescue Foundation, an animal fostering group, in Los Angeles, that established a veterinary triage and temporary shelter in a private school near the levees in New Orleans, grew up in South Africa. She says that when she was a child, wildfires would pass through the wildlife farms where her family lived, and Amanda and her family would form rows to knock out the fires. She says, "Our grandfather had seven sons and one daughter with many grandchildren. He would call everyone up when there was a fire. Almost one hundred cousins and nephews and other family members would come. We walked the dusty black line at the end of the evening, putting out fires and protecting the animals. That was always part of our indoctrination: we were supposed to save the animals."

If you heard about Dan Maloney's childhood, you might not be surprised that he grew up to become a zookeeper at the Bronx Zoo and eventually vice president and general curator for the Audubon Zoo, in New Orleans, responsible for 1,500 zoo animals during and after the hurricanes. Dan says, "I had all kinds of creatures, even growing up in a North Jersey suburb. I raised ducklings, squirrels, herps, snakes, turtles. There were lots of patches of cemeteries with woodlands in my neighborhood. When I was in junior high, during snow days, I'd take an old pair of binoculars, a canteen from Boy Scouts, and *Peterson's Field Guide to Eastern Birds*. Then I'd hike by myself. I liked it that way. I could see a lot more creatures."

Laura Maloney, who married Dan Maloney and is the other half of New Orleans's animal-rescue power couple, is the executive director of the Louisiana SPCA. Hurricane Katrina demolished her animal shelter. Still, Laura and her staff were in charge of saving the lives of as many of the city's animals as possible while trying at the same time to get the help they desperately needed from beleaguered city and state officials and national animal organizations.

Her childhood seemed custom-made to prepare her for living in the animal world and negotiating with officials and bureaucracies. Laura says, "I grew up on a farm in Charles County, Maryland, which was tobacco country. Animals were always part of my life. My mother was a supervisory paralegal specialist in charge of the correspondence unit, in the criminal division of the U.S. Department of Justice. Since both of my parents worked in DC, I had city and farm friends. When I'd try to share my excitement about animals with my city friends, they didn't understand my fascination. So I had to learn to live in the city and political atmosphere while growing up in the country with the animals I loved."

Michael Mountain, president of Best Friends Animal Society, in Kanab, Utah, supported the organization's executive director, Paul Berry, in forming a temporary animal shelter in Tylertown, Mississippi. It became the safe refuge and friendly pit stop for thousands of rescued animals. Hurricane relief and its resultant chaos seemed to be in the cards for Michael, especially when you consider the names he gave to his childhood kitties in England — Siegfried, Psycho, and Catastrophe.

Susan McLaughlin volunteers at the headquarters of United Animal Nations (UAN), in Sacramento, California. She volunteered at the temporary shelter that UAN set up in Jackson, Mississippi, after Hurricane Katrina. Susan says, "At my wedding my father said to my husband, 'I hope you realize you are marrying a woman who has inherited an absolute passion for animals. She will be feeding the animals before she feeds you.'"

## Why They Rescue Animals

Many people wonder what motivates others to rescue animals. We asked the people we interviewed why they do this work, and they offered reasons as varied and colorful as their childhood experiences with animals had been.

For many people, rescuing animals recharges their batteries. Barb Prindle says, "Rescue work is not tiring. It's incredibly energizing. Sitting around at a coffee shop is tiring. Dealing with boorish, self-important people is tiring. Traffic jams are tiring. Meaninglessness and doing things that don't matter are tiring. Saving lives is not tiring."

Pet sitter and dog trainer Laura Munder, from Roswell, Georgia, agrees that animal rescue work can be energizing. She says, "Each animal's life I touch and improve, even if in the slightest way, is a victory. Each animal who finds a home [counts as] a victory. No matter how many adoptions I make, it will never be enough. That's what keeps me going."

Jane Garrison coordinated rescue teams as a volunteer for the HSUS in New Orleans and later cofounded Animal Rescue New Orleans. She worked in the area for months, continuing to keep animals alive. Jane says, "I have a really strong purpose to help animals. It is so deep within me, such a part of my life and who I am, that I don't even think about it. Stopping never crosses my mind. People live their whole lives not knowing what their purpose is and how to contribute. For me, it's so clear. This is both a gift and a curse. I can never put it aside. I can't turn my back to animal suffering without doing something. My motivation is so strong."

## Why Not Help People?

In spite of their honorable aspirations, animal rescuers rarely receive the respect and gratitude they deserve. They get no paid leaves of absence to carry out their noble deeds; they are not awarded keys to the cities of the shelters where they donate their time and resources. One reason is the erroneous notion that many people have about them. Often animal rescuers are viewed as eager to help animals but indifferent to human suffering. They are asked, as an implied criticism: Why do you care so much about animals when people need help?

Jane Garrison eloquently expresses what we heard from hundreds of rescuers: "It is not a matter of choosing animals over humans. If I were coming across a person and an animal, I'd help both. What I do for animals doesn't diminish my feelings for humans. And I *am* helping humans. Every animal I rescue helps a whole family. A lot of people have lost everything. When they have their animals back, they are so happy."

Almost every one of the hundreds of animal rescuers we interviewed also donates time and money to other causes. They are Big Brothers or Big Sisters. They work for VISTA or help people with AIDS; they assist people with chemical dependencies. It is the rule rather than the exception that people who help animals also volunteer for human service organizations.

Ramona Ruhf from Bethlehem, Pennsylvania, says, "I donate to the Girl Scouts and Diabetes Foundation. I helped raise money and items for the troops in Iraq and for rescue workers of the Twin Towers after 9/11. I have helped with letter-writing campaigns for sick children with cancer."

Most animal rescue workers will tell you that the lives of animals and people are inextricably intertwined. They also will say that to help animals you have to deal with people too. It takes the skills of a diplomat and the discernment of a sleuth to figure out how to get an animal into or out of unsafe situations when humans are involved, which is often the case. Animals and people go together. In animal rescue work, if you help an animal, you are helping a person.

## A Gold Star Animal Rescue Volunteer

One of the most memorable animal rescue volunteers we met demonstrates the grit, compassion, and determination needed for saving animals from disaster. She uses her skills and life experiences to better the lives of both humans and animals.

Candice King-Palgut is forty-seven years old. She is married to a man who has learned not to argue with her when she says she's going to help the animals. They live in Orlando, Florida, which was hit with three hurricanes in six weeks during the summer of 2004. Their neighborhood sustained a great deal of damage. In downtown Orlando the storms downed huge one-hundred-year-old oak trees. A year later houses were still being gutted.

Twelve years ago, after a bad car accident, Candice underwent six back surgeries and now needs to use a wheelchair. She can walk very short distances but is in chronic pain. She was a glassblower for twenty-five years, but the accident ended that career. Now she calls herself a "domestic goddess and estrogen engineer." She makes quilts for the preemie unit at her local hospital and does clicker training for dogs, a gentle persuasion form of teaching obedience skills.

Candice says, "I have days when I don't get out of bed. I use a cortical stimulator, with wires and electrodes implanted in my spinal column. This causes electricity to play back and forth across my spinal column and blocks pain signals. I still take pain medication, but I am cussed independent. I have been on my own since I was fourteen years old. I grew up fast and hard, with determination to make it. This upbringing gave me a strong work ethic. When I want to do something, you might as well get out of my way. It will be easier on everybody. I'll go around or over you if I have to."

Always an animal lover, Candice had worked for a veterinarian when she was a teenager. After Hurricane Katrina hit, she watched the news on television, cringing at the sight of so many animals suffering. A segment on CNN about an organization called Noah's Wish caught her attention. She emailed the organization, saying, "I'm in a wheelchair. I can scoop poop with the best of them. I'll sit in gas lines and free somebody stronger to do things I can't." Candice was invited to come to Slidell, Louisiana, where Noah's Wish had set up a temporary shelter.

Candice made an appointment with her pain clinic to get medications for a month. When neighbors and friends found out about her plans, they decided to sponsor her. An organization called Pet Rescue by Judy gave her pet supplies. Candice's eighty-eight-year-old mother-in-law donated a tank of gas. A quilting partner, Beth, offered a hundred dollars for expenses and used her garage as a supply depot. Beth and Candice's neighbors loaded the van and baked goodies to send to the volunteers as morale boosters. With her power wheelchair strapped to the carrier on the back of her minivan, Candice was ready to go.

Her husband wasn't thrilled about his wife's determination to volunteer. Candice says, "He's a really good man, the wind beneath my wings. I'm stubborn and hardheaded. This wasn't a fight he'd win. So all he said was, 'Don't do anything stupid, please.' "

Candice knows how to rough it and considers herself street smart. "Besides," she says, "I don't set myself up for trouble. I was going, even if the city had looters. Call me naive or crazy. I really don't have a whole lot of fear. I believe in angels, or whatever you want to call a positive guiding force in the universe. I come from a Buddhist background. Maybe it's good karma built up. I'm not invincible. But I'm not a little mouse in a corner either. I've had lots of bad stuff happen in my life; there is tremendous opportunity to grow and learn, even from a huge disaster."

Those courageous thoughts would have to hold Candice in good stead when she caught her first glimpse of Slidell. Exhausted after driving twelve hours straight, she arrived at the end of the day — the busiest time for Noah's Wish, when animals were brought in from the day's rescues and staff people were trying to wrap up for the night. Six hundred dogs barked nonstop, a horrendous din. Generators pumped. People ran back and forth. It appeared to be total chaos. Candice thought, "Oh, my god, what have I done!"

No one had time to welcome her. This was her first night in a strange city under martial law, and Candice had to make her way to the volunteers' lodgings, a warehouse in the back of a furniture store. Lights were left on all night to prevent looting. Candice and the other volunteers slept on the warehouse floor. "We were human bug food," she says. "It was hot, nasty, and dirty. No air moved. I was being eaten alive by mosquitoes."

About her work Candice says, "Originally I was supposed to check in volunteers, but they were woefully short of help with intake. So I got my trial by fire. The first three days were absolutely maddening. I was trying to learn complicated procedures for the job while a never-ending sea of people and animals arrived. Most of my career, I have been able to keep intensely concentrated on one thing at a time. In this setting, I was constantly interrupted. I spent two weeks being completely frazzled. And, honey, I hate paperwork! That's all I did for two weeks was paperwork."

Better than the paperwork was her direct contact with the animals. Candice enjoyed providing comfort to what were known as the "failure to thrive" dogs. While sitting at the intake table, she held the dogs on her lap and snuggled with them. These little animals were so traumatized, withdrawn, and depressed that they couldn't adjust to being at the shelter and were refusing to eat. Candice's attention helped them to perk up and learn to love and trust again.

Each day Candice listened to evacuees, many of whom were searching desperately for their pets. Candice says that the hardest part was watching people who had to surrender their pets because they were leaving the state for an unsteady future or had to move in with families who didn't want the pets. The happiest times, of course, were when people were reunited with their pets.

She says, "This was a roller coaster that never stopped. It was brutal. Many days I'd have been happier in the back, scooping poop, than having to go through all that pain with people. I gave what I could. I would call my girlfriends, blubbering, 'I can't keep doing this. I want to come home.' Then I'd tell them, 'It's all right. I just needed to get it out.' "

Candice had a method for dealing with the stress. She says, "One of two things happens. You get away at the end of the day and cry, process it, let it out. Or you hit times during the day when there is no more sucking it up. Then you have to duck around the corner and boo-hoo. If you don't look at anybody, they leave you alone. If you make eye contact, someone comes over and gives you a hug."

Candice wanted to stay in Slidell for three weeks, but she had a serious infection the whole time and was taking antibiotics. When she felt herself getting crabby, she realized that she had reached her limit and should leave. Feverish and exhausted, she stopped at a hotel on the way home and spent a much-needed night alone to process the experiences.

She says, "I had run everything out of my system. I had nothing left. It threw me into a major fibromyalgia flare. I could hardly walk or move for six weeks. I had really bad nightmares for weeks. By the time I was able to get up again and go out, everything seemed surreal. I would walk around the Wal-Mart store and feel this weird sense that I should be doing something else. I couldn't relax and get back into a normal routine. To this day I can't watch anything about animal rescue on television."

After Candice returned home, she created a quilt with a backing of bandannas that the Noah's Wish volunteers had worn in Slidell. She says, "I dug through my stash of brightly colored dog and cat prints. I put the animal quilting blocks topsy-turvy in the body of the quilt. I chose that pattern because the animals' lives were turned every which way. There is a light blue border that symbolizes the floodwaters. In the outer green border, I quilted hearts alternating with handprints. I named the quilt Hearts Guiding Hands."

Candice did such a great job with her volunteering that Noah's Wish founder Terri Crisp offered her a scholarship to attend the formal training that would make her an official volunteer. Terri says, "Before Candice left she said, 'I cannot tell you how this has changed my life. I felt I was useless, that there was nothing I could do. Everybody at home wanted to do everything for me. When I worked as a volunteer at Noah's Wish, there was no hovering [in the background]. I have my confidence back.' "

Candice donated the quilt to Noah's Wish and took it to the training that Terri Crisp held for volunteers in Savannah, Georgia, in February 2006. The quilt was raffled ten times over the next weeks, during each of ten trainings offered by Noah's Wish in the United States and Canada.

Terri also planned to match the $6,000 expected to be raised through the raffle. Candice says, "I hope the money will be set aside for a special fund for travel expenses for cash-strapped volunteers. A lot of these volunteers made two, three, or four trips to Slidell at three dollars a gallon. It was a hardship on them financially. But they kept coming back."

After we interviewed Candice, she wrote that although the volunteer experience was hard, often brutal, on mind and body, it was so rewarding that she would not hesitate to volunteer when she is needed again. She keeps two large plastic tubs filled with all her gear, ready and waiting for the call to action.

# CHAPTER THREE

# Katrina to Katrina

Few people know that there is a group of truckers who call themselves the Underdog Railroad. They drive dogs across the country to families who will adopt them, arranging pickups with other truckers. At truck stops you can see them walking the dogs in their care. One of the most moving stories of rescuing animals from New Orleans involves some truckers who similarly opened their hearts — and their rigs — for a cat who needed their help.

Barbara and Keith Nicholson are bartenders and waiters. Keith is also a nonfiction book author and novelist. On July 20, 2002, the two were hungry for a burger and a beer after getting off work and decided to stop at Fat Harry's, a little restaurant and bar where college students hang out. It's just up the street from their house in the Uptown area of New Orleans. As they walked toward Fat Harry's, Keith and Barbara looked inside a gated parking lot and spied a skinny, dark-gray tabby cat with white paws and white chest running toward them. With this first glimpse of the cat, they began a friendship that would weather the biggest storm of their lives.

Despite the roar of the bar next door, the cat brazenly flopped down, rolled over on his back with arms and legs skyward, and exposed his white tummy. Then he twisted his neck to look at them in that catlike way that says, "I'm here! What are you going to do about it?"

Barbara, a lifelong animal lover who has been "owned" by dozens of cats, was instantly charmed. Keith, for whom cats were his least favorite animal, was indifferent. Barbara explained to Keith that the cat had placed himself in a vulnerable position and was making it obvious that he wanted to be petted. Keith says, "I looked down at the little cat, and for some reason, my eyes watered up. He rolled one way. Then the other. He looked at me the entire time. He had the biggest green eyes in the world. He was very skinny and, although he appeared to be an adult, was very frail."

Keith noticed a closed drugstore across the street and got an idea. Kneeling down, Keith promised the cat that if he was still there the next morning, Keith would go to the drugstore and buy him something to eat.

Keith and Barbara entered the neighborhood bar and enjoyed their burger and beer, then headed home, past where they had met the cat. This time the cat jumped through the iron gates of the parking lot and ran to the street corner ahead of them. Keith called out, "I'll bring you food." As they neared the corner, the cat looked over his shoulder and waited for them to catch up, then darted to the right. They remarked on how cute it was that the cat seemed to be going in the same direction they were.

The couple continued their late-night walk home with the cat leading the way. Keith says, "All along the street he jumped stairs, went underneath houses, crossed the street a time or two, then went to the next corner of the block. He stopped and waited for us, then turned his head to look over his shoulder. He knew exactly where we lived." The cat led them all the way home. "That's the night," they say, "that Kitty-Kat adopted us."

At home, Barbara took her waiter's apron and wrapped the cat in it, fearing he would paw and scratch her. They examined him more closely and concluded that he was so emaciated he would not live much longer without their help. They tried to feed him soft food, but he couldn't keep it down. They noticed he was wearing an old, faded collar and had been neutered (unusual in New Orleans), so they knew he had been someone's pet. They assumed he was left behind by one of the college students who moved back home or graduated, unfortunately a common practice in this neighborhood.

Still concerned about their new friend, they went to bed that night talking about how to save the cat's life. The next day their lives were upended. Both found out that they had lost their jobs. Now, nursing Kitty-Kat back to health became an occupation that for a while took their minds off their dual unemployment.

Even though Kitty-Kat was not playful like a kitten, he teased Keith to get Barbara's attention. The cat had a habit of barging in on Barbara in the bathroom, never wanting her to be out of his sight. Once in the bathroom, regardless of what objects were lying around, Kitty-Kat picked Keith's hairbrush to bat into the sink. The cat also took over wake-up calls. No matter what time Keith set the alarm clock, Kitty-Kat always woke him up by jumping on the nightstand and mewing right before the alarm went off. This earned him the nickname "alarm clock Kitty-Kat." As Keith said later, "This cat taught me what love means."

Fast-forward to August 28, 2005, the day before Hurricane Katrina hit the Gulf Coast. Keith and Barbara planned to evacuate the city with Barbara's family but learned when the family arrived that everyone would be staying in a single hotel room in north Louisiana. Keith was taken aback. He imagined the still-frail Kitty-Kat trying to cope with five adults, a teenager, and a pair of fully grown dogs in one room. Rather than risk Kitty-Kat running off or getting hurt, he decided to stay in New Orleans until the storm blew over and Barbara returned home.

Barbara and her family left for the safety of the hotel. The hurricane descended upon the city. The front door of Keith's house blew open, and electrical wires wrapped around the gutters. Keith fought his way to the door trying to shut it without being electrocuted. Kitty-Kat, who usually ran and hid under the bed at the first loud noise, followed Keith to the door. He lay down at Keith's feet and placed his front paws on top of Keith's shoes, as if trying to hold him down and keep him from being blown out the door. Keith was hit in the face three times by the electrical cables and gutters, breaking his nose and chipping a tooth. He was trying with all his might to get hold of the door and shut it. Through all this, the timid Kitty-Kat hung on to Keith's feet. Scared as he was, his love compelled him to stay through the storm with Keith.

After the winds stopped, Keith held Kitty-Kat in his arms and said, "I will never abandon you."

Then the levees broke and the floods came. National Guard soldiers tried to evacuate Keith's neighborhood. Keith says, "I was told by some National Guardsmen that after my neighborhood area was cleared of civilian residents, it would be more humane for them to shoot the animals on sight because they would starve or dehydrate without citizens to care for them. The animals would decay and cause disease or pestilence. As a result, I refused to evacuate the city without taking Kitty-Kat."

Keith and Kitty-Kat stayed in their apartment with the temperature rising to 115 degrees at night. He listened, terrified, to looters breaking into neighboring apartments, gunshots being fired, and the sounds of glass breaking. Kitty-Kat seemed to know that he had to stay quiet. Keith says, "Had he screamed or meowed, let out cat calls, or scratched at the door, the looters would have known we were in the apartment and we would not have made it out of there alive."

## Almost Two Weeks after the Hurricane

After the storms, Keith and Barbara lost all communication with each other. Keith didn't know where his wife was, and she didn't know if her husband and Kitty-Kat had survived. Every two hours the National Guard troops assigned to Keith's part of town passed by on patrol. They were looking for "pet-loving holdouts." Keith reported to them that he was still alive and had not vacated yet.

The troops tried to let Keith use their cell phones so he could call Barbara, but the phones always failed; cell phone towers had blown down. On the twelfth day after the hurricane, Keith finally got through to the hotel where Barbara was supposed to be staying. But Barbara and her family were no longer there. Alarmed, he called Barbara's daughter, who reported that the hotel had sustained heavy wind damage, and because of the lockdown of New Orleans she had not been able to return home.

Barbara and her family had driven all the way to Springfield, Illinois, to her brother's house. Keith finally reached Barbara in Illinois, and this was the first that his wife knew he was alive.

Keith told us of the ordeal that took place after he reached Barbara:

At many different times people were told to evacuate, but when they got to the parish lines, the other parishes would not allow them to enter. We were all in flux. Even those who wanted to get out, who had cars and money, could not.

I was flown from a National Guard evacuation center by helicopter. When we flew over the city, snipers shot at us. The helicopter swayed and rocked from side to side. We had to return to where we had boarded originally. Though I was in fear of being arrested, I sneaked off with Kitty-Kat [toward home]. There was *no way* I was going to go through that again!

I walked between hurricane-damaged houses and fought my way through entire streets that were nothing but green jungles of century-old broken oak trees and branches. Power poles, house porches, and roofs littered the street. I navigated around downed power lines and struggled not to be seen by the police department, National Guard, and the criminals.

After I returned home I stopped at a neighborhood store that was occupied by its owner. The store owner's cell phone started to work. He allowed people in the neighborhood to make calls. When it was my turn for the cell phone, I spoke with Barbara and told her about the helicopter. Right then, the National Guard troops came to the store. They told all of us that we had to evacuate *right then* or be arrested. If that happened, I knew I would not be able to keep Kitty-Kat, so I had no choice. I was in tears. I had promised Kitty-Kat I would not abandon him.

While I was on the phone with Barbara, I told the National Guard guys, "I am not going!" She heard all eight of them when they clicked their machine guns and said, "You're going!"

They said I would be escorted, once again, to the evacuation center where I had been the day before. I could bring only what I could carry in both hands. This turned out to be a cat carrier with Kitty-Kat in it and a suitcase.

    As I was waiting for them to take me away, a neighbor, who was with the Louisiana State Air National Guard, saw me getting on the back of the transport truck. He put me and the cat carrier in the back of his truck, drove us across the lake, and left me at an Army National Guard station. From there, I was further evacuated north of the city and away from the chaos.

Keith's rescuers gave him a couple cans of cat food. They also handed him a bus ticket so he could rejoin his wife in Illinois.

Keith arrived at the Hammond, Louisiana, Greyhound bus station, which sits next to the Central Truck Stop. In almost two weeks he had not shaved, showered, or had much to eat or drink. He was hot, frazzled to the core, and definitely not up for any more bad news. To his shock, the bus driver refused to let him get on the bus with Kitty-Kat. This was more than he could bear. He broke down, crying on the parking lot. He could hear a man and woman asking someone in the crowd what this guy's problem was. Someone answered that Keith was an evacuee from New Orleans and he wasn't being allowed to take his cat on the bus.

The couple came over to Keith. With gentleness in their voices, they introduced themselves to him as a husband-and-wife truck-driving team. They had just stopped to get a bite to eat at the truck stop next door. They offered to take Keith's cat from him so he could get on the bus. But there was a problem: they had a dog who also rode with them in the truck's air-conditioned cabin. They wouldn't be able to keep both their dog and Kitty-Kat in there. If the cat had to ride in the truck, he might die in the scorching heat.

Another truck driver, Bobby Haynes, had also parked at the truck stop. A driver for Central Hauling, Bobby lived in Plumberville, Arkansas. He is an animal lover who understood Keith's bond with Kitty-Kat. When he was a child, Bobby and his mother had survived a house fire that destroyed everything. He was moved by Keith's plight and said to him, "Follow me." When they reached Bobby's truck, he called his dispatcher, Charlotte Williams, working out of Little Rock, Arkansas, and asked if she would take care of Kitty-Kat until Keith and Barbara could get on their feet.

Another animal lover with two dogs and two cats, Charlotte heard Keith crying so hard over the thought of being separated from Kitty-Kat that he couldn't speak. Charlotte says, "I knew then and there I would eventually have to take Kitty-Kat even though I didn't know how he would adjust to me and my 'zoo.'"

Bobby says, "I got off the phone thinking that when my ex-wife and I used to ride together, we carried a cat and a dog with us. I knew how to take care of a cat and would make sure everything went fine." So Bobby told Keith, "Charlotte has other animals at her home. She'll take Kitty-Kat if nothing else works out. But if Kitty-Kat likes my truck and gets comfortable, I'll let him stay with me until you can get him back. That way he won't go through so much upheaval again."

Keith felt wretched over breaking his promise never to abandon Kitty-Kat. But now he could board the bus for Illinois, reunite with Barbara, start rebuilding their lives, and work toward the day when their whole family would be together again. He gave Bobby his cell phone number and a business card, which said, "Keith Nicholson, Bartender, Author, & Ne'er do well."

With a mixture of gratitude and trepidation, Keith handed Kitty-Kat over to Bobby. Then he boarded the bus and continued his journey with a heavy heart. After a thirty-two-hour trip with eight transfers and a lot of dirty looks because of his appearance and smell, he was reunited with Barbara in Springfield, Illinois.

Bobby settled his new passenger in the truck, then drove down the road and spent seventy dollars buying a litter box, dry and canned cat food, cat treats, a few toys, and a cat bed.

Later Bobby said, "Truck drivers get a bad reputation. But most drivers have big hearts. We're out here running down the road for a living. We see nice things and a lot of things nobody likes to see. Most truck drivers love animals. They have good hearts."

Although Bobby opened up his heart to Kitty-Kat, the cat wasn't happy with the new arrangement. Bobby says, "The first day in the truck cabin, he hid. He wouldn't eat. I bought soft cat food and put it in his mouth to get him to eat. I was scared to death of losing him. He was real lethargic. He couldn't move. He would look at me and pant a little bit. I tried to get him to drink water. I put water on my finger and tapped it onto his tongue. Finally he ate and drank."

Eventually Kitty-Kat lay on the truck's countertop, but he wouldn't use the kitty litter box. Instead, he peed on himself and he peed on the carpet. Later Bobby had to replace all the carpet in his truck to get the odor out. But he understood that the cat was traumatized. Bobby believes that Kitty-Kat blamed him for taking him away from Keith. After a couple of days Kitty-Kat finally started using the litter box. At night he lay beside Bobby's bed until Bobby fell asleep. Then he would prowl the truck. He began to get more comfortable in the cabin, climbing up into the cabinets and lying on Bobby's clothes. Bobby left the top bunk down for the cat and allowed him to move freely. But Kitty-Kat stayed away most of the time, only occasionally letting Bobby offer an ear scratch.

One of Bobby's favorite memories is the night he practiced guitar. "I was playing a beginning song from my guitar book, like plucking strings for 'Jingle Bells.' Nothing elaborate. Kitty-Kat came down from his cubbyhole in the cabinet and curled up beside me and watched me play. After I put the guitar up, he climbed back to his perch. It felt like he was saying hello to me but he would like it if I played something a little more upbeat."

About two weeks after Kitty-Kat moved into the truck, he started hissing at Bobby and not using the litter box again. Bobby called Miss Charlotte, and she agreed to take Kitty-Kat to her home and hoped he would adjust to her and her other pets.

Meanwhile, Barbara and Keith had reunited, but they had no long-term plans yet. They were merely surviving day to day. They worried that Bobby Haynes might think they just didn't want Kitty-Kat back, but nothing could have been further from the truth. They missed their cat terribly. Now, though, they had no permanent place to live, no car, no jobs, and no money. Keith says, "We feared that we would never see Kitty-Kat again. Did he understand that I had to leave him at the bus station? Was he afraid? I had constant nightmares, thinking that Kitty-Kat believed I'd lied to him, had abandoned him."

## Months after the Hurricane

Charlotte Williams, the dispatcher, put up a baby gate in her home to keep Kitty-Kat safe from her menagerie. For the first few days at Charlotte's house, Kitty-Kat slept under the bed. Over time he started to eat, drink water, and use his litter box.

After three weeks Kitty-Kat was comfortable and even affectionate. But one day Charlotte noticed that his behavior was changing; he was becoming lethargic. Worried, she took the cat to her veterinarian. Kitty-Kat was diagnosed with a severe urinary infection, which eventually escalated into kidney failure.

Charlotte called Keith and Barb, who authorized the (expensive) treatment, hoping that they would somehow find the money to pay for it. Charlotte was thinking, "This is all Barbara and Keith have of their past life in New Orleans. I can't let anything happen to Kitty-Kat."

Kitty-Kat spent four days at the vet's office on IVs. After Charlotte brought him home, he had to be given a special diet and medication. He pulled through like a champ, improving steadily. Charlotte took up a collection at work to help pay Kitty-Kat's vet bill.

Back in Illinois, reporter Mary Wicoff caught wind of the story. She wrote an article in the *Danville Commercial-News* about Barbara and Keith's long journey and their attempts to keep Kitty-Kat alive. At the end of the article, she gave the veterinarian's address in Little Rock, Arkansas, where Danville readers could send a donation. The vet bill was paid in full.

Kitty-Kat was becoming calmer. He seemed to realize that Charlotte and the other strangers were helping, not hurting, him. To reassure him even more that he had not been forgotten, Barb and Keith talked to Kitty-Kat on the phone each time they called Charlotte.

## Will They Be Reunited?

The last leg of Kitty-Kat's journey involves another trucker, Kat Pate, who drives for Bobby's company and also gets her assignments from Charlotte

Williams, the dispatcher. On Wolf Ranch, her twelve acres in Plumberville, Arkansas, just a short distance from Bobby's home, she has seven dogs, three cats, and three birds, all of them rescues. She'd been kept up to date on Kitty-Kat's plight in her conversations with Bobby and Charlotte, and she sympathized with Keith and Barbara. Kat says, "If I lost any of my animals, I'd be heartbroken."

Two months after Charlotte took Kitty-Kat into her home, Keith and Barbara were ready to ask for their cat back. Charlotte received their request for Kitty-Kat's return with mixed emotions. She knew Kitty-Kat needed to be with them, but, she says, "I kept Kitty-Kat living. He slept next to me. We became very close. It was hard when it was time for him to go back." Another member of Charlotte's family also felt the pain of separation. One of her cats had developed a massive crush on Kitty-Kat.

When Charlotte called Kat Pate to ask her to drive Kitty-Kat to Illinois, Kat says she was happy to do it. But she had one question. She asked Charlotte, "Are you sure about me taking Kitty-Kat back to them? After all, my full name is Katrina. How will they react?" Charlotte replied, "Oh, my god, I never thought about that!"

Barbara was philosophical about the synchronicity. She said, "Katrina took Kitty-Kat away from us, but Katrina brought him back." Charlotte took off work on the day she placed Kitty-Kat into Katrina Pate's safekeeping. She said, "I cried when I put him in his crate and the truck. I was glad he was going home, but I loved him too."

Kat drove off with the cat in her cabin. She opened the door of his carrier. He walked back to Katrina's bed, curled up there, and went to sleep. Katrina thought, "It is almost as if he knows this time not to worry."

Charlotte kept calling Kat from work that night to check on where Kat was, while Charlotte's cat ran around the house calling for his lost friend. On the twelve-hour drive, the gray tabby with the neon green eyes also enchanted Kat. She says, "They are the most beautiful eyes I ever saw on a cat." After a long nap, Kitty-Kat walked to the front of the cabin and jumped onto the seat next to Kat. Kitty-Kat listened as Katrina told him, "I'm taking you home to your mom and daddy. We're almost there." Kitty-Kat meowed in reply. He finally climbed onto Kat's lap. She petted him. He raised his body and put his paws on her chest. Kat says, "I was thinking that this cat understands everything I'm saying. He is really smart. I don't need to talk in cat language to him."

After their heart-to-heart talk, Kitty-Kat went back to bed. Katrina says, "He sat there like he was an old pro at riding a truck." Kitty-Kat kept staring out the window, waiting.

Near Bloomingdale, Illinois, Kat pulled her truck off at Exit 169 and went inside the Truckers of America restaurant. Barb and Keith knew immediately who she was. Kat says, "They were so happy to see me. They were fixin' to get their cat back. They came running up, hugging and thanking me so many times. I told them how Kitty-Kat was doing. It was late at night. We went out to gather him up. I climbed inside the cabin and got the cat from behind the driver's seat where he had made himself at home. I said, 'Your mom and daddy are outside, but you can't go until you get back into this cat carrier.' He walked right into it."

Barbara stood at the door of the truck, and Kat handed Kitty-Kat's carrier to her. Kat observed later, "Once Kitty-Kat was back in Barbara's arms, he was meowing and meowing, like he was telling them all the things he went through while he was gone. He seemed to be saying, 'I'm so happy to be back with you. Let's not ever do a rerun of this.'"

Barb and Keith didn't dally at the truck stop. They said good-bye to Kat, hurried to their car, and drove home. When they arrived, Keith says Kitty-Kat seemed frightened. "He had been through hell and was suffering from separation anxiety and stress from all the driving. We worried it had been too much for him. But the first morning after we got Kitty-Kat

*Keith and Barbara Nicholson and Kitty-Kat, together again.*

back, he played a practical joke on me, just like when we were a family in New Orleans. At 6:45, I heard my hairbrush clang against the inside of the bathroom sink. Then I looked up and saw Kitty-Kat meowing at the top of his lungs while staring at me from his perch in front of the alarm clock. That's when I knew everything was going to be okay. I think this was his way of telling me that he was not angry and that he knew I hadn't abandoned him."

Today Keith is writing a children's book about Kitty-Kat and Hurricane Katrina titled *The Adventures of the Cajun Kitty Kat*. He says, "I already have one PTA president and two school boards chomping at the bit for us to do readings for elementary schools. I hope it will serve as an inspiration for others, and people will understand that pets are members of families."

Since their reunion, Keith says that Kitty-Kat has become more affectionate. He lets Barbara and Keith hold him for extended lengths of time. He constantly leaps on their laps and sleeps on top of their stomachs and chests. Barbara says, "He is now the lap cat I always wanted him to be."

Keith says, "Yes, he missed us and is thankful to be with us again. Kitty-Kat tried to save my life during the hurricane. But now he saves my life every day. He gives me love like I've never known."

# CHAPTER FOUR

# The Doctor, the Actor, the Journalist, and Oprah

What do Oprah Winfrey, Matthew McConaughey, and Cokie Roberts all have in common?

They are all linked to New Orleans's fifty-six-year-old anesthesiologist Dr. James Riopelle. When Hurricane Katrina hit, he was a Louisiana State University faculty member whose department provided anesthesia services for patients at the Lindy Boggs Medical Center Hospital, one of the leading transplant hospitals in the country. Lindy Boggs is named after Corinne Linda Boggs, the first Louisiana woman elected to the House of Representatives, after the death of her husband, Thomas Hale Boggs Sr., who previously held the seat. Lindy Boggs is also the mother of journalist Cokie Roberts.

Where do Oprah and Matthew McConaughey, *People* magazine's Sexiest Man Alive for 2005, come into the picture? And what do they all have to do with the animals? Read on!

## Before the Hurricane

Dr. James Riopelle is known in Louisiana for being an animal advocate. He and his wife, dentist and part-time professor of dentistry Dr. Jamie

Manders, have been married since 1982. Dr. Riopelle moved from Madison, Wisconsin, and has lived in Louisiana since he was in eighth grade. His wife is a native. They have fed (and neutered) as many as twenty stray dogs and cats at a time at their home on the West Bank of New Orleans. Before Katrina hit they lived there with two frail and elderly housecats, Butterscotch and, Jamie's favorite, a Persian named Calista, who would place both of her paws in one of Jamie's hands as they fell asleep each night.

Dr. Riopelle is the past president of Coalition of Louisiana Animal Advocates, a statewide animal organization. During his tenure there he organized protests against cockfighting and tried to get legislation passed at the state level to ban the activity. He also cowrote a bilingual Cajun American children's song, "Don't Crow, Little Red, Chante Pas, 'Ti Rouge," with verses alternating between Cajun French and English. It was based on a newspaper clipping that a friend sent to him about a little boy who tried to save his bird from being put into a cockfighting pit. The boy sings to the bird and warns him not to crow so he won't be found. The song was played on Cajun radio stations all over the state. Dr. Riopelle's efforts have not been successful so far, and Louisiana is one of the few states where this violent activity remains legal.

On the day before Hurricane Katrina was expected to make landfall, Lindy Boggs Hospital invited the staff to bring their families, human and animal, to the facility. This had become standard practice during hurricanes in order to keep the hospital adequately staffed. Dr. Riopelle took his wife, her mother, and Butterscotch and Calista to Lindy Boggs for the hurricane. The two cats needed daily medical care, especially Butterscotch, who was suffering from renal failure and required subcutaneous IV fluids. Dr. Riopelle left five other cats the couple was caring for on the second story of their home with a week's worth of food and water.

The hospital staff and all the patients made it through the storm in their sturdy building with no problems. They had electricity, plenty of food and water, and enough medical supplies. The day after the hurricane, though, they noticed that although the weather was clearing up, water was streaming toward the hospital. Unaware that the New Orleans levees had broken, they were puzzled by this turn of events. Worry grew to alarm when water rose and eventually flooded the basement of the hospital.

Everyone at the hospital believed that the government authorities would soon be sending a boat to evacuate them. But they started hearing word that snipers were shooting rescuers and that police were confiscating any boats to prevent unauthorized persons from entering the area. Hospital staff thus could not call friends and neighbors with boats to come and evacuate the patients.

The staff moved all the patients to the second floor. Then the emergency generator failed. Suddenly they were without water and electricity. The staff switched patients on breathing apparatuses to special oxygen-powered machines that required no electricity. Food was running out. The chief of emergency medicine contacted the hospital administrators at Tenet Louisiana and told them that they had to evacuate the patients. The strategy was that the sickest patients would go first.

After a few days the Shreveport Fire Department arrived at the hospital with different priorities. They were under instructions to tell the staff that the sickest patients wouldn't be taken out at all. Instead the staff and families would leave first, along with patients who could climb into a boat or helicopter on their own. The other patients would not be evacuated for the foreseeable future. Dr. Riopelle says, "The entire city needed evacuation at that time. Tens of thousands of people were trapped. No one was talking or even thinking about evacuating the animals that were at the hospital."

The staff now had to tell terrified patients and families that the sickest ones would be left behind. It was a heart-wrenching task. Dr. Riopelle says, "The hospital people had patients as the priority. The government authorities got their way."

Jamie and her mother, who has Alzheimer's and was incapable of evacuating on her own, prepared to go with the hospital staff. They caught a ride with a stranger to Baton Rouge.

The staff all hugged each other and cried over having to leave their patients and pets behind. They gave their resident animal lover, Dr. Riopelle, instructions for the pets' care. They handed him master keys for rooms so he could move the animals around in the building as needed. Dr. Riopelle told them he would stay as long as necessary to take care of their pets. He promised he would not fail, short of being arrested, handcuffed, and physically removed from the premises by authorities. Now there was plenty of food and water. Tenet human resources director Sherry Amberson had had food helicoptered to the hospital roof. Five of her dogs also were at the hospital.

One of the local firemen was keeping ten animals in an adjacent building but had moved them to Lindy Boggs after the storm. He gave Dr. Riopelle a gun and told him to use it if looters invaded the hospital.

## Most of the Patients and Staff Leave

Now only Dr. Riopelle, nurse Cheryl Martin, respiratory therapist Jody Pattison, Catholic priest Father Ignatius Rappolo, about twenty patients, and sixty or seventy animals remained at Lindy Boggs. One of the transplant surgeons, Dr. Thiagarajan Ramcharan, left the hospital to find a boat and retrieve two of his patients and their family members. Jessie LaSalle kept vigil with her husband, Carl LaSalle, who had just had a liver and kidney transplant. Elaine Bass waited with her daughter, Laticia Young, a twenty-eight-year-old woman with liver disease who was in the hospital awaiting a new liver but was too unstable yet to receive one. Both patients were critically ill. Dr. Riopelle offered Elaine Bass a small dose of morphine to ease Laticia's pain. Afraid that the morphine might kill her daughter, she refused. These remaining family members feared that their loved ones had been left in the hospital to die.

The pharmacy was locked, which was standard evacuating procedure. The only medication available was enough morphine to euthanize the forty-five dogs, two guinea pigs, and fifteen cats that the staff and patients had left at the hospital should this drastic measure become necessary to end their suffering. In the coming days Dr. Riopelle would do everything in his power to make certain it did not.

Dr. Riopelle tells what happened next.

We split up the work. Wendy Smith, a nurse anesthetist, worked with the animals in other parts of the building. The priest and I did as much as we could for the patients. There was not much we could do except give the patients water and keep them clean. Every day Father Rappolo would say prayers for them as we went from patient to patient. Being an agnostic, I just added, "Amen."

Cheryl and Jody organized the animal sheltering and set up two large dog runs. I collected leftover peanut butter and bread for the dogs' dinners at night.

Wendy called her sister who is a pharmacist in Lafayette. She told the staff how much bleach to use to make the water potable. We drained all the water left in the building and cleaned and filled large trash cans with it. We put the required amount of bleach in and covered the cans. The water would be usable within twelve hours.

On the third day that we were left there, one of the ICU patients died. It was beastly hot at over one hundred degrees in the daytime and the high nineties at night.

All around, there were signs of human effort and great heroism. The sky was filled with what looked like a swarm of giant mosquitoes. Thirty to forty helicopters flew in the air all day and late into the night.

I heard a loud noise outside my windows. I saw a helicopter hovering just above the treetops. This little line came down. A guy bound a small woman or child with ropes, like a spider wrapping up a fly, and then he gave the up sign to the pilot. The helicopter lifted the soldier and his charge, and they flew away. Great heroism went on all around. At no time did I feel like we were unique. All around, people were in horrible situations, and they were doing wonderful things to help. The spirit of the moment was very positive.

On Thursday, September 1, Dr. Ramcharan had commandeered a boat and came back with it to the hospital with one of the administrators. They helped his two patients onto the boat. Jessie LaSalle ventilated her husband, Carl, with a ventilation bag.

Soon the pilots from Aviation Services and DynCorp, Tenet's private security force, came back for the rest of the staff and all the living patients. I was ordered to leave along with Jody, Cheryl, Wendy, and Father Rappolo.

Dr. Riopelle refused to leave. He had made a promise to take care of the animals. Plus, his two cats needed him.

Prior to this last group of staff and patients leaving, most of the staff had evacuated earlier and some had left their animals in Dr. Riopelle's care. At that time, an unfortunate decision was made that haunts him to this day. He could not assure everyone that their pets would be absolutely safe. After all, looting and shooting were taking place and fires were breaking out, and no one knew how long this dangerous situation would last. Dr. Riopelle could get injured or killed. The animals could be burned if the building caught fire or die if he became injured.

These concerns led a husband and wife to insist that Dr. Riopelle euthanize their two dogs for fear that after they left, the animals would suffer if something went terribly wrong. Dr. Riopelle repeatedly pleaded with the couple not to take this preemptive action, but they explained that they had considered the factors very carefully and had agonized over the decision. They believed it was the only humane thing to do. Dr. Riopelle says, "Everything was going from bad to worse. If I had known that help would come in time to save the animals, it might have been different. As it is, I regret acquiescing to their request. I could not promise any of the pet owners anything other than that through the dark and scary times, I would stay and take care of the animals as long as I was physically able to do so and not forced to leave."

Now that all the patients and families were gone, he and the animals were alone, hoping that help would soon be on the way.

## Alone with the Animals

Dr. Riopelle was concerned about several things. He had to run up and down stairs, often in the dark, to care for the animals, and he could fall. This would have tragic consequences. He feared that looters might overtake the building. But most frightening were the fires breaking out on every horizon. Natural gas lines had broken. If the hospital filled up with gas and ignited, it would turn into a torch. He was also concerned about dysentery, since human waste was everywhere. He was careful never to touch his face or food without first using a sanitary wipe.

He had been able to communicate with Jamie about his decision to stay. Thirty seconds each day he used the push-to-talk function on the cell phone. Since the battery was low, with no way to recharge, all communication had to be to the point and practical. Jamie was worried but understood and supported him. Now in Houston, she was going on the Internet and writing to everyone — hospital authorities, animal groups, government officials, media, anyone who would help — to get her husband and the animals safely out of the hospital.

Meanwhile, Kent Glenn of Aledo Veterinary Clinic, outside Dallas, was making arrangements with the Tenet Louisiana officials to evacuate Dr. Riopelle and the animals by air. It was to be very expensive, involving a hundreds-of-dollars-per-minute helicopter and private security guards.

On the day the chopper came, Tom Uglialoro, head of Aviation Services, and Dr. Riopelle along with staff of DynCorp loaded all the animals onto a metal boat and took them to a makeshift landing at the post office parking lot. Dr. Riopelle called this place Post Office Island. They worked against time, racing up and down the stairs from the fifth floor, where the animals were housed, to the boat to Post Office Island. It grew later and darker. They had to maneuver the boat through shrubs, trees, signs, fire hydrants, and submerged objects. They couldn't move forward more than ten feet without getting sucked into the debris and having to use the boat's oars to break free. It took many trips to bring all of the animals to the island. Dr. Riopelle was exhausted but relieved that the ordeal was about to end.

He and Tom stood on the loading dock at the back of the hospital facing the island and watched the helicopter arrive. Another helicopter was taking off from this landing pad while theirs was coming down. The downwash from the exiting chopper caused the landing helicopter to tip over on its side and hit the ground. To their horror, the chopper's engine exploded. They feared that the pilot had been killed, but he managed to get out and run to safety.

Demoralized and totally exhausted, Dr. Riopelle and Tom had to return all the animals to the hospital that night. Dr. Riopelle says, "This was probably my emotional low point. I didn't know if there would be another helicopter. When the pilot and Tom left, they didn't say they would be back tomorrow for any future rescue efforts."

Dr. Riopelle was left alone with the animals on the first floor of the building. Upstairs, they'd had dog runs and separate spaces, but now they were in cages. All night long police boats salvaged valuable equipment from the crashed helicopter on Post Office Island. Dr. Riopelle tried to find a cool area to sleep in by lying on the deck of a metal boat that was tied to what used to be a truck loading dock at the back of the hospital. Feeling sorry for the animals, he started letting them out of their cages, allowing the dogs to move about the loading dock and a large adjacent room in the hospital. The dogs were stressed and began fighting with each other. One of them fell into the water near the boat. Dr. Riopelle reached down to pull him up. He heard his glasses plunk into the water but in the dark was unable to find them. He dried off the dog just as it started to rain.

Dr. Riopelle had to rearrange the dogs, cats, and two guinea pigs into rooms, putting together the animals who would be compatible. There was nowhere for them to relieve themselves except on the floors. The stench grew unbearable. He couldn't risk trying to return so many excitable and strong animals to the fifth floor in the dark since they could escape into the general hospital building and miss out on feedings and waterings. If he fell and broke a leg on the wet staircase as the big dogs pulled him along, he would die of thirst before anyone found him.

He checked on his old friend, Butterscotch. She was frail but hanging in there. By two o'clock in the morning, Dr. Riopelle thought he had the animals settled and would be able to sleep. At least he could rest until dawn, when the animals would wake up and need to be fed.

The next day he was awakened by the sound of a helicopter landing on the hospital's roof. He ran up and was greeted by a man he thought must be a reporter because he was asking a lot of questions. This turned out to be the actor Matthew McConaughey. Oprah Winfrey was doing a show on location from Mississippi. She and Tenet Louisiana had gotten together to send Matthew and a cameraman, as well as an Aviation Services crew and men from DynCorp. They were there to bring Dr. Riopelle and the animals out of the hospital.

With the camera rolling, Matthew said, "You're the doctor that's been here over a week. You've stayed here with the dogs. Said you weren't gonna leave until you got the dogs out safely."

Dr. Riopelle said, "And cats."

"And cats," Matthew agreed.

"I heard you're taking them all," Dr. Riopelle said. "I'm so deeply grateful. I'm tired. I wasn't sure I could go much longer. I'm mighty glad to get out. It's been exhausting. Extremely glad to be rescued."[1]

Now the process started all over again. Time was of the essence; Dr. Riopelle didn't want any animals left behind. With Matthew's and the DynCorp security men's help, Dr. Riopelle made as many as twenty trips up and down steps and from room to room, racing at top speed and carrying animals and loading them onto hospital boats to take them to Post Office Island landing for airlifts. He says, "The DynCorp guys were major players in the animal evacuation. Despite their thick black uniforms and very heavy weaponry, they ran up and down the hospital stairs, carrying animals. It was a beastly task." About Matthew McConaughey, he says, "Matthew was quiet and very good at driving the boat. Much better than I was."

They packed the animals into the Huey helicopter and tied them to seat posts, since there wasn't enough room for cages. Dr. Riopelle's two cats were among those loaded onto the helicopter.

This long day there was a torturous wait as the helicopter took the first load of animals to North Shore Hospital in Slidell and then returned for another load. Meanwhile, one of the DynCorp guys put out liquid illuminators to help the helicopter land safely. The last airlift of animals took place in the pitch-dark.

## After the Airlift

Dr. Riopelle and Jamie's cats were brought to North Shore Hospital in Hattiesburg, Mississippi. Unfortunately, the stress of the evacuation had been too much for the sickly Butterscotch, and the cat died en route. Calista, Jamie's special friend, was dehydrated. A doctor saw the cat looking extremely agitated and gave her Valium, thinking this would calm her. It had a disastrous effect on the tiny three-pound cat, and she began staggering around. The veterinarian who next examined Calista didn't know about the Valium and thought she had suffered a stroke from the trauma of the hurricane. Believing Calista was suffering, he euthanized her.

Later Dr. Riopelle told us, "Of all the animals that I kept at the hospital, only our two cats died. I felt nauseated when I heard what happened. I don't hold it against the doctor or the vet. They made an ill-advised judgment call. Everybody felt like they did what they had to do amid all the chaos." His wife, Jamie, is still in mourning. She is sorry that her husband ever let their cats out of his sight.

Dr. Riopelle was also airlifted to North Shore Hospital, where a bizarre twist to this story occurred. Although he was recovering physically, the hospital doctors refused to let him leave and ordered him to be evaluated by a psychiatrist. Still grateful that Tenet Louisiana had airlifted the animals and him out of Lindy Boggs, he cooperated fully with the evaluation but was startled and somewhat amused by the conclusions.

Dr. Riopelle says, "I believed they were keeping me at North Shore because they thought anybody who stayed with the animals must be nuts. I was upset because my wife had asked me to get back to New Orleans to bring more food and water for our own animals, and I couldn't leave without a competent adult to accompany me. The psychiatrist told Jamie he was concerned that I might be obsessing about our cats."

Jamie called her sister Alison, who is married to the St. Tammany Parish coroner, Dr. Peter Galvan. Dr. Galvan came to help Dr. Riopelle get released from the hospital and flew him in his private plane to Texas, where he was reunited with Jamie. Meanwhile, she had contacted their neighbors in New Orleans and learned that they were using a key she had given them to feed and water the five cats left at home, and the cats were all in good shape.

After Dr. Riopelle was released from the hospital, he got a call from Bob Davis, a reporter writing a story for *USA Today* about the drama of keeping critically ill patients alive at Lindy Boggs Hospital. Dr. Riopelle recounted his story. By this time, *The Oprah Winfrey Show* had been televised, showing Dr. Riopelle and Matthew McConaughey's segment.

After Dr. Riopelle did the interview, Bob Davis's reporter partner called back. He said, "It must have been really awful having to kill all those patients at the hospital. It's got to be hard for a doctor to euthanize patients."

Dr. Riopelle asked, "What patients?"

He was thinking back to the time at the hospital when he and the priest, Father Ignatius Rappolo, went around every day bringing water and changing bed linens. He recalled that the patients were frightened about not being evacuated. He realized that some of them must have gotten the idea that they were going to be killed. Since he was the last doctor there, an anesthesiologist, they must have jumped to the conclusion that he would become Dr. Death.

When Elaine Bass, whose daughter, Laticia, was awaiting a transplant, saw Dr. Riopelle on the Oprah show, she screamed that he was the one who was going around to all the patients and giving them the needle. Since he had offered the bit of morphine to ease her daughter's pain, she must have assumed that she had to protect Laticia from him.

Dr. Riopelle says, "That was the mental attitude of the place. That's how scared people were." He adds wryly that sometimes "no good deed goes unpunished."

Now Dr. Riopelle had to deal with accusations that while he was working to keep the animals safe and the remaining patients alive, he was actually murdering sick people. He needed to talk to the authorities in Baton Rouge, meet with the attorney general's office, convince the reporters at *USA Today*, and rely on the corroborating testimony of the transplant surgeon, Dr. Ramcharan, and the Catholic priest that he was only changing people's linens, not trying to kill them. The *USA Today* article, when it was published on September 15, said, "Riopelle and Ramcharan say the dosage [of the morphine Dr. Riopelle offered to Elaine Bass for her daughter] was small and would have caused no harm. But both understand why the women might have feared otherwise. Having already been passed over and with no rescue in sight, the families believed they had been left there to die."[2]

Dr. Riopelle was cleared of any and all suspicions. He says, "Every time you think this story is over, there is some kind of weird act coming on."

Soon Dr. Riopelle and his wife were able to return to their home on the West Bank. It suffered rain damage but no flooding.

He says, "What I did was nothing in comparison to what the volunteers did and continue to do. Pam Leavy and her husband drove to New Orleans from Baton Rouge every day and put out food and water for the animals in the northeast and continue to do so. Volunteers flew in from all over the United States and Canada to walk, feed, and find homes for the animals. They spent months searching house to house for people's pets. This is awesome. They often slept on rocks or concrete. They worked long hours. They are the people who deserve the greatest credit. That my story has certain interesting, dramatic features gives it a disproportionate appeal. These people make me proud to be a person."

Today Dr. Riopelle continues to be part of the large Louisiana Tenet health care system. In the course of doing hospital work, he meets people who went through Hurricane Katrina and says about them, "They all have incredible stories to tell."

# CHAPTER FIVE

# What It's Like to Rescue Animals in Disasters

Rescuing animals in disasters can provide thrilling experiences like nothing else in life. Repeatedly rescuers told us of chasing fleeing animals or being threatened by frightened, territorial ones only to later hold these animals in their arms and watch them morph back into somebody's pet. Dogs lean against a rescuer's chest and heave a sigh of relief at the loving experience of being embraced in the arms of someone who cares. Gratitude fills the eyes of animals who drink and eat for the first time in days or even weeks. There is absolutely nothing in the world quite like it.

In the aftermath of a disaster like a hurricane, flood, fire, or earthquake, animal rescuers are peeking behind bushes, carrying catchpoles that look like oversized butterfly nets, and crawling underneath houses and buildings. They are climbing ladders, shoving in air conditioners to get inside windows, forcing their way into houses where pets have been stranded. While people rescuers are attuned to human voices — shouts, whimpers, weeping — animal rescuers listen for barking, growling, mewing, chirping, squawking, neighing, clawing, and cawing. They look for paw prints, not footprints. They walk and drive through city streets that may be so silent not even a bird is chirping. Most often, people describe the experience as surreal.

The following stories offer an overview of what animal rescues and reunions feel like for the people who facilitate them. The stories hardly begin to communicate the drama, the joy, the heartbreak experienced by those who rescue animals from disasters.

## Spirit of the Animals

Karen O'Toole is a screenwriter from Paradise Valley, Arizona. Her screenplay *Wild Horses* won the prestigious Nicholl Fellowship from the Academy of Motion Picture Arts and Sciences. She is a member of the Writers Guild of America and was the production manager for the Golden Globe–winning and Academy Award–nominated film *Transamerica*, among many others. When we spoke with her, Karen talked about the lifelong work she has done and continues to do for animals and humans. She is on the board of the International Society for the Protection of Mustangs and Burros. She works for orphaned children in Cambodia and rescues wildlife in the Amazon and Asian elephants in Thailand.

Karen told us, "I'm trying to give you insight into a rescuer's time in New Orleans and the animals we touched and how they touched us. Ask me anything about the spirit of the animals. We have lived and breathed the world of the animals, alone with them all day, all night. They were animals in their most concentrated state, when the purest of the animal was visible. Naked, desperate, this is no longer a pet going through its normal daily routine. This is now an animal lost in the wilderness. The same with the rescuers. We were people lost in a torrid, uncharted land. Animal and human alike, we all had our souls sticking out through torn, burning holes in our hearts."

In New Orleans Karen worked first as a freelance rescuer with the groups that set up shop in a Winn-Dixie parking lot. Later she turned into a premier volunteer with the MuttShack Animal Rescue Foundation operation at Lake Castle Elementary School. She earned the nickname "GI Jane" from a fellow rescuer and F-18 fighter pilot Mike Pagano for her proficiency at swiftly pulling out trapped animals from flooded and destroyed homes and apartments. Her first trip to New Orleans lasted seven weeks. She returned there several more times.

She writes,

> This is a city full of dying animals. Often you could be the only person who will find a certain pet. All of us have stories about the animals we "accidentally" stumbled across. You'd get lost and find a mother and puppies. You'd go to the wrong house and find rabbits trapped in their cages on the kitchen table. It was often serendipity or fate that rescued the animal.
>
> I remember following a cat into a backyard and noticing a small wooden shed in a neighbor's backyard. Suddenly a head popped out of a tiny hole gnawed in the bottom of the door. A dog had dug himself a hole just big enough to stick out his head and watch the world go by. If I had not been in New Orleans, it's probable that he would never have been found. We all *had* to be there.

One of Karen's most profound memories is when Tami, a twenty-three-year-old pregnant woman, approached her in a parking lot in St. Bernard Parish. Tami asked Karen for help with her dog, Sasha. She said that she had rescued Sasha before the hurricane. Sasha and Tami had been living in a car for two months.

Tami cried as she handed Karen the beautiful black-and-white dog who was licking the tears off her face. She said that she could no longer keep the dog because she needed to start living in the FEMA tents. She didn't want to put the dog in "the system" and hoped that Karen would help her find a permanent home for the dog, who had become such a good friend.

Karen didn't know what to do. How would she find a home for this dog when everyone she was meeting in this city was now homeless?

Karen got busy on her phone, calling everyone she could think of. One connection led to another, and she got through to a woman named Tina, who lived twenty-five miles outside the city. Tina was having many troubles herself but she said that she wanted to help the poor young woman. So Tina generously offered to foster Sasha.

After driving the twenty-five miles to bring Sasha to her new foster mom, Karen found Tina waiting for her. Karen opened her car door. Sasha, still on her leash, took one look at Tina, jumped out of Karen's car, and dragged Karen toward Tina's car. Karen heard Tina screaming with delight.

Turns out, Tina had lost her dog six months earlier. Heartbroken, she had searched for the dog everywhere. She had assumed the dog was dead and that she would never see her again.

Who was the dog she had agreed to foster? None other than Tina's very own lost dog, Gabby. Karen says, "Tami found the dog, took her in, loved her, and had to give her up. Tina decided to foster the dog. This decision led to the dog's original owner being reunited with her lost dog. In all the world, that these two should find each other again was miraculous. Tina could have refused to help Tami. She would have stayed heartbroken. She would have hung up the phone and never known that I had her dog, Gabby."

## Let's Hear It for the Quiet Heroes

Many of the volunteers we spoke with found satisfaction, even joy, in caring for the physical and emotional needs of animals who had been through so many traumas. Volunteers unloaded trucks and sorted supplies. They drove vans and trucks and lifted crates with animals in them onto airplanes. They made phone calls and spent hours on the Internet searching for clues to evacuees' and lost animals' whereabouts. They also often had the thrill of seeing people and pets brought back together. Universally, everyone was grateful for the pooper scoopers, cage cleaners, intake coordinators, and dog walkers of the animal rescue scene.

Melissa McGehee Smith, an engineer from Lubbock, Texas, says, "The greatest feeling in the world is to rescue an animal. No matter if it's a dramatic rescue in a devastated area like New Orleans or happening upon a neighborhood stray who has been hit by a car. You've gone beyond yourself to help in a situation for which you may never get a thank-you. But you know that the animal you have helped has another chance at life. This makes the effort totally and completely worth it."

Nikki Morris is a Wachovia bank systems analyst who volunteered with both Animal Rescue New Orleans, on Magazine Street, and the Best Friends temporary shelter in Tylertown, Mississippi. She writes about the important work of caring for the animals who are brought in to a temporary shelter.

The animals, especially dogs with frightened, hopeless eyes (kitties try to hide their feelings) — just give them time, when the daily duties are done. Try to find the right word or words. They tremble and are afraid to come out of their crates. And to go back in.

My first trip to New Orleans was seven weeks or more after Katrina. It hadn't rained in that long. No puddles to drink from. Few residents, so not much garbage for the homeless animals to scavenge.

I met a brindle pit [bull]. They said it would take two to walk him. He was in a weakened condition and had a band underneath his bottom to keep his legs up and walking. I was in front of him. I asked that the band be removed and to leave us alone, finally, to talk.

"What did your human say to you? 'Good Boy'? 'Who wants a biscuit'?" Just words, but hoping I'd strike the right chord.

We spent at least an hour. "Remember the smell of grass before the bad thing happened? Look! There's the moon, just as it was. Remember being loved? You were, and you are still. Do you want to take me for a walk? And remember smells? (No, it's not about being the alpha here.)"

The dog got up. His back legs shook and wobbled, but he gained strength. He sniffed this and that. He even got some spring into his step.

I was so happy. Yes, I will admit to being happy.

The gang all came out and clapped. The Dog Whisperer, they called me. Fun and cute. But the truth is, he is the one with the secrets and memories that he can't share.

Another diligent cage cleaner, Ann Jordon from Oakboro, North Carolina, writes,

I walked dogs, cleaned kennels, fed, transported, networked, and supplied food for locations in New Orleans. I can make a difference, even

if it is only for one more, then one more after that, and so on. I like seeing the animals' eyes light up when I come to feed and clean their
cages. They know they are going to be taken care of and get a little
attention. I also like seeing them reunite with their owners.

Quiet moments filtered throughout animal rescue as people gained
the skills of seasoned detectives in the privacy of their own homes. Marilyn Knapp Litt, a bold Texas woman who isn't easily dissuaded from
whatever she wants to accomplish, formed a band of Internet sleuths she
calls Stealth Volunteers. After the hurricanes, their ranks swelled to as
many as one thousand. Marilyn says,

We were even able to educate the animal shelters. We would call a
shelter to tell them that we had found the owner of one of the animals
they brought back from Hurricane Katrina. They would ask how we did
it. I'd tell them I went to LexisNexis and found a family obituary from five
years ago. Then I found the out-of-state relatives mentioned in it and
traced the animal's owner. This was revolutionary. We were not waiting
for owners to find us. We were doing research, and I think we helped
with a lot of reunions, some that we never knew about.

## The Climbers and Crawlers

Trained animal rescue crews, decked out in safety equipment and sweltering in the New Orleans and Mississippi heat with their hip waders,
cargo pants, and heavy boots, were a hardy lot. They carefully followed
safety-first procedures and took care of themselves and the animals in the
process of rescuing them.

Many other people, though, did not go through training but came to
help with the best of intentions. They experienced unforgettable things
that, to a person, they said changed their lives. They found in themselves
unidentified strengths, new muscles, and nerves of steel. They weren't always
as careful as they could have been, but they were certainly determined.

Rachel McKay Laskowski is an antique art dealer from Collegeville,
Pennsylvania. One of the highlights for her was when she gave a belly rub

to a rottweiler whom neighbors considered vicious and showed that the dog was really a sweetheart.

Jane Blythe, a volunteer from Florida, explains what it was like for a sixty-year-old woman to be on an animal rescue team in New Orleans. She says,

> We would jump out of the car, run through debris-filled lots, set up plastic-covered wire netting around the places where the animals were cowering (usually under houses, sometimes in bushes). The two older men and one young woman would crawl under the filthy buildings — petting, stroking, gently pulling out the dogs. It took endless patience and love, and the trau-matized dogs would calm down so quickly. One time we found starving dogs running in a deserted schoolyard, trying to get away by jumping over the six-foot-high wire fences that were capped with barbed wire.
>
> After we would catch the animals, we would place them in cages, transport them back to the site. They would be fed and watered, given TLC, and delivered to a sanctuary in Mississippi that night. The fright-ened animals responded beautifully to kindness and love. I felt it was an honor to meet the extraordinarily dedicated volunteers who saved their lives. They are true animal lovers.

## Frustrating, Tiring Work

Animal rescuers, when they sign up for the joys of the work, also open themselves to its hardships: lack of sleep, bone-wearying fatigue, guaran-teed horror, and overstimulation of every one of their five senses. In rescue work nothing ever goes quite as planned. After Hurricane Katrina, this principle couldn't have been more true.

Laura Brown, manager of domestic animal and wildlife rescue and information for People for the Ethical Treatment of Animals (PETA), felt frustrated by the delays that rescuers had to endure when they desperately wanted to move into the city to save animals. She says of her work,

> In the first couple of days of our rescue work, I used a crowbar to pry open a boarded-up home and pull out a starving, terrified dog who somehow survived for two weeks on old garbage. While fighting

nausea from the stench of contaminated floodwaters, I spotted a terrified chow chow with his left eye missing. He hid in sewage collected under his crushed home. I coaxed him to safety. While military helicopters roared overhead, I gathered a starving dog in my arms and gave her her first drink of fresh water in more than a week. I waded through waist-deep, noxious water to reach an emaciated pit bull stranded on a feces-covered porch. I fed fifty lovebirds and finches I found standing on the remains of their cage mates. And I searched for telephone bills in these homes, hoping to find numbers that would lead to the people who were surely frantic about their animals.

Then there is the sheer relentlessness the work requires.

Terri Crisp, founder of Noah's Wish, is a two-time book author and veteran of seventy disasters. She created the Emergency Animal Rescue Service in 1988 for United Animal Nations and continues to help animals during disasters through Noah's Wish. Many volunteers and staff people from animal organizations told us that they got into animal rescue work after reading one of Terri's books or attending her trainings. Her experience with Hurricane Andrew, as told in her first book, *Out of Harm's Way*, was typical of Hurricane Katrina volunteers as well:

Hurricane Andrew taught me the true meaning of being tired. After three weeks at the MASH unit I was exhausted, both mentally and physically. At the end of the day, which usually arrived around 3:00 AM, I would collapse on one of the bunks in the motor home, thinking, I'll never be able to get up at five.

But I did.

The dogs were our alarm clock. All it took was for one of the early birds to begin stirring, and then the rest of them would start in with their relentless barking. Any attempt to drown out their pleas to be walked failed.

Half awake, I'd roll out of bed, still wearing the clothes I'd fallen asleep in just a few hours before. I'd yank on my knee-high rubber boots as I stumbled out the door. I always considered it quite an accomplishment when I managed to get the correct foot in the correct boot. There were a couple of times, though, that I'd gone through half a day before I realized I'd gotten my shoes on the wrong feet. It was easy not to notice the discomfort. When your entire body aches, you lose the ability to pinpoint pain.[1]

## The Dog Who Rescued Her Animal Family

Kathryn Armand and her husband, David, lived in Chalmette in St. Bernard Parish. They had to stay through the storm because David worked for the St. Bernard water and sewage system as an environmental lab technician, a position considered essential in an emergency.

At the time of the hurricane the Armand household included their sixteen-year-old son, Kraig, who has birth defects and severe asthma and allergies, and a Lab-mix puppy, Katie, a gift to Kraig from his older brother. Fortunately, Katie hadn't set off Kraig's allergies, and the two were the joy of their home. The teenager delighted in teaching the smart puppy how to give high-fives, jump through a hula hoop, ring a bell, and play fetch — all through hand gestures. The family also included a blue-and-white beta fish named Nemo, a red lovebird named Tweetie, whom Kathryn had raised by hand-feeding, and Bandit, a fourteen-year-old black Chihuahua with hardly any teeth or fur left. The Armands always considered Katie to be a loyal friend but had no idea how far this virtue would extend until it was put to the ultimate test.

When the hurricane and flood hit, the Armands hunkered down in their second-story apartment with Katie and the rest of their pets. After five feet of water reached their floor and then flooded it deep, the Armands helped other people who floated out of their apartments and were swimming into the Amands' second-story windows. The people were being trailed by biting garfish. When rescue boats arrived, the Armands realized they too had to evacuate. Kathryn's husband had had heart surgery a few years prior, and Kraig was having an asthma attack. One of the rescuers, a deputy Kathryn knew, advised her and her family to leave immediately. It was pitch-black. Anything could go wrong. The Armands put pet food out for the two dogs and hoisted the birdcage and fishbowl onto the highest part of the attic. With great trepidation and sorrow, they left their beloved animals behind.

The Armands' journey took many twists and turns. By the time Kathryn spoke to us, from San Antonio, Texas, the wonderful Renee Harris at the San Diego Humane Society and SPCA had facilitated the Armands' reunion with Katie. Sergeant Loy, a San Diego HS and SPCA officer, brought Katie to the Armands' door in Texas.

Katie had been rescued on September 16 and taken to the Lamar-Dixon Expo Center, where San Diego HS and SPCA employees and volunteers staffed the intake center. Katie was critically ill with parvo virus. After Katie was transported to the San Diego shelter, she was nursed back to health with blood transfusions, medications, and supportive therapy. Renee also located Nemo, Tweetie, and Bandit, the Armands' other pets. San Diego HS and SPCA had the satisfaction of facilitating the reunion of this entire animal and human family.

The reason this story has such a happy ending, though, is not only because of the generosity of so many human rescuers. Katie is the one who made it all possible.

Rescuers told Kathryn Armand that when they came to the apartment building and found Katie, the dog refused to get into the boat with them. The old Chihuahua, Bandit, scurried right in; he was worn out by the ordeal and hanging on by only a thread. Katie, though, kept scooting deeper into the apartment. This forced the rescuers to follow her. That's how they discovered the apartment's attic, where the Armands had placed Tweetie's birdcage and Nemo's bowl on a top shelf.

The bird and the fish remained silent. Katie knew that the rescuers would have no way of knowing they were there. It was only after the rescuers brought Tweetie and Nemo out, where Bandit was already getting comfortable, that loyal Katie followed the rest of her family into the boat. Kathryn says, "Katie is our little hero!"

In the next chapters you will discover how the three largest and most influential animal organizations in the world affect your life in ways you may never have imagined.

## CHAPTER SIX

# Over a Century of Making a Difference

Many groups are devoted to protecting animals and advocating for their welfare. But three of them have become the largest animal welfare and protection organizations in the world. We call them the Big Three.

Even if you don't live near New York, Washington, DC, or Colorado, where these groups are headquartered, you and your animal friends are still benefiting from their work. If you buy pet food, they make sure the ingredients are safe. If you like films that feature animals, they contribute to your moviegoing pleasure. If you eat bacon, eggs, milk, or anything that could have been raised on industrialized factory farms, they are vigilant in ensuring that the animals were treated humanely prior to their deaths. If you have a dog or cat or horse or chicken or iguana — any kind of animal that could be found in an American home, ranch, or farm — these three groups influence how you treat them.

Along with other national animal welfare and animal rights organizations like PETA, the Doris Day Animal League, and others, the three giants protect and defend animals by lobbying for laws that govern what you can and cannot do to an animal entrusted to your care. They provide education packets to teachers of your children so the next generations will be kind to animals. They help politicians get elected who will pass animal welfare and protection laws that they support. The Big Three are the American Society for the Prevention of Cruelty to Animals, the American Humane Association, and the Humane Society of the United States. In the next three chapters we'll take a closer look at each of these groups.

## The Great Meddler

In 1866 Henry Bergh won a nickname that millions of Americans today who love animals and fight for their welfare would proudly wear. Henry Bergh was known as the Great Meddler. On a warm April evening that year, Henry Bergh was strolling the streets in New York City when he saw a man unmercifully beating a team of horses. Bergh stepped up to the man and informed him quietly that as of that day, April 19, 1866, the man was breaking the law by beating his horses. The man was dumbfounded; treating your own animals however you liked had been part of American life as long as anyone remembered. But Bergh had proof: just that day the New York State legislature, after months of lobbying by Bergh, had passed an anticruelty law.

Bergh was a wealthy man who had traveled in Europe and been a diplomat at the Russian court of Czar Alexander II. On his way home from this assignment, Bergh had visited with the Earl of Harrowby, president of England's Royal Society for the Prevention of Cruelty to Animals, an organization the earl had founded in 1840. Armed with the earl's knowledge of how a nation's animals could be protected, Bergh returned to the United States and spoke eloquently in New York, convincing Manhattan's business and government leaders that cockfighting and slaughterhouses were immoral. Power brokers such as John Jacob Astor Jr., Horace Greely, Horatio Potter, and Thomas Seton, among others, signed Bergh's "Declaration of the Rights of Animals."

Soon after he garnered this influential support, Bergh convinced the New York State legislature to charter the American Society for the Prevention of Cruelty to Animals. Nine days later they passed the anticruelty law and granted the right to enforce it to the ASPCA.

Bergh would continue for decades to "meddle" in the lives of Americans, campaigning tirelessly for kinder treatment of animals. Writer Pune Dracker, in a 1996 issue of the ASPCA's *Animal Watch* magazine, quoted Henry

Bergh as telling a reporter, "Day after day I am in slaughterhouses, or lying in wait at midnight with a squad of police near some dog pit. Lifting a fallen horse to his feet, penetrating buildings where I inspect collars and saddles for raw flesh, then lecturing in public schools to children, and again to adult societies. Thus my whole life is spent." By 1894 the ASPCA became New York City's premiere animal control organization, offering stray and injured animals shelter from the storms of life.[1]

## Continuing the Work of Kindness

Today the ASPCA is one of the largest animal welfare and rescue organizations in the world. It runs an animal adoption facility, the ASPCA Bergh Memorial Hospital, in New York, and an animal poison control center with a twenty-four-hour hotline. The ASPCA supports and trains animal shelters around the world with information and grants. It works with federal lawmakers to ensure that animal protective legislation is passed.

The ASPCA promotes humane education for teachers, providing them with lesson plans and materials they can use in the classroom to bring a working knowledge of animal welfare into the educational process. The ASPCA keeps on eye on animal cruelty around the globe, including monitoring the Internet for criminal behavior toward animals. On its website the ASPCA offers information on animal behavior and leads grieving people to the pet loss services it provides. Staying true to its roots in Henry Bergh's work to end cruelty, especially to horses, the ASPCA operates a full-blown equine rescue and education program. To inspire corporations to manufacture humane products, it offers the ASPCA Seal of Approval program.

As an organization, the ASPCA works hand in hand with other animal welfare groups. Julie Morris, senior vice president of national outreach for the ASPCA, heads five departments at the organization's main office in New York City. She says, "I feel strongly that it is important to work with everybody for better animal protection. I don't get bogged down in what organizations to the right or to the left of us are doing. Politics has no place in this. We have a nondenominational approach. We make it a point to hire people who can work with anybody. They can have personal views about issues, but those views can't interfere with how they do their work here."

Humane law enforcement officers from the ASPCA have peace officer status in New York State, which gives them the right to arrest animal abusers as well as enter secured areas at times of disaster. On 9/11 they were the only group allowed to recover animals stranded in apartment buildings near the World Trade Center site.

To further the goals of protecting animals from disastrous situations, the ASPCA is part of the Iams International Animal Care Advisory Board and does surprise site inspections at the company's research facilities to ensure that animals are being treated humanely.

Julie Morris told us that since Hurricane Katrina she has worked closely with the Louisiana SPCA (LA/SPCA), the Humane Society of South Mississippi (HSSM), and the St. Bernard and Jefferson Parish animal shelters to help them dig out from their massive losses and build for the future. The ASPCA hired advisers to do strategic and long-range planning with Laura Maloney, executive director of the LA/SPCA, and Tara High, executive director of the HSSM. These mentors are helping Laura and Tara rebuild and prepare for annual hurricane seasons. The ASPCA donated Katrina funds to Mississippi and Louisiana to build new animal shelters and create high-volume spay-neuter clinics and voucher systems. Laura Maloney says, "The ASPCA has been remarkable. I have grown to admire and respect them in new ways. I was overwhelmed with their responsiveness and their caring about animals and our staff. I learned a lot from Julie Morris. It has been a life-changing experience."

The list of activities the ASPCA is involved in goes on and on. The organization is widely trusted because it strives to be reasonable in its approaches and to foster nonjudgmental attitudes, which enable it to make friends and form coalitions with other organizations. You can go to its website to become a member or volunteer and to receive its weekly online newsletter.

As you will see in the following chapter, the ASPCA has a slightly younger sibling that started off in the animal welfare movement about the same time. The next of the Big Three, the American Humane Association, offers a unique approach to animal rescue and to promoting and protecting the human-animal relationship.

## CHAPTER SEVEN

# Protecting Children and Animals

While Henry Bergh was forming the ASPCA to protect animals, Etta Angell Wheeler, a Methodist mission worker, was trying to free ten-year-old Mary Ellen from the abusive home of her mother, Mary Connelly. After many failed attempts, Wheeler turned to Henry Bergh for help, and Mary Connelly was convicted in a very public trial.[1]

After Mary Ellen's case drew public attention in 1873, the first Society for the Prevention of Cruelty to Children was formed. Four years later the American Humane Association was founded to bring unity to the many organizations protecting animals or protecting children. It is the oldest national nonprofit organization working for the welfare and protection of both children and animals.

Marie Belew Wheatley, president and chief executive officer of American Humane, says, "Working for children and animals is really about creating a more humane and caring society. If people were operating at their highest level and demonstrating caring and compassion, children wouldn't be harmed and animals wouldn't be abused. People wouldn't be mistreated. American Humane speaks for those who can't speak for themselves."

Since Marie grew up on a family farm, she is especially tuned in to creating a healthy environment for farm animals. She says, "Producers, ranchers, or farmers tend their cows to produce milk or raise their chickens for laying eggs or to be slaughtered as food. We have scientifically set standards for these animals to be treated humanely. They need to have access to an atmosphere that is normal for their species. They need to be humanely treated. Our Free Farmed program means that animals are free from hunger, pain, and distress. They are not confined or uncomfortable in battery cages or inhumane conditions."

In addition to protecting farm animals, the organization promotes animal population control, animal adoption, better sheltering services, legislation to protect animals, and education about animal issues; it conducts disaster relief and animal emergency services training; and it monitors filmmaking on sites where animals are used as actors. With the Second Chance Fund that American Humane provides in partnership with Bayer Animal Health, member organizations can apply for up to two thousand dollars for medically treating abused and neglected animals. These animals are then prepared for adoption into permanent homes.

The division of American Humane that monitors film and commercial production has its office in Los Angeles but sends a certified animal safety representative to motion picture sites all over the country. When you see the words No Animals Were Harmed® in the end credits of a film, it's because a Certified Animal Safety Representative has ensured that the filmmakers could make that claim. It means that the filmmakers adhered to American Humane's guidelines for the Safe Use of Animals in Filmed Media.

On the child protection front, American Humane is a national leader. The organization holds presentations and trainings and publishes papers to show family service workers, law enforcement officials, medical personnel, educators, and parents how to treat children better and how to detect and prevent child abuse. It also educates the public and professionals about the link between the abuse of animals and violence toward humans. Through its National Center on Family Group Decision Making conferences, it focuses on including family and extended family in making decisions about youth at risk.

Currently American Humane has more than 100,000 members,

including 2,000 rescue, animal care and control, and humane societies. Its database includes 9,000 people that the organization can reach readily with messages about animal and child welfare issues and with calls for support and advocacy action.

American Humane provided disaster relief after Hurricane Katrina by activating the organization's enrollment of trained volunteers, sending five emergency vehicles, renting additional RVs, and deploying the group's eighty-two-foot semi with bunks for twelve people, rescue boats, horse slings, cages, surgical tables, communication modules, satellite phones, and the best emergency communication systems available. The Humane Society of the United States and Louisiana SPCA with the help of American Humane and other animal organizations ran the Lamar-Dixon animal sheltering operation.

Because American Humane also has strong ties to policy makers, the organization created the National Emergency Animal Response Coalition and sent an open letter to Congress about including animals as part of the family and not leaving them behind in a disaster.

American Humane sponsors conferences that bring together national and local animal organizations and federal and military health officials. It hosted the National Emergency Management Summit, in Orlando, Florida, in January 2006, a conference that allowed the key players in the animal disaster relief to meet face-to-face and hash out what went right and what went wrong in their Hurricane Katrina response efforts. Everyone we talked with who attended this conference said, "It was a good start." Summits such as this one solidify the understanding that groups and individuals need to coordinate their efforts and figure out how to organize for future disasters. According to Marie, the animal organizations will have to agree on credentialing volunteers and standardizing training procedures.

Marie Wheatley worked formerly as CEO of the American Red Cross chapter, in Denver, and was a level 5 disaster officer for public affairs. She went through Hurricane Andrew, the biggest disaster the country had ever seen at that time. She finds that using the National Incident Management System during her fifteen years with Red Cross disaster response puts her in a unique position to help promote its use for improving disaster response in the animal welfare community.

Marie admires the National Voluntary Organizations Active Disaster program, which is critical to American Red Cross's community disaster preparedness. If local animal shelters and rescue organizations get involved in the program's planning sessions, they can become part of preparing for disasters and not be operating alone or shut out in emergencies. Marie says, "You have to get to know each other and how you will work together before disaster happens. All responding organizations need to know who will be there and what they will be working on."

Crucial to American Humane's role in responding to disasters, the organization's memorandum of understanding with the American Red Cross has recently been renewed. It calls for locating animal shelters alongside Red Cross shelters for humans.

In our opinion this type of arrangement goes a long way toward avoiding the stress and danger for humans and animals by making it easier for them to stay near each other while remaining safe in a disaster.

In the next chapter we explore the role of the Humane Society of the United States, the young giant of the Big Three. It only came into being in 1954, yet this organization affects almost every aspect of the human-animal connection.

# CHAPTER EIGHT

# New Kid on the Block

Among the Big Three, the Humane Society of the United States is the new kid on the block. It's a very vocal kid, though. Established in 1954, the HSUS says it has ten million members and according to its website is "the nation's largest and most powerful animal protection organization, working in the United States and abroad to defend the interests of animals."[1]

The organization focuses on four major issues: factory farming, animal fighting and other forms of cruelty, the fur trade, and inhumane sport hunting practices. It also spearheads campaigns to close down puppy mills, end the ownership of exotic animals as pets, stop greyhound racing, and oppose unacceptable animal research and testing practices. The group also runs sanctuaries, wildlife rehabilitation centers, and mobile veterinary clinics.

To put it mildly, the HSUS acts like a keg of dynamite in its efforts to persuade legislators to pass laws favorable to animals. It has been engaged in a protracted battle to end the slaughter of horses and the transporting of horse meat to Europe and Asia for human consumption.

To help animal shelters improve animal care and network with each other, the HSUS hosts the Animal Care Expo each year. Experts in animal care and control hold workshops on topics such as humane education, volunteer management, and planning and responding to disasters. They call it the "premiere international educational conference and trade show for animal sheltering professionals," with as many as 1,500 participants from 50 states and 30 countries.[2]

A unique aspect of the HSUS is its Urban Wildlife — Our Wild Neighbors® program. The purpose of this project is to help people resolve conflicts between humans and wildlife so that people who think wild animals are encroaching on neighborhoods can learn about other options besides killing off the animals. The organization explains how to humanely end a standoff between humans and the geese or deer or coyotes or black bears who used to live on the land now taken over by houses. In addition, the HSUS offers information on creating wildlife sanctuaries in your own backyard, including how to install bird feeders and what to do if you find an injured animal.

In its quest to be the protector of all animals on the planet, the HSUS focuses on marine mammals as well. The organization's report on marine mammals, which is coproduced with the World Society for the Protection of Animals and titled "The Case Against Marine Mammals in Captivity," opposes supporting zoos and aquariums that exhibit captured marine mammals publicly but do not work to conserve the species. This publication tells about the brutal killing and capture of dolphins and whales, driven by a public that wants them for display, for entertainment, and for petting or swimming exhibits.

The HSUS has its main headquarters in Washington, DC, and also runs eight regional offices. Dave Pauli is the regional director for the HSUS North Rockies Region. Talking to him is like listening to a veteran of the animal wars. From his many travels around the country he has lots of stories to tell, such as the time he had to check an alligator as cargo on the plane and had a tortoise as his carry-on luggage.

Dave told us that disaster relief is something the HSUS has been involved in throughout the world — the tsunami in the Indian Ocean, the Red River floods of North Dakota and Minnesota, and Hurricanes Opal, Ivan, and Charlie, to name a few. When the number of animals needing to be rescued from Hurricane Katrina far exceeded anything the Louisiana SPCA's destroyed animal shelter and decimated staff on Japonica Street could handle, Laura Maloney called the HSUS. She asked that the organization's disaster department take over managing the rescue operation. Dave Pauli was appointed incident commander at the Lamar-Dixon Expo Center, the temporary shelter that housed thousands of rescued animals.

Jane Garrison worked as a volunteer with Dave Pauli to bring thousands of stranded animals to safety. Jane became well known to the media as camera crews followed her and her team through disease-infested waters on rescue missions. Lt. Randy Covey, an executive at the Oregon Humane Society and a highly trained animal rescuer, did such exemplary work at Lamar-Dixon that the HSUS recruited him to be its new director of disaster services.

Not only was the HSUS operating the biggest and most complex temporary shelter for animals after the storms, it also collected the most donations because of its widely acknowledged expertise in handling publicity and the media. When the HSUS ran Lamar-Dixon Expo Cen-

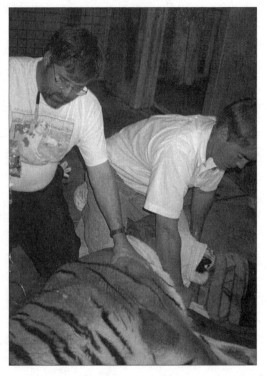

*Dave Pauli (left) of the HSUS during zoo evacuation of a big cat.*

ter, documentarians video-recorded and photographed the entire process. With thousands of volunteers wearing HSUS T-shirts and Wayne Pacelle, president and chief executive officer of the HSUS, holding press conferences, the organization's presence was noted in virtually every newscast and documentary about animal rescue.

Solidifying the HSUS's preeminence as an international animal welfare organization, the annual Genesis Awards show offers an Academy

Awards–style television event that airs on the cable network Animal Planet. Gretchen Wyler, vice president of the Hollywood office of the HSUS, was the events chairperson until 2006. An array of animal-loving celebrities serve as presenters or on the Genesis Honorary Committee. The Genesis Awards go to members of the media and media organizations that present animal-friendly and animal-advocacy programming.

While other organizations might struggle to be even a blip on the screen of public recognition, the HSUS remains expert at drawing attention to animal issues. The HSUS website offers an impressive wealth of information, inspiration, and practical applications on every aspect of animal health, welfare, and protection. The organization gives public recognition to legislators who work with them on targeted animal welfare issues. With its massive membership, the HSUS has political clout and the ability to sway public opinion. It wields this power deftly and joins in coalitions with other organizations to push animal agendas through Congress.

A number of organizations form a second tier of influence in the animal welfare and protection community, and we have more information about them in later chapters. Although they were shining stars long before the hurricane hit, these organizations became more visible to the public as they were given attention in the press for the work they did along the Gulf Coast.

When organizations and volunteers from all over the world arrived in the Big Easy, they found a culture that mixed animal and human life in ways that were unique and even unsettling. In part 2 we explore ways that cultures clashed during animal rescue efforts along the Gulf Coast. Although much of the information in part 2 of this book is specific to Hurricane Katrina, it is relevant to how future disasters are planned for and handled. Animal rescue organizations and volunteers come from all over the country and the world to help out in a disaster. What can we all learn from Katrina about dealing with cultures, philosophies, priorities, and procedures that differ from our own? How does the uniqueness of a disaster impact making decisions for fulfilling the two-pronged mission of saving animals' lives and reuniting them with their families?

# PART TWO

# CLASHES OF CULTURES
# AND HURRICANE KATRINA

*Photos on previous page, left to right:*

Candice King-Palgut's wheelchair
and van for volunteering at Noah's
Wish.

At Lamar-Dixon, an animal worker
gets a kiss from a mother dog.

A rescued cat in an overhead bin
during Continental Airlines Operation
Pet Lift.

## CHAPTER NINE

# Animal Life in the Big Easy

New Orleans is known for its jambalaya, a spicy mixture of rice and meats and seafood, and one could say that in the culture of the Big Easy animals and humans mix also in spicy ways. Before Katrina the city of New Orleans had a population of 485,000. If the national statistics hold true, we can extrapolate that six out of ten of its homes contained at least one pet. In addition to the number of owned animals in New Orleans households, Laura Maloney, executive director of the Louisiana SPCA (LA/SPCA), estimates that New Orleans had about 26,000 stray animals, or 144 per square mile. The strays ate out of garbage dumps; local restaurants and residents fed them scraps. Estimates are that 250,000 stray and owned animals were left behind when the city evacuated.

The LA/SPCA is a private nonprofit organization that has been chartered since 1888. Its home on Japonica Street was overcome with floodwaters and rendered uninhabitable in the hurricane. A new facility will be built with funds donated by the HSUS and ASPCA, among other sources. Under Laura Maloney's leadership, the LA/SPCA coordinated the city's surrendering, fostering, and adopting of pets. In addition, the LA/SPCA offered obedience-training classes for dogs and visited schools to educate children about humane animal care. The shelter included a low-cost veterinary clinic for both the public and shelter animals.

Laura says that in 2004 her organization was able to spay and neuter only 5,000 animals from the area. Animal overpopulation and irresponsible pet ownership remain as two of the biggest problems the organization must deal with on a daily basis. Also in 2004 the LA/SPCA's return-to-owner rate was 4 percent. Few animals had pet identification — microchipping, collars, or tags. In the storms and floods, veterinary offices lost all their records, making it even more difficult to reunite pets and people. Many of the animals who were sick or boarding in these facilities died.

Heartworm and parvo diseases are rampant among dogs in New Orleans. Typifying the clash in cultures that would occur when volunteers from around the country came to rescue animals, Valerie Schomburg, an animal control officer from Orange County, California, observed, "When I came back home, I saw the difference. My vet had never treated a heartworm-positive dog."

New Orleans has a law, a standards of care ordinance, against tethering animals as a primary means of confinement, and the law is actively enforced, but the LA/SPCA has only six officers, who must work around the clock. In this warm southern climate, people distinguish between yard dogs, the ones they keep outside — often chained to a porch, fence, or balcony — and house dogs, inside pets with whom they socialize. The practice of keeping cats as indoor-only is uncommon. Feral cat populations had exploded in the Louisiana parishes. Animal abuse cases were rarely prosecuted. The city has a contract with the LA/SPCA to handle animal control, but the contract pays for only those six officers to do cruelty investigations, stray collection, and code enforcement.

## Cockfighting and Dogfighting

Two states in the entire country do not ban cockfighting, and Louisiana is one of them, although animal organizations continue to work toward establishing such a law in the state. Cockfighting is a statewide money-maker with gamblers betting high stakes on the outcomes.

Dogfighting, although illegal, is also highly profitable. The purse in a dogfight can run as high as $50,000. Champion fighting dogs are sold for $10,000 or more. Pit bulls are trained to kill each other for this blood sport. Six months before Hurricane Katrina, Laura Maloney was instrumental in having rings of dogfighters arrested. For interfering in these lucrative operations, Laura received death threats. Still, animal rescuers noticed as many as a third of the pit bulls they found were scarred and highly dog-aggressive, signs that are indicative of fighting dogs.

## Beloved Pets

In spite of the violent aspects of the region's relationship with animals, in most Louisiana and Mississippi homes pets are as loved and pampered as anywhere else in the nation. Best Friends Animal Society of Kanab, Utah, set up an emergency animal rescue operation in Tylertown, Mississippi, headed by Paul Berry, Best Friends' director of operations and chief executive officer. Paul was born and raised in New Orleans. He says, "People in the South make pets part of the family. Local Southern folks get this. It is a celebrated tradition. When I was a child we would wake up on Christmas morning with the dogs and cats right there with us. When I talked to local military and police about reuniting pets with their owners, it wasn't a stretch for them at all. They knew what animals meant to these families."

## Laura and Dan Maloney Prepare Animals for Disaster

Before the hurricanes hit, Laura Maloney had set in place evacuation procedures for dealing with a Category 3 or higher hurricane. Laura's plan at the LA/SPCA named two events that would trigger evacuation: a declaration of precautionary evacuation by the City of New Orleans, and the activation of the Emergency Operations Commission. On August 27 the LA/SPCA activated its prearrangement with Patti Mercer, executive director of the Houston SPCA. Laura rented two refrigerated trucks. She and fifteen members of her staff drove to Houston with their personal pets and the 263 healthy LA/SPCA animals and their paperwork, photos, supplies, and medications. They expected to return to New Orleans a few days later, as they had many times before.

In the wealthy Audubon area of New Orleans, Laura Maloney's husband, Dan, also put into effect disaster preparation plans at the zoo. As the general curator of the Audubon Zoo, Dan was responsible for keeping alive the 1,500 animals housed at the zoo with the aid of fifteen staff members. He told us that his main objective was for the zoo to be operational and to stay safe for up to two weeks. By then he hoped he could get other zoos to help replenish supplies and transport animals needing evacuation. And they did.

Dan's preplanning included crucial decisions for sheltering each type of animal, considering the sturdiness of their exhibits and the behavior specific to each animal. For example, having the flamingos stay outdoors instead of inside, where they might be frightened and hurt themselves, saved the birds' lives.

Out of the 1,500 animals, only two young otters and a raccoon were lost. Dan says of the oasis that the zoo became, "We built the ark and trained the animals to walk two by two into its doors."

Thousands of animals in the Big Easy didn't have an easy time before the storm, much less after it. Although Laura Maloney asked volunteers to put up posters that showed a puppy inside a tornado funnel cloud with the words, "Take your pet with you," hurricane-weary residents didn't heed or couldn't manage to follow that advice.

The next chapter offers stories about journeys that pitted the forces of nature and the follies of humankind against survival for the animals.

# CHAPTER TEN

# Why Did People Stay?

After seeing residents trying to survive in the flooded streets and homes of New Orleans, the nation wondered, Why did people stay when they knew a deadly hurricane was coming? Captain Scott Shields, who came to prominence for his work after the World Trade Center bombing, told us a story that provides one answer to that question: because of the animals.

Captain Shields and his golden retriever, Bear, searched through rubble at the Twin Towers after September 11, 2001. They became legendary for leading firefighters and rescuers around Ground Zero. The United States Army honored Bear for "extraordinary service to humanity." Bear was also honored at the United Nations as Hero to Humanity. His portrait hung there during World Peace Month. The subject of Captain Shields's book, *Bear: Heart of a Hero*, Bear died of complications from injuries he sustained while working at the World Trade Center. He was buried as a firefighter, and a memorial for him is at the Fire Department of New York Emergency Medical Services Academy.[1]

On August 30 Captain Shields, the former director of marine safety for the New York City Urban Parks Search and Rescue Team, received authorization from Louisiana Governor Kathleen Blanco to deploy member Search and Rescue (SAR) teams of the Bear Search and Rescue Foundation. The foundation deployed a total of twenty-two teams for Governor Blanco in response to Hurricane Katrina, including the first FEMA CERT (Community Emergency Response Team) to ever see action from Battery Park City next to the World Trade Center. Captain Shields brought with him Theodore, his new dog, a relative of Bear, to do search and rescue in the flooded streets of New Orleans. For two weeks Captain Shields led five volunteer SAR teams from the Bear Search and Rescue Foundation that worked with Colonel Brian Owens, commander of the 3rd Brigade's Army 82nd Airborne division. The military's designation for the units from the Bear Search and Rescue Foundation was "Bear's Navy."

Lieutenant Roberto Turner of the 82nd started the first animal rescues with the 3rd Brigade. His actions led to the citizens evacuating instead of refusing to leave their houses. The 3rd Brigade, with the support of Bear Search and Rescue Foundation teams, rescued 847 people and transported 4,106 people and hundreds of animals.

*Captain Scott Shields in action.*

Captain Shields spoke to us about the people who rescued animals. He said that the 82nd Airborne's special boat units passed by houses where most people were out on their patios or balconies and had refused to leave.

While in a flooded neighborhood, Captain Shields used his cell phone to call the chief public affairs office of the U.S. Secretary of Health, asking that during this crisis their office change the policy of not allowing pets and people together in rescue boats. He believed that the policy was a failure and was leading people to refuse evacuation. Many of the people who remained in the city would not leave their pets alone and had no way of taking them or were being refused transport with them. Now they were refusing to get into the rescue boats for the same reasons.

Residents watched Captain Shields from second-story windows and roofs as he made the phone call. He yelled to them, "Will you go without your pets?" Everyone yelled back, "No!" He held up the phone for the government official to hear the residents shout, "Could we take our pets with us?"

Lieutenant Turner had a choice to make. He could follow guidelines, or he could allow people to get into the boats on their own with their pets. If he didn't let pets and people evacuate now, boats with local authorities would have to come through later and force the residents to leave. He decided to throw a roll of silver duct tape to the houses' front porches for people to create makeshift dog muzzles as a safety precaution for the rescuers. Residents who had been avoiding forced evacuations began to emerge. At that moment, Captain Shields says, "The cell phone went dead. The 82nd Airborne team evacuated the animals and the people. I think that Lieutenant Turner is a national hero; his actions changed everything. His method won out the day."

Later the crew on the naval ship *Tortuga* sheltered the rescued animals with the help of veterinarians from New Jersey's Red Bank Animal Hospital. In the article "A Witness to Katrina's Tragedy," by Sharon Schlegel, Captain Shields is quoted as saying, "Hundreds of people died because they loved their animals more than themselves and wouldn't leave them."[2]

Captain Shields says, "My fondest memory is seeing 82nd Airborne trucks riding around with the logo of the Bear Search and Rescue Foundation on their trucks. I hope my epitaph includes the title

*Army 82nd Airborne, 3rd Brigade, doing rescue work with dogs.*

we were given by the men and women of the 82nd Airborne down in New Orleans: Admiral of the Navy for the 82nd Airborne."

## Other Reasons People Didn't Leave with Their Pets

If you have a job that makes you responsible for the health and safety of your community, during an emergency you are considered essential personnel and in most cases you must stay at your post. Captain Cindy Machado, animal services director at the Marin Humane Society, in northern California, shared a story about a reunion that her facility made possible for essential personnel. A deputy sheriff in St. Bernard Parish called Marin Humane looking for her dogs. The woman said that she and two hundred other deputies were living on a boat with no electricity or running water. Her three dogs went missing after she had to report to duty. Fortunately, Marin Humane had the woman's Lhasa apso and promised to keep searching for the other two dogs as well as animals the woman's colleagues had lost.

Other residents refused to leave because they never evacuated during storm warnings. Older residents of New Orleans, often called the Elders, have seen hurricanes come and go. Typically they refuse to evacuate out of a belief that they have survived every other storm and will make it through the current one. Also, they have their regular practices for holding down the fort while younger people flee the city. Kerry Ermon, a New Orleans resident, sent us a copy of a letter she emailed to friends after the hurricane. She wrote, "My ninety-five-year-old neighbor, Miss Miller, knowing that I was panicking about my two feral cats, graciously fed them food and fresh water every day I was gone."

Laura Cortese, a New York fashion stylist, volunteered in New Orleans and was charmed by an Eighth Ward resident, Elder Barry Chissell, who had survived the storms. The day that Laura met Elder Chissell, he was ringing a little brass bell to beckon his animals for lunch. He told Laura that the house had been in his family for almost one hundred years and he was proud of the fact that it was made of good quality wood and no cheap materials. That is why it was still livable after Katrina when many of his neighbors' homes weren't. Laura asked him if he knew of any animals in trouble. Elder Chissell told her, "How could there be? I'm taking care of them all." He explained that the helicopters overhead had scared his pets silly, and the *Dallas Morning News* had mentioned his name in an article. Laura left him with fifty pounds of dog and cat food for the animals he fed. At Christmas that year she sent him a box with a photo she had taken of him, some dog and cat toys, flannel pajamas, and a new pair of slippers to replace the ones he says his cat always attacks.

## Scott and Kyle Radish and the Cairn Terrier Rescuers

One of the most unusual and harrowing stories we heard concerning why people stayed came from Scott Radish, a builder and landlord who lives with his wife, Kyle, in Orleans Parish. Scott's mother performs generous deeds for dogs every day, and when she and her son needed help, it came from an unexpected source.

Scott and Kyle Radish lived with their two dogs in the upstairs section of a duplex they were rebuilding. Tulip, a mutt, was then four years old and Corduroy, a fifty-five-pound dog, looks like a cairn terrier mix. Two weeks before Hurricane Katrina, Scott's mother, Deirdre Bailleu, went out of town to visit her elderly mother. She asked Scott to keep her three cairn terriers, Tia, Kringle, and Honey, an old rescue dog with only three paws, two teeth, and one and one-half ears. Since Deirdre also cared for Buttons, a shih tzu who belonged to Scott's brother, he agreed to take that dog also.

Deirdre is a dedicated volunteer for the Col. Potter Cairn Rescue Network. She and her Internet buddies call themselves the Aunties. They rescue the breed from puppy mills and shelters and take in unwanted dogs. They transport rescued dogs to new adoption and foster homes. A rescuer named Colleen keeps the dogs who are still healing or are not adoptable at her Camp Lonestar ranch in Texas.

Cairn terriers — think Toto in *The Wizard of Oz* — are known for their fearless tenacity. At the time this story begins, Tia, Kringle, and Honey were about to join Buttons along with Scott and Kyle's two dogs and black cats, Deek and Jelly Bean, on an adventure that surpassed anything Dorothy and Toto encountered when the tornado swooped them up from Kansas.

## Staying in the City

Asked why he decided to stay in New Orleans through the hurricane, Scott gave reasons we heard repeatedly: "There is always the forecast of doom and gloom one or two times every year," he says. "We had already evacuated for four hurricanes that didn't hit or were weak. It's such a pain with 1.3 million people trying to take the same highway out of town. We just stopped listening to the warnings." The couple also suspected that trying to leave town with six dogs and two cats would present its own unique challenges. Were they ever right!

Through the early morning storm, the Radishes stayed in their upstairs duplex, ten feet above ground. Scott had replaced all the house's studs and felt confident in its sturdiness to withstand high winds. He hadn't considered that the levees might break. When Katrina blew all the shingles off the roof, the couple saved carpet and furniture by placing buckets under ceiling leaks. By mid-morning they assumed the worst was over and took the dogs for a walk. By dark of that day, the broken levees had flooded nine feet of water over their cars and spilled over their front porch.

Through the next days the Radishes managed to take a neighbor's boat, get the dogs and cats over to railroad tracks that run along top of the old levee, and find refuge in a three-story-high Baptist church. But ultimately they were refused a ride on a Coast Guard boat that wouldn't take their animals, forcing them to walk through one-hundred-degree heat to an evacuation site.

In the broiling August heat, Scott wore a backpack that he filled with dog food, a few toiletries, bottled water, a jar of peanut butter, and some energy bars. He carried Honey in his arms. The dog had tried to keep up but only managed to wobble on her three paws with her tongue hanging out. After a hopeless struggle, Scott said to Honey, "Kyle and I will walk to the site, drop off the cats, and I will come back for you." With a terrible foreboding, he left Kyle and the other animals at the evacuation site so he could keep his promise and return to get Honey. After he had retrieved her, a man with a boat carried them back to the evacuation site.

Scott says later that he and Kyle must have "looked like lunatics" with all their animals. They rode in the back of a rental truck, as well as in a church van, a fire truck van, an army personnel carrier, and a school bus with a couple of empty seats, all in an effort to get to the Red Cross shelter at Nicholls State University (NSU), in Thibodaux, Louisiana. Kyle carried the two freaked-out cats in a bag. Scott lugged Honey and the backpack. They relied on loyal Tulip to lead the pack of dogs alongside them. On the bus Scott fed peanut butter to the severely weakened Buttons, their dehydrated little dog who had been running to keep up with the rest of her family.

The Red Cross wouldn't let the Radishes or the other people who had brought birds, dogs, cats, and a potbellied pig out of the floods with them into the shelter. Scott says, "I am a man with my own business. I have vehicles, money in the bank, and credit cards. But because I have animals, I'm sitting on the side of the road and can't get into the Red Cross shelter."

The Reverend Jim Morris, pastor of St. Thomas Aquinas Catholic Center on the NSU campus, heard about the situation. An animal lover himself, the priest had a Labrador named Blue who lived at the church. The Reverend Morris invited the fifty-three evacuees to sleep on the church's terrazzo floor that night. The Radishes slept on the library floor with their brood, where, as Scott says, "we literally let the cats out of the bag."

Although the church had no electricity, the Reverend Morris managed to get word about the evacuated pets to his parishioners, who arrived in droves with dog and cat food and kitty litter. Scott and Kyle dined on peanut butter and jelly smeared over hot dog buns. The next morning the generous church people brought piles of food for the human evacuees.

Scott walked to the next parish, which had its own phone system, and learned from his mother, Deirdre, that both his and Kyle's relatives had been trying to rescue them but all the highways into New Orleans were shut down. Scott asked Deirdre to get on the Internet and find someone in Louisiana who belonged to the Col. Potter Cairn Terrier Rescue Network. She located Joan Aycock, a retired schoolteacher living in nearby

New Liberia, Louisiana. Joan's son and daughter-in-law drove to St. Thomas church, loaded up the Radishes with all their animals into their SUV, and drove them to a Wal-Mart. Scott says, "When we were back in civilization, I walked into the store, looked at the toothpaste, deodorant, and clean underwear, and started to cry." Joan welcomed the Radishes to her house with a bed, a shower, a safe place to sleep, and a big box of fried chicken on the kitchen table.

Joan took the Radishes' cairn terriers in her car and met fellow cairn terrier rescuer Colleen halfway to Colleen's Camp Lonestar, in Texas. There the Col. Potter Cairn Terrier Rescue Network paid for vet care for the Radishes' dogs. Deirdre's dogs, Honey, Tia, and Kringle, and the brother's dog, Buttons, all returned safely home. It would be one month until Scott and Kyle could retrieve Tulip and Corduroy from Camp Lone-star and return with the dogs to New Orleans. The Radishes dropped off their two cats, Deek and Jelly Bean, at Kyle's mother's house, in Ohio, and picked them up again on their way back to New Orleans.

Scott and Kyle are now at home, fighting with insurance adjusters and trying to get their lives back together. We asked Scott what he learned from this ordeal. He says, "Obviously animal rescue is very important. These are nationwide networks of do-gooders. They are kindhearted people. Although they mainly rescue animals, they are all angels and saints unto themselves for their many layers of goodness."

Scott gets quiet for a minute then adds, "And don't ever be sitting for your mother's four dogs with a hurricane coming."

It will become painfully clear from reading this book that evacuating with your pets makes much of animal rescue unnecessary, even though there will always be unforeseen circumstances causing animals to have to fend for themselves after a disaster. As many people have told us: "If it is un-safe for you, it is unsafe for your animals."

In the next chapter you will have the opportunity to understand more about the surprising ways people and animals were separated. Hope-fully these cautionary tales will help you do everything possible so that similar crises don't occur for you and your animal family.

# CHAPTER ELEVEN

# How Were Animals and People Separated?

After Hurricane Katrina hit the Gulf Coast, people were separated from their pets for a variety of reasons. It was a policy not to allow animals into Red Cross shelters or onto buses, boats, or helicopters. Yet there were individual exceptions. Anderson Cooper of CNN commented in an interview, "This thing...about pets is a huge deal. Some people are being told you can bring pets.... I've seen pets being loaded onto helicopters; others are being told, 'No you can't,' and they're staying."[1] Heidi Brasher, community outreach manager at the Houston SPCA, says she noticed that people were smuggling small animals onto buses. A huge man arrived at the animal shelter with a tiny black-and-white cat he had hidden on an evacuation bus. When the man came back to the Houston SPCA to pick up his cat, whom he had left there for safe-keeping, Heidi was touched to see him sit for twenty minutes in the lobby, lovingly greeting the cat. We heard reports of birds and other small animals making their ways into evacuees' purses and bags.

Whether animals were allowed to accompany their people seemed to depend on who was in charge and how much power or mercy they dispensed. Stephanie Jehle, founder of Operation Underdog Rescue in

Dallas, Texas, says, "There was a woman who came up to Lamar-Dixon to look for her animal. She told a rescuer that when she was told to leave her pet behind, she refused. The next thing she remembered was waking up in a boat. She had been shot with a Taser [electric shock] gun by the individual and put into the boat without her pet."

Few such extreme stories surfaced, and to be fair, rescuers thought they were saving human lives by forcing people to evacuate, even without their pets. But confusion reigned over every aspect of the animal rescue efforts. Rescuers assured people that if they got into boats with their animals, they would be able to keep their pets. When the people arrived at the Superdome, though, they were made to release the pets outside. The little boy who cried so hard that he vomited when his dog, Snowball, was torn out of his arms before he was forced onto a bus tugged at the nation's heartstrings and brought a swarm of animal rescue volunteers to Louisiana and Mississippi.

A rescue boat came to Julie Morgan's steps when waters rose to six and one-half feet. The rescuers said Julie had to leave, but she wouldn't go without her animals, so they went too. She says, "I went with my animals on two boats and two army trucks to get to I-10. When they wouldn't let me on the buses with my pets, I tried to go back home but couldn't get back into New Orleans." Julie stayed all night with her animals in a vacant house that had no doors. The next morning she struggled to carry two cages with her animals in them through what she called the "muddy slop" back to I-10, where people sat on the ground waiting to be picked up and taken who knows where. One cage contained her cat, Mew, and a ferret. The other cage held her two small dogs. She kept her old, injured greyhound on a leash. When animal rescuers from Jefferson Parish Animal Shelter Department came by to see if people wanted to surrender their animals for safekeeping, Julie signed what she thought were papers that would allow her to reclaim her pets for up to two years.

After Julie got on the bus to Houston without her animals, she started calling the people she had given them to, asking about them, and was told they were fine and all kept together. She called almost every day and returned to New Orleans specifically to get her animals back.

Later Mew, a special cat Julie's husband had given to her before he died, got mixed up in the system and sent to Second Chance Cat Rescue in Flagler County, Florida. Months later the rescue group's owner, saying that Julie had relinquished ownership of Mew, refused to let the bereft New Orleans resident have her cat back.

Reporter Jim Witters, in his article about this incident, writes, "Morgan's animals were among an estimated 13,000 pets that owners officially turned over to rescue workers following Katrina's August 29th devastation."[2] Julie told us that in February 2006 her story was featured on *Naomi's New Morning Show*, hosted by Naomi Judd on the Hallmark Channel. This didn't bring her much joy, though, because no mention was made of Mew on the show, only about the fact that she had met and married her new husband, Howard, as part of her evacuation journey.

Julie says, "The first thing I told Howard was that I have all these animals, and my cat Mew sleeps by my chest every night. He said that was fine with him. I didn't realize I wouldn't be able to get my beloved Mew back. Now I feel so depressed at times that I wish I had stayed here and died with the animals. At least I wouldn't have lost Mew."

Julie Morgan had to make yet another decision before getting onto an evacuation bus. Because her greyhound was old, in poor health, and hostile to strangers, she feared that he would get hurt or bite somebody, so she signed papers allowing the dog to be euthanized. We heard from several people who had to make that life-and-death choice in the moment of crisis.

Several people we interviewed said that residents often did not understand what they were signing or what rights they were surrendering when they turned their pets over to temporary sheltering services. They were sometimes shocked to find that their pets had been sent to other parts of the country or that records had been lost or that the animals had been euthanized.

On the other end of the spectrum were pet owners who foolishly left animals tethered to fences or porches or locked inside cages where they starved to death before help could arrive. We heard eyewitness accounts from rescuers who saw residents return to their homes, pick up their belongings, and leave nearly dead pets on trash heaps or in garbage cans. To say this appalled animal rescuers would be an understatement. The crisis definitely brought out the worst as well as the best in human nature.

New Orleans residents who evacuated without their pets told us they thought this hurricane would be like all the rest and they would be gone for only a day or two at most, so they put out plenty of food and water for their pets and left. Some had tried to evacuate with animals previously and couldn't find pet-friendly hotels to stay in. Others had far too many pets to fit in their cars or had to leave with relatives or friends who didn't want, were allergic to, or had no room for pets. Sometimes they were going to relatives' or friends' homes where pets were unwelcome.

It was tough for some animal rescuers to refrain from passing judgment, especially if they did not talk with the people whose animals they had saved. Veterinary technician Chris Robinson, from Ontario, told us, "I find judgmental attitudes frustrating. People who think they would never leave their pets probably haven't considered that many residents did not have the means to get out of the city easily. Even though many people and animals were later separated, initially the people did everything they could to stay through the hurricane with their animals. There are animal rescuers who don't understand what some people went through and how hard they tried to keep their animals with them. Some even died trying. The stories are heartbreaking."

## Mixing Animal and Human Rescue

Dr. Melissa Hunt, associate director of clinical training in the psychology department at the University of Pennsylvania, mentioned another reason why human rescuers refused to let people onto boats with their pets: dogs' and cats' claws can puncture inflatable airboats. Animals can get excited or agitated and bite or scratch.

The "people first, animals later" philosophy of disaster rescue isn't going to fade away until solutions such as simultaneous rescue become widespread. Dr. Hunt says, "As a nation, we haven't figured out how to devote resources appropriately to animal rescue. We have to overhaul the system. You can't say it's okay to bring along a companion animal to the Red Cross shelter. It's not possible for them to manage animal feces and urine there. It would be a public health hazard. There are asthmatics in these shelters. Volunteers can't deal with the risk of bites or scratches. Lots of public health reasons rule out the Red Cross as a place for pets. But rules aren't the problem. We aren't providing resources to fund enough temporary [animal] shelters alongside human shelters. There's no need to convince the pet lovers. It's the ones who don't care that much about animals who need to have these issues framed in terms of human economic costs."

Chapter 15 shows how placing temporary shelters adjacent to or near Red Cross shelters is highly effective at reducing human economic and emotional costs. This type of practical solution resolves the life-and-death issues that arise when people with pets must evacuate a disaster zone.

## Mama Gloria and Her Babies

Gloria, a senior citizen, did everything humanly possible not to be separated from the dogs she loves. Although she had suffered a stroke six weeks before Hurricane Katrina and now walks with a cane, Gloria says, "I am the youngster on the block." At the time of the hurricane she lived among the eighty-year-olds of her Lower Ninth Ward neighborhood, in a home her mother had built fifty years earlier. She had installed a plywood floor in the attic of the house for extra storage.

Gloria's brother John, a traveling registered nurse in California, had dragged his sister kicking and screaming into the modern world of computers when, a year earlier, he gave her a laptop. It sat unopened on Gloria's desk for four months. After finally learning how to use it, Gloria made email buddies, never dreaming that in the coming year her ability to use the Internet would save her life.

Gloria's three dogs, her "babies," are Polobaby, Jazz, and Mynini. She's always communicated with them constantly and tells us, in her slow Louisiana drawl, about life with the dogs. "I never tell Polobaby that he is a pit bull mix," Gloria says. "He's primarily a yellow Lab with gold eyes and a faint gray stripe down his back. Polo wouldn't leave my side while I recuperated from the stroke. I promised him he would always have a good home."

Gloria and Polo took a walk every morning. Each day a neglected border collie named Spices waited at the street corner for them. It wasn't long before Polobaby and Spices fell in love. An elderly neighbor started calling Spices a Jezebel because the dog chased after Polobaby so brazenly. At Polo's insistence, Gloria adopted the dog. Her nine-year-old niece dressed up the two dogs and held a wedding ceremony for them. This made Jezebel an honest woman. Gloria changed the dog's name to Jazz but still called her a "flirt." Gloria offered the bride some advice:

> The reason Jazz wanted to come live with us is because Polo lied to her. Polo told Jazz that this was his house, and I was his maid. For six months, Jazz wouldn't listen to me. Every time I said something to her, she would look at Polo. Finally I said to Jazz, "Baby, men lie. Polo lied to you. This is my house. I put the money in here. I take care of you." After we had that little talk, she still loved Polo, but I didn't have any more trouble with her listening to me.
>
> I often did demos for pet food at PETCO and PetSmart. They would put little outfits — hats and scarves — on the dogs. Jazz loved it. She is a high-heeled-shoes mama.

Mynini is a German shepherd–chow mix. She has short, thick, lush, silky blond fur, with dark brown–black marks on her face and a hint of a diamond shape on her forehead. Gloria's neighbor had adopted Mynini for her young granddaughter, but the girl was too young to take good care of the puppy. Mynini befriended Jazz, and Gloria agreed to adopt her too despite Polo's initial objections.

The dog soon became Gloria's close companion. She says, "For two years Mynini slept in my bed in the small of my back and drove with me to work. She was the only puppy that I actually chose as my own."

Polo and Mynini worshipped Jazz, whom Gloria refers to as "the diva."

## During the Storm

Gloria didn't watch much television and wasn't aware that a serious hurricane threatened the Gulf Coast. She was taking medication and still enduring the effects of the stroke. Although she wanted to leave, her plans fell through, and given her poor health she was not strong enough to quickly find alternatives for evacuation. It was a decision she came to regret, but at the time she was too ill and disoriented to make better choices.

Gloria didn't know it, but the levees had been breached on Monday evening, August 29. By Tuesday morning 80 percent of the city was under water. Polo woke up Mama Gloria after water flooded her house, up to Gloria's ankles. She ran to get her purse and laptop. Now the water was up to her waist, and she had to leave the computer behind. The dogs all climbed onto the floating bed. She put them on top of some high furniture. The window broke. The water outside was now higher than the water inside.

Furniture crashed and splintered into pieces. Gloria doesn't know how she found the strength, but she hacked into the ceiling and pulled her babies onto the plywood rafters in the attic and lifted them all, and herself, to safety. Mynini jumped onto her lap and put her paws around Gloria's neck. The dog let out a big sigh of relief.

Suddenly the roof tore away from the house. Gloria and Polo were caught in the rafters. Jazz, frozen in fear, was blocking the hole Gloria had to crawl through to get onto the roof. Gloria says, "I leaned over and said, 'Jazz, Mama loves you. But, baby, if you don't move, Mama's gonna die. Mama's gonna drown.' This is the one who don't care what Mama wants. She looked at me, and the next thing I knew, Jazz jumped out of that hole onto the roof."

Gloria prayed that her babies wouldn't suffer. She believed the pampered Jazz couldn't survive adversity. The wind blew so hard it nearly knocked her off the roof. She thought the water was still rising, but actually her roof was sinking. Dressed only in a thin cotton night shirt, Gloria recalls, "The freezing rain felt like tiny pieces of icy gravel."

Mynini fell in the water. When she heard Gloria screaming, the dog redoubled her efforts to swim back onto the roof. Her rabies tag and collar were lost, but she managed to return to Gloria's arms.

Hours later Michael Knight, Gloria's neighbor, was rescuing people with his private boat. Too weak to climb into the boat, Gloria had to let men on the boat drag her, on her stomach, into it. She recalls, "I can't remember anything in my life that was harder than leaving my babies. They're my children, my family. They didn't think I was abandoning them. They thought people were taking me away."

Michael left Gloria at a church on, of all places, Flood Street. Hours later on that same day, the people in the church moved to a new two-story schoolhouse where people from the Department of Wildlife and Fisheries found them and took them to a bridge. Gloria says, "I had to walk across that hot cement bridge in scorching heat. One of the men was kind enough to wrap my feet in towels."

Two generous strangers, Rufus and Vonelle Richards, drove Gloria and others on a bus they had commandeered to Houma, Louisiana. Gloria went to the Red Cross shelter there and later walked to the library to get on the Internet. This is how she contacted her sister and an old friend in Tyler, Texas. Her friend Jackie sent money, and Gloria traveled to Texas. As soon as she settled in at her friend's home, Gloria's sister Joan registered Polo, Jazz, and Mynini on Petfinder.com. The search was on. She had nothing else left in this world.

## Help from Far Away

Thousands of miles away in San Francisco, Tom Strother, a dot-com entrepreneur with a degree in mechanical engineering and an MBA, was watching the horror of the hurricane unfold on the news. He contacted the Humane Society of the United States and volunteered to help rescue animals. He was assigned to the temporary shelter set up at Lamar-Dixon Expo Center, in Gonzales, Louisiana.

Tom says, "It was hard, dirty work in a hot and difficult environment. The volunteers there were amazing. They didn't complain about the heat. They did things you couldn't pay the average person to do."

Tom walked dogs, cleaned crates, and did the grunt work. One day a dog arrived and was placed in a crate in the area where Tom spent most of his time working. With this dog, unlike with any of the other dogs, a name came to mind — Lucy — and he started calling the dog by this name. For the next few days Lucy became the first dog he walked each day and the last one he said good-night to. When he had imagined adopting a dog, he had pictured one who looked like Lucy.

Tom had signed up to volunteer for one week and a second if he were needed, and he was indeed needed. During that second week he had Lucy transported to San Francisco with a group of pit bulls. His friends picked the dog up at the airport and took care of her until Tom returned.

Lucy was wearing a collar but no tags. He had the address where she was rescued. The sponsoring rescue organization had posted a photo of Lucy on Petfinder.com and PetHarbor.com.

By this time Polobaby had made it safely to Lamar-Dixon and was transported on a Continental Airlines plane to the San Diego Humane Society and SPCA. Polo's rabies tag was still attached to his collar.

## The Reunions

The San Diego Humane Society and SPCA is the kind of place that believes in doing everything necessary for the health and well-being of animals. Renee Harris, senior director of animal services, along with staff and volunteers, conducted searches for the owners of the animals who arrived at their facility in ways that were worthy of a skilled private detective. The San Diego shelter, or campus, as Dr. Mark Goldstein, executive director, calls it, provided pet owners round-trip airline tickets to San Diego, accommodations at pet-friendly hotels, and supplies, including PETCO gift cards, to help people restart their lives with their pets after reunions at the shelter.

As they got off the plane, with warmth and open arms Renee Harris welcomed each person soon to be reunited with a pet. At first some were wary. Dr. Goldstein says, "It is as if they are waiting for the other shoe to fall. Where's the hitch? It is hard for them to believe that we want noth-ing more than to care about them and their pets."

Renee did everything to make the San Diego shelter's guests com-fortable. She told them to order whatever they wanted from the hotel's room service menu. She prepared them for the fact that the dogs might not recognize them right away and that owners should not take this per-sonally; their dogs would not hold any ill feelings. She listened to the sto-ries of their sad journeys.

In Gloria's case, Renee had read Polo's rabies tag and put the address information together with where the dog was found, a couple miles from Gloria's home. She managed to trace Gloria to the First Christian Church, in Tyler, Texas. Gloria had given the church her contact number.

While Renee searched for her, Gloria was on a new computer she had bought even before replacing her clothes. She hoped that having this laptop would help her find her babies. When she received the call that Polo was at the San Diego Humane Society, she cried so hard that she got a headache and had to go to bed.

This is the reunion in Gloria's own words:

When I signed in at the San Diego hotel, they knew Polo was coming back with me. They said I had to give them a credit card in case he did any damage. I said, "Okay, that's no problem. But who you going to get to sign for me? Because Polo is neater than me. You want him to sign for me? He doesn't make as much mess as his mama." Everybody at the desk fell out. I have more clutter around than he does.

When they brought us to the Humane Society building, Renee warned that Polo might not recognize me. They have the cutest little vis-itors' room for the animals and their families with chairs and pillows. When I first went to the room, Polo was against the opposite wall. He was kind of going, Rrr-rrroo. I started crying. Renee hugged me. She said, "This is normal, baby. He's got to smell you."

But Polo is a child who can't stand to see his mama cry. He started smelling me. I was calling his name. He finally came over.

The news media was there. Polo and I carried on like long-lost soul mates. He's a big dog, but Polo sat on my lap. There was a picture window glass between the hall and where the people were. They were watching Polo kissing his mama. Polo posed for them.

Later, Polo walked into the hotel like he owned it. People recognized him.

I said, "How?"

They said, "From the news."

Polo walked around like, "I've been doing this all my life. Staying at a hotel." I ordered my baby a room service hamburger. It was a happy ending.

Two days after Gloria and Polo returned to Texas, Renee called again, to say that she had found Jazz. Gloria says, "Renee is an angel. I don't know how she put Jazz and me together. That had to be God. She didn't have a picture of Jazz. She only had what was on Petfinder.com."

Jazz was living in San Francisco with Tom Strother. Renee explained that Tom would call Gloria to talk with her.

Tom says, "After I came home from Louisiana, I searched through thousands of postings on the Internet, looking for the dog's owner. By this time I was very attached to Lucy. It was obvious that her previous owner took good care of her. I felt that I had to make sure that Lucy's owner had an opportunity to find her. When Lucy and I went for a walk, she pulled at the leash if she saw another dog. I had the feeling that she was looking for her family. It broke my heart to see it."

There was a photo and description of Lucy posted on Petfinder.com and PetHarbor.com, but as was the case with most postings, the photo was not very clear. Tom took additional photographs of Lucy and posted them under every breed of dog that someone might judge Lucy to be — border collie, Australian sheepdog, English shepherd, and so forth.

Less than a week later Tom got an email from Renee, who told him that Gloria had lost everything and the one thing she wanted was to have her three dogs back to restore her family. Tom says, "I was a mess all day. For several hours I procrastinated calling Gloria. This was right before Thanksgiving. I was already grieving over losing Lucy from my life even though I wanted a happy ending for her owner."

In Gloria's version of the phone call, Tom grilled her for information. Rather than becoming offended, she was convinced that Tom loved the dog and wanted to be sure that Gloria was really Jazz's mama.

Tom says, "Gloria said things like, 'Jazz is so sweet. She walks like she's on high heels.' I'm an engineer. I wasn't looking for personality traits. I wanted Gloria to describe physical attributes and things that she couldn't have seen in the photo. Finally she said that Jazz had a bump on her chest and another on her tail. I had to say then, 'She's your dog.'"

Gloria listened to the whole story of how Tom brought Lucy/Jazz home from Lamar-Dixon and how the dog had become a wonderful part of his life. She says, "Sure enough, they found Jazz in a safe house where people were bringing food and water for her. I think she charmed somebody into bringing her across the bridge."

After their phone call, Tom sent Gloria an email complete with photographs he had taken of Lucy/Jazz at Lamar-Dixon and from the time that she had spent in his home in San Francisco. Gloria became convinced that Tom, who looks like a younger version of her brother, was providing Jazz with a great home and that he loved the dog very much. In the photos Gloria saw Lucy/Jazz looking flirtatious and content. Gloria had always suspected that Jazz, a "high-maintenance woman," wanted to be an only child. After much soul-searching and prayer, she decided that it would be in Lucy/Jazz's best interests to allow Tom to keep the dog. She wrote an email to him that began with the words, "To my baby's daddy," and told him of her decision. Tom was ecstatic.

Tom and Gloria made plans to meet when he returned to New Orleans for an animal rescuer reunion. He continued to send photos of Lucy to Gloria. Tom joked that Lucy attracted so many women in the dog park that he thought this might be how he would find a wife.

Gloria has not yet found Mynini. She searches for her every day. She says, "I'm real poor right now, but if I had a choice between winning the lottery and getting my Mynini back, I would take Mynini." Gloria suspects that someone has Mynini but is not willing to do the right thing and return her, as Tom was willing to do.

Gloria closed the interview with us by saying, "You don't even have to like animals to respect and treat them right. I don't care if you call it Buddha, Goddess, whatever, there's a supreme being tied in to every one of us. If you have respect for yourself, you got to respect everything on this earth.

"Well, we're gonna go get a newspaper now," Gloria says. "Mama and Polo are gonna take a walk."

# CHAPTER TWELVE

# The Volunteers Who Came to Help: What Were They Thinking?

W hat were they thinking?

The people who volunteered after Hurricane Katrina were thinking that the animals needed them.

While millions evacuated, animal lovers headed toward the ravaged, toxic Gulf Coast. Later they would remember that it felt as if they were answering an inner call. Many would say, "It was not a decision. I had to go. I couldn't stand by and do nothing."

Some stayed for a week or two weeks. Some returned repeatedly as if addicted to the drug of selfless service. Some used up all of their vacation time. They lost or quit their jobs rather than leave fellow rescuers to battle on without them. They gave each other nicknames like Boston Bob or Possum Lady. They found like-minded people and formed friendships that will last a lifetime.

When they least expected it, they were aided by corporate giants like Winn-Dixie, Wal-Mart, UPS, PETCO, PetSmart, Continental Airlines, and T. Boone Pickens. National Guard and Coast Guard personnel, police officers, and firefighters carried puppies to them or showed them where animals were trapped in flooded houses.

Animal lovers toughed out Hurricane Rita and refused to abandon the thousands of animals who still needed them. They grew angry, cantankerous, and vocal. Most learned to work together with people who did not share their approaches and philosophies. Some became frustrated with the slowness of bureaucracies and splintered off to form their own organizations. Some broke laws and made up their own rules. Months later they still did not know the work others had done in different parts of Louisiana and Mississippi. They may never know the rewards and consequences of their actions for themselves and for other people and animals.

## New Partnerships Formed

In federal documents prior to Hurricane Katrina, evacuation and rescue planning referred to animals as "nuisances." Animal evacuation plans, if there were any, fell under the jurisdiction of the state departments of agriculture and the state veterinary offices, with little regard for pets as members of families and for the deeply felt warmth that exists between people and animals who share homes. No national regulations allowed for the significance of the human-animal bond. Those who went to help after Hurricane Katrina did not realize that senators, congressional representatives, and CDC, FEMA, and Homeland Security officials were trying to make disaster relief better and more humane for farm animals, wildlife, *and* pets.

After Hurricane Katrina hundreds of state, city, and national organizations cooperated in unprecedented ways. Media coverage made stars out of animal control officers and independent rescuers. Television crews followed them around; filmmakers and photojournalists documented sanitized versions of their "adventures" in animal rescue.

The staff of local and state animal shelters and veterinary clinics set aside worries about their own families and their own destroyed homes to transport animals in their care and to set up makeshift triage centers. With cell phones and land lines gone, they had little communication from the outside world or with their loved ones. They hoped that others, elsewhere, were mobilizing help for them.

Volunteers and animal organizations from the United States and Canada as well as visitors from other countries sweated together in 100-degree temperatures and 100 percent humidity. They waded through poisonous waters, leaped over barbed-wire fences to face the snarls of frightened dogs and the claws of terrified cats. They wore face masks, wader boots, and plastic gloves. They fended off mold, rot, sunburn, mosquitoes, snakes, and alligators. They endured the unforgettable stench of death and decay while crawling under houses, climbing onto rooftops, or stepping over human and animal remains.

They drove miles and miles trying to find addresses on streets with no signs. They spray-painted messages onto houses for other rescuers and pet owners to find. They rooted through mail looking for cell phone numbers to call. Many of them followed with military precision the Incident Command System, the national structure that is part of the National Incident Management System and provides an approved set of disaster response protocols.

## What No One Else Would Do

Volunteers scooped tons of poop and kitty litter. They hoisted twenty-five-pound bags of food and lugged thousands of gallons of bottled water, constantly reminding each other to stay hydrated. They vowed never again to eat another granola bar or military ration meal. The vegetarians and vegans among them used the meat from prepackaged meals to lure hungry dogs into crates.

Animal lovers tried to call home when an occasional phone worked. They got busy and forgot to take prescription medications, yet everyday aches and pains disappeared. They felt adrenaline rushes and helpers' highs. Sitting around late-night campfires, they wondered how they could return to mind-numbing day jobs and cluttered cubicles. Some resolved to find more meaningful work that would allow them to keep on saving animals.

In the few hours they slept, many lay on cots in FEMA tents, on the concrete pavement of parking lots, or in the backseats of their cars and minivans. Many endured nightmares of images that had been seared indelibly into their minds. Some showed symptoms of post-traumatic stress disorder. Some stayed longer than they were effective and had to be told by others to go home.

Some volunteers took one look at the devastation and burst into tears. Feeling horrified, saddened, and defeated, they immediately fled to closed airports where they waited for the next flights out of stricken areas.

What were they thinking?

They were thinking that the animals and people needed to be together again.

The following story shows the amazing connections between people, animals, and the Universe. These invisible golden threads awed those who participated in saving the animals from disaster.

## Her Name Was Sweetie

Forty-four-year-old Dwayne Blackman is the only child of Viola Blackman. Viola has been through all the storms. When Dwayne, a traveling businessman who lived in Wichita at the time of the hurricane, tried to persuade his mother to evacuate, she refused. She knew that human shelters wouldn't take animals. She felt safe at home with Sweetie and Ming, her two Belgian shepherds.

Sweetie and Viola were very close. Dwayne's friend Dean had given Viola the first dog as a puppy. After looking into her loving eyes, *Sweetie* was the only name that came to Viola. This dog had deep emotions and expressed them freely. Her expressive face clearly showed when she was sad or happy.

When Dwayne lived in New Orleans with Viola, Dean gave the second puppy, Ming, to him, and the dog became Dwayne's good buddy. Ming followed Dwayne everywhere, never letting him out of her sight. She is very strong and protective and doesn't like being around strangers. Viola called the two dogs her babies. She always made sure that Dwayne remembered to lock the front gate. She asked him to take her babies for rides in the park. The dogs were well cared for and had collars, current rabies tags, and regular vet care.

A few years before Hurricane Katrina, Dwayne built an attic loft on Viola's home. His mother always questioned its necessity, but when the floods came, this attic helped to save her life.

Dwayne says, "Normally people say, get batteries, tape up the windows, have flashlights. This time, the Elders attempted to do so, but the worst happened. They weathered the storm and were ready to go about their day when the water started rising rapidly. They were sixty and seventy years old. Nothing like this had ever happened. Mother went to bed, thinking she would rest, and the storm would be over. The dogs came swimming to her and woke her up. The furniture was floating. Mother grabbed some paperwork and climbed into the attic loft with Sweetie and Ming. They stayed there together for four days. The water was breast-high. She wore the same clothes all that time."

Dwayne's friend Dean came on a boat with rescuers to pick up Viola. The rescue boats would take only humans in them. Sweetie and Ming looked at Viola as if they couldn't believe she was leaving them. They cried and whimpered, breaking Viola's heart. Sick and weak, she wept for her babies. Dean promised Viola that he would come back and get the dogs.

Viola was brought to a staging area and evacuated to the Houston Astrodome. By this time she had lost all contact with Dwayne, who was frantically trying to find her.

Dean kept his promise and took Viola's dogs to his mother's home. It was on higher ground and had only two feet of water and very little damage. He put the dogs in the dry, fenced-in backyard where they could lie in the garage and wouldn't be overheated in the baking sun.

By this time Dwayne had had no contact with Viola for four days. He was frantic. He says, "I was weary and nervous. My inner spirit needed a battery charge. I opened up the Word and prayed. Within a half hour the phone rang. It was my friend Jackie. Mother had left the Houston Astrodome and gone to a motel, where she had remembered Jackie's phone number and called her. Jackie told me where my mother was and a number to reach her. Mother was now in New Orleans. She had attached herself to a large young family of our relatives, and they took

Mother with them to a motel. She was well cared for." Dwayne brought Viola back with him to Wichita.

## An Animal Volunteer from Seattle

Carla Dimitriou is a painter and potter from Seattle, Washington. The day after she watched television news stories of the evacuation and saw people taken to the Superdome in New Orleans, she got a call from Redwood Animal Hospital, the place where she regularly volunteered. The shelter was sending a team to New Orleans to work with Pasado's Safe Haven, a sanctuary in Sultan, Washington, that had set up a temporary shelter near New Orleans and was looking for volunteers to help with animal rescue.

Mark Steinway, who founded Pasado's with his wife, Susan Michaels, had gone to Lamar-Dixon and watched it fill up until it was only intermittently taking rescued animals. Frustrated, he made inquiries until he found a generous donor in LaFourche Parish named Louis St. Martin, who allowed Pasado's use of his large barn in Raceland to temporarily shelter and medically triage rescued animals. At Raceland the group could set up a record-keeping system with tag information and photographs to post on Petfinder.com and other Internet sites. From Raceland the group transported unclaimed animals to Seattle for foster care until their owners could be found.

When Carla Dimitriou decided to answer the call for volunteers, her husband, owner of Dimitriou's Jazz Alley, worried about his wife going to an area that looked unsafe on the news reports. But he supported her by paying her airfare to the Oregon airport where Pasado's volunteers were gathering to leave for the Gulf Coast.

When Carla arrived at the airport, she wondered what people's reactions would be when they saw her wearing a T-shirt labeling her as an animal rescuer. She felt gratified when strangers approached to thank her for volunteering to help the animals.

At Raceland, Mark Steinway instructed his volunteers to go into New Orleans and find all animals that were alone and needed to be rescued.

Carla had had no formal training in animal rescue other than her volunteer work with Redwood Animal Hospital. Mark warned his rescue team to be careful about packs of dogs.

These weeks after the hurricane, former pets had banded together into odd-looking packs of large and small dogs, reverting to instinctual behavior for survival. Frightened dogs were looking for food and running away from or attacking people. And of course, the thousands of perpetual strays were now getting very little food and clean water from residents who usually fed them.

Carla says, "We found a German shepherd loose inside a garage behind a house that didn't have much damage. Unlike most of the dogs we saw, she had a collar and tag. This was my first rescue, and my interpretation of our instructions was to take all dogs out of the deserted city. I loved this dog the moment I saw her. She was frightened and looked depressed. We nicknamed her Sweetie. The name just seemed to fit her."

Sensing that Sweetie was a well-cared-for dog, Carla kept asking that she remain close to New Orleans and not be airlifted to Seattle. Besides, Sweetie had become so depressed that she had stopped eating and drinking and had to be given IV fluids. Carla feared that Sweetie would get lost in the system or be too sick to survive air transport. She asked Mark Steinway if she could foster the dog, and he agreed. She says, "I put my name on Sweetie's cage, and we moved her away from the dogs that would be picked up and moved out. Sweetie had a lot of people looking out for her. We often said that angels were saving the world here, one dog at a time."

## An Animal Volunteer from Close to Home

Belinda Thibodaux is a dosimetrist, or X-ray technician, at the Cancer Center, in Thibodaux, Louisiana. Her husband is a sheriff's deputy. She decided to volunteer at the temporary shelter in Raceland operated by Pasado's. When she arrived for her first day on the job, she met Carla Dimitriou and Sweetie. Carla had spent four days doing animal rescue and was returning home the following day. She told Belinda that she was concerned about taking Sweetie home with her. The dog was severely depressed and weak from not eating. Carla told Belinda, "Shepherds are like that. They can die of a broken heart."

Belinda was touched by Sweetie's obvious devotion to someone she suspected was missing this dog as much as the dog was missing her owner. She called her seventy-seven-year-old mother, Ellen DeSoto, who used to raise and show German shepherds, and asked if Ellen would care for Sweetie until Belinda could find the dog's owner. Her mother agreed to help.

Belinda used the information from Sweetie's rabies tag, went on the Internet, and began trying to trace the address and phone number. She figured out that the dog belonged to Viola Blackman and that Viola had been taken to Houston.

Belinda found Contact Loved Ones, a website started by Dan Schoeffler in New York, where people could leave messages in hopes of locating each other. A woman who twenty years earlier had worked with Viola in New Orleans was also using Dan's service to find her friend Viola and offer help. By putting the messages from Belinda and Viola's friend together, Dan helped Belinda locate Viola, who was now in Wichita, Kansas, living with Dwayne.

Later, when we asked Belinda to tell us about the most positive volunteer experience she had, she said, "Finding Viola and hearing the voice of someone who had just found out that her loved one made it through the storm and was safe and waiting for her."

## Reunions

Dwayne and Viola drove back to New Orleans to retrieve Sweetie from Belinda and her mother. Along the way, they stopped at other temporary shelters and rescue operations to look for Ming. Dwayne talked with people at the various organizations and asked for their help. One of them was Barbara Williamson, a public relations person and volunteer for Best Friends at the shelter in Tylertown, Mississippi. Barbara offered to help search for Ming.

Dwayne had heard from Dean's neighbors that well-meaning animal rescuers came into Dean's backyard while he was gone, thinking that the dogs had been abandoned. While they were checking on the dogs, Ming had escaped, eluding the rescuers who pursued her. By the time Carla had found Sweetie in Dean's garage, Ming was long gone.

When Dwayne and Viola arrived at Belinda Thibodaux's home, Sweetie warmly greeted Dwayne. But the dog was having a hard time forgiving Viola for leaving her behind. When Viola tried to hug Sweetie,

*Dwayne Blackman and his mother, Viola Blackman, reunite with Sweetie.*

the emotional German shepherd backed away, rolled her eyes, and looked away. For almost a month, she allowed only Dwayne to feed her and would not bark or be affectionate with Viola, increasing Viola's trauma. Slowly, over several weeks, she began to warm up again to Viola.

Before Viola and Dwayne took Sweetie back with them to Wichita, Belinda suggested they have calls from their old New Orleans number transferred to them at Dwayne's home in Kansas. They were grateful for the suggestion because this is something they hadn't thought to do.

A strange thing happened after a few more months of Viola's exile in Wichita. Dwayne continued to search for Ming but had no luck. A week or two prior to the day that Dwayne thought he would have to give up finding his beloved dog, he experienced a vision of Ming cuddled up to a large black dog. Soon after Dwayne's vision, Viola's phone rang and a man's voice asked, "May I speak to Ming?"

Dwayne told the man that no one there was named Ming but they had a dog by that name. The man said that he had been unable to read the dog's tags, but today he had scraped the rust off and discovered the rest of this phone number. He said he went to New Orleans to help with animal rescue and found Ming roaming around the streets there. He fell in love with the dog. They stayed in New Orleans after Katrina, and the man had taken Ming with him to help with Hurricane Rita rescue. Then he took her home with him to Texarkana, Arkansas.

Dwayne asked the man if he owned a large black dog. He said that he didn't but that Ming liked to play with a large black dog who lived across the street.

They made arrangements for Dwayne and Viola to drive from Wichita to Texarkana and be reunited with Ming. Prior to leaving Wichita, Viola called the number the man had given her, and a woman, the man's mother, answered. When Viola told her that they were coming to retrieve Ming, the woman hung up. Viola tried again with the same results. Finally Dwayne got through and received directions to the house.

Dwayne suspected that the man and his mother had become attached to Ming. He wondered if they really did find Ming's phone number only recently. Perhaps the man had twinges of conscience until he finally did the right thing and called Dwayne.

Dwayne wasn't exactly sure how to find the man's house, but he seemed to be operating on an inner radar. Unknowingly, while looking for the place, he stopped in front of the man's house. When he saw a red truck parked in front, he noticed it had a sign on it that said, U.S. Emergency Disaster Team. This assured him that they were at the right place.

The man came to the door looking sad. When Ming saw Dwayne, she jumped on him, and the two rolled on the ground in unbridled joy. Ming was skinny but healthy, and she bonded right away with Viola as well. It was a happy drive back home.

Now Dwayne, Viola, Ming, and Sweetie are all back together in New Orleans. Dwayne is helping his mother rebuild and is answering the seemingly obvious questions posed by insurance adjusters, such as, "What caused damage to the house?"

He continues to be grateful and says, "If it wouldn't have been for those who took their time and money to come down here and help, we wouldn't have our dogs back home."

## Volunteering and Marriages

Since we are a husband-wife team, we were curious what spouses of volunteers thought when their husband or wife announced that he or she was going to the Gulf Coast. Were they concerned about safety and health?

Valerie and Tom Schomburg, from Newport Beach, California, went to New Orleans together. Valerie is an animal control officer, and Tom is a police officer. Tom was only intending to accompany his wife to New Leash on Life's staging area in the Winn-Dixie parking lot, in New Orleans, but when he went to the first briefing meeting with her, he decided that he too would volunteer as a safety officer on the search-and-rescue teams.

Dr. James Gardner and his wife had to face the separation and possible dangers of one of them doing rescue work. Dr. Gardner is a clinical psychologist and active environmentalist who protects a two-thousand-acre Atlantic rain forest in Brazil. He and his wife supervise the reforesting and protection of fragile ecosystems and help to sustain the music tree, which produces the only wood used for making violin bows. Dr. Gardner says about rescuing animals, "It was very rewarding. Nature dealt them a bad hand, and for a few hours, a few days, I can enrich their lives. I think of it as a small island in a sea of despair. Sometimes all I do is hold an animal. They give a big sigh and collapse in my arms. I stroke them. Caress their faces. Play with their mouths. The biggest, baddest dog becomes a small puppy. Other times I am enabling them to play with other animals. To be dogs again. Dogs are social animals. They lose this in the kennels. They regain it in the Bark Park, a dog-walking area that I helped to make for them."

As Dr. Gardner started planning his second trip to volunteer, he said, "My wife got worried that I had a girlfriend down there. By the third trip, she was sure I had something going on. But the animals and other volunteers needed us to come back and help them."

Jennifer Shirley is an American Airlines flight attendant who joined the Oregon Humane Society's animal rescue team on its second trip to New Orleans. Jennifer told us, "I thought, These animals need our help. Their humans are not there to rescue them. This dog I saw on television news is somebody's companion. These are living, breathing life forces. I wanted to do whatever I could to improve their situation — give them food and attention, walk and love them."

Jennifer talked to her husband, Bruce Hazen, about Oregon Humane's request that she deploy as a volunteer. Bruce says, "My initial thought was that she must not be asking what I think she just asked. I was concerned about her returning from such a mission unharmed. The news from that area was dire. I wanted to know more about the conditions where Jennifer would be going. When she called me from Lamar-Dixon right before Hurricane Rita was supposed to hit, she said, 'I may have to go if the siren goes off while we're talking. It means that tornadoes have been reported in our area again. I'll run into the lavatory which is the only concrete building that's here to be used as a shelter.' Oh, yeah, I was feeling pretty good after that phone call!"

But both Jennifer and Bruce were pleased with how her volunteerism paid off. Bruce says, "Jennifer's confidence and energy were noticeably higher than I've ever seen them, and she has a deeper commitment to making a difference by working with animals."

We also asked people we interviewed what responses they received from friends and coworkers when they announced that they were going to the hurricane-ravaged coast. A lot of volunteers didn't tell anybody, thinking that no one would understand or that concerned friends would try to talk them out of going. Chris Cutter, at International Fund for Animal Welfare, says that his friends made comments such as "Be careful," "That's awesome," "Tell me what it's like." When he returned they asked, "Did you meet Anderson Cooper?"

He didn't.

But you will meet many of the people that Anderson Cooper and other journalists covered as animal rescue and reunion faced its greatest challenges after Hurricane Katrina.

# PART THREE

# RESCUES AND REUNIONS
# AFTER HURRICANE KATRINA

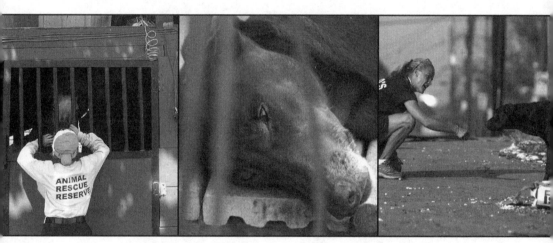

*Photos on previous page, left to right:*

Denise Gove, San Diego Humane, checks on a horse at Lamar-Dixon.

Luana Maria Rathman and Margie Wilmoth's dog Noodle rests after a long journey home.

A Pasado's Safe Haven volunteer entices a dog with food.

# CHAPTER THIRTEEN

# Lamar-Dixon Expo Center: Emergency Shelter for Animals after the Storms

After Hurricane Katrina, organizations and individuals banded together to try to save the lives of more than a quarter million New Orleans–area animals who were struggling, often alone, to survive the storm. Throughout Mississippi and the Gulf Coast, millions more had died or were in danger of dying. The riveting accounts of the largest emergency animal rescuing, sheltering, and reuniting process in history offer unprecedented insight into saving animals from disaster.

On Tuesday, August 30, the day after Hurricane Katrina, Laura Maloney, executive director of the Louisiana SPCA (LA/SPCA), returned from the Houston SPCA, where she and her remaining staff of fifteen, out of the original sixty-five, had evacuated 263 animals in climate-controlled trucks from the shelter on Japonica Street. The staff had lost everything. Two had no idea where their family members were, including one who couldn't at first locate the children who had stayed with her ex-husband. With all they were going through, these staff stayed and worked every day to rescue animals. Laura's husband, Dan Maloney, general curator at the Audubon Zoo, was caring for the animals there and staying with his staff. Friends from the Houston Zoo took care of the Maloneys' four dogs.

After conferring with the State Department of Agriculture, Laura started the sheltering operation at Lamar-Dixon Equine Exhibition Center in Gonzales, Louisiana, sixty miles north of New Orleans. Eventually, Laura says, 8,500 rescued animals moved through the facility.

## Trivia Question: Who the Heck Are Lamar and Dixon?

Before we go further into what happened at the facility that became the pivot point for animal rescue experiences after Katrina, you may be wondering, as we were, What is the history of this place?

Mary Lee and Bill Dixon are multimillionaire philanthropists. Bill Dixon is a professional horse trainer and competitor. Mary Lee is the daughter of Charles Lamar Jr., founder of Lamar Corporation, an outdoor advertising business. In 1997 the Dixons built the Lamar-Dixon Equine Exhibition Center, which seats several thousand people, and gave it to Ascension Parish as a nonprofit organization. The Dixons intended it to be a venue for equestrian and other events, such as 4-H exhibitions, and to be used as a resource for economic development of the community; it was not to be a commercial venue. The Lamar-Dixon website adds what in hindsight looks ironic considering what you are about to read in this chapter: "Our aim is to attract diverse entertainment to the community in a safe, user-friendly environment."[1] When the place was transformed into an emergency animal rescue operation following Hurricane Katrina, little remained that was entertaining, safe, or user friendly. With the unexpected deluge of animals entering the facility, it quickly turned chaotic and unmanageable.

## The First Days after the Storm

At first Lamar-Dixon appeared to be the perfect place to set up shop and receive animals brought in from the ravaged New Orleans areas. Laura Maloney says, "It was a large horse-show facility with bathing stalls and space for campers. When we arrived it was a virtual ghost-barn." Dave Pauli, regional director for the HSUS, who became incident commander at Lamar-Dixon, describes the facility: "It was excellent with drainage and capacity for cleaning and weather protection. It was better than 99 percent of the fairgrounds I had used in previous disasters."

Laura says, "Lamar had five barns available to house animals. These would become landmarks for us to navigate the site as Barns 1 through 5. Each barn had thirty to forty stalls that could hold four to five wire crates for individual animals. In the first days we used only half of Barns 1 and 2. By the time we left, we had outgrown all the designated barns and created Barn 6 out of a separate area." The facility's management set a limit of 1,300 animals. It could hold 2,000. Dave Pauli says, "At its peak, we had 2,700 animals there."

To set up emergency rescue operations Laura needed funds, but the local Whitney National Bank was now under water, so she had no access to the organization's cash or credit. She called Julie Morris and Laura Lanza at the ASPCA. Julie wired $50,000 to a nonlocal bank so Laura could buy cages and other necessary items and start the sheltering functions. Because no apartments or hotel rooms were available, Laura and her staff stayed at Laura's father's house in Baton Rouge. In the two or three hours at night that they slept, the staff used sleeping bags and air mattresses, even the dog's couch, as beds.

To accommodate her staff while they worked at Lamar-Dixon, Laura found a house for sale in nearby St. Amant by a woman named Angel who wanted to sell it to someone doing something important. At the same time, BellSouth was buying up huge blocks of property for its people to live in, and prices were skyrocketing. Laura told Julie, "I need $150,000 to buy a house." The money got wired to her. Local SPCAs from around the country sent more than a thousand veterinarians, animal control officers, and activists to help with the disaster relief.[2] Laura says, "I have grown to admire and respect the ASPCA in ways that I never imagined. I was overwhelmed with their responsiveness, their caring about animals. Our staff learned a lot from them. Julie Morris called me every day. It was a life-changing experience."

Initially upon opening the animal sheltering operation at Lamar-Dixon, Laura was the incident commander. On Wednesday, August 31,

Laura and her staff began rescuing animals in Jefferson Parish. They picked up pets from interstate highways where evacuating people had been forced to leave them behind. Laura says, "The first day we entered the city of New Orleans, on September 2, military police forced us to pull out after only a couple of hours. The reports of shooting and other rampant crimes had turned it into a virtual war zone." When the shelter staff was finally allowed into the city, the shock of what they saw there started to penetrate — thousands of residents evacuated, their pets left at home or in the care of neighbors.

Laura activated a cell phone in Baton Rouge and released the number to the public. Calls poured in from frantic people who couldn't get back into the city to rescue their pets. Cajun Clickers, a group of volunteer computer whizzes, logged the handwritten rescue requests into a database that had to be updated every day by midnight. These requests were then converted to lists for animal control officers and rescuers to use by 6:00 each morning.

Because HSUS's Disaster Animal Rescue Teams had experience in large-scale disaster management, Laura, realizing that Katrina was far larger than anything the Louisiana SPCA had handled in the past, asked them to manage the operation at Lamar-Dixon. The HSUS had sent Dave Pauli to Gonzales, Louisiana, where he was expecting to do field rescue on a boat, but his role soon changed. He says, "At my first meeting, Laura asked if I'd relieve her as incident commander so she could work with her agency. I thought it would be a short-term assignment. It turned into a blur of crisis management and logistical planning for survival." He asked Dick Green of AHA and Barbara Callahan, a specialist in oil spills (formerly with IFAW), who were already at Lamar-Dixon, as well as representatives from other national groups such as the ASPCA, IFAW, and Code 3 to help him manage the operation.

Dave Pauli served two stints of twenty-four days, starting on September 7, at Lamar-Dixon. He worked a total of fifty-one days on other aspects of the rescue effort, which included trapping animals, attending debriefing meetings, and focusing on other Katrina-related duties that took him away from his home base in Montana. He says,

Normally if I come to an event, by day seven I would find a well-oiled machine. This one had neither a machine nor oil. We had to think what we would do for the next hour or two to help these animals. It was hard to even find a table where we could do planning. It wasn't until day eight that we got an RV to use for an office. We had been sitting on a golf cart and using a pallet as a desk. This was an equine facility that was supposed to house eighty to one hundred horses and grew to house 1,500 dogs. Having enough volunteers to pick up animal waste was a major issue. We had to design ways to control dog-doo problems. That hadn't been on my hundred-item checklist during previous disasters.

Andrea Kozil of In Defense of Animals–Africa had no shelter experience but was put in charge of running Barn 5, where intake occurred each night as rescue teams brought in their day's catch of animals. She described her experience for us:

We had several hundred animals to care for and not enough supplies. We needed more cages, food, water bowls. The problems were constantly shifting. I had volunteers crying and animals who were in shock, frozen in fear, and sitting in filthy cages in the intense heat. Some animals were family pets; others were terribly neglected backyard dogs. Some were biting at their cages, trying to break free. Tiny dogs shivered in cages next to huge dogs. Some pit bulls had scars and wounds from being forced to fight.

I had to organize volunteers and try to communicate with the outside world to let people know how desperate we were for the things we needed.

The dogs never stopped barking.

I met some of the most inspiring people I have ever known in my life. I tried to make a difference. I tried to do whatever I possibly could to help the terrified, hungry, confused, and sick animals. Some dogs smothered me with kisses when I was able to have short visits while walking them; others were too miserable to care. Their whole lives had been turned upside down.

Because all the animal organizations were calling for volunteers, ready and willing people with much experience or none began spilling in by the hundreds, then the thousands. The HSUS put out calls for volunteers on its website, asking everyone to come and help. When invited volunteers arrived, they were given HSUS T-shirts, and everyone, including the Louisiana SPCA volunteers, wore them. Laura says, "The T-shirts implied credibility for people who may or may not have been skilled. Volunteers showed up in flip-flops. We got hammered by the military because some animal rescue people weren't wearing proper clothing. The HSUS T-shirts and spray-painting LA/SPCA on their vehicles got volunteers through military checkpoints into New Orleans. We had always had good relationships with local police."

From many accounts we heard, the police and military couldn't tell who was legitimately sanctioned by the LA/SPCA or qualified to rescue animals and who wasn't. Since so many thousands of animals needed emergency help, many officials at checkpoints figured it was a moot point or didn't know what kind of credentials to accept, so they waved through those who identified themselves as animal rescuers.

Also, volunteers would show up or call the HSUS and other animal rescue organizations, wanting to be on rescue teams like the kind they were seeing on television — in boats or going from house to house to find animals. In some cases, if the volunteers weren't credentialed by HSUS or another national organization that offers training, they could work at Lamar-Dixon as cage cleaners or do other tasks but were not allowed to serve on rescue teams.

Because Dave Pauli understood that volunteers came to Lamar-Dixon with images of themselves walking out of destroyed houses carrying animals in their arms, he occasionally rotated some of the untrained volunteers to do field work with skilled animal rescue teams. Yet there was still the issue of volunteers who arrived at Lamar-Dixon or called the HSUS to volunteer and were told that, being untrained, they would not be allowed on official animal rescue teams. This policy, a standard throughout all of the national animal organizations that offer training, caused some volunteers to become frustrated and angry. It motivated them to establish their own operations or join other animal rescue groups working inside New Orleans and in other Louisiana parishes. More about this appears in chapters 14 and 15.

*Ron Silver planning rescue strategy.*

Local police were pitching in to help with rescue efforts, as you'll see throughout this book. Ron Silver, a filmmaker from Nebraska, did rescue work with HSUS's DART. He says, "Armed security guards stopped us while we were working in the Garden District in New Orleans. These were a group of guys with machine guns. They said they had rescued an animal in the hotel where they were staying. They brought out a hamster and said that they had named him Killer. On the way back to Lamar-Dixon, Killer gave birth to six babies. I was thinking, I hope the crooks don't know what a bunch of softies these guys are. They all had dogs and cats at home."

## Special Expertise Was Needed

Laura soon realized that Lamar-Dixon was primarily a sheltering-dispatch operation, and as such, its roles were to provide veterinary care, micro-chipping, and photographing and to prepare animals for adoption or reuniting. To increase the help that Laura Maloney and Dave Pauli were getting from the Big Three and other animal organizations, HSUS called upon the Society of Animal Welfare Administrators, a professional association whose members manage animal shelters. United Animal Nations, whose staff are experts in setting up temporary shelters, stepped in to help the national groups with sheltering and coordinating efforts through daily telephone conference calls. The national organizations called their animal shelter members around the country and asked them to send trained staff. Arizona, Boston, Connecticut, Denver, Houston, Nashville, New York, Oregon, and San Diego Humane Societies and SPCAs were among the top-notch teams that traveled to Lamar-Dixon and places in Mississippi to organize sheltering operations and perform technical types of animal rescue with boats, gear, and ladders.

Laura set up command in the city's Emergency Operations Center, at the Hyatt Hotel, where she occupied a desk in the hotel's ballroom along with FEMA, the Red Cross, and other agencies. She made daily trips between New Orleans and the Lamar-Dixon Expo Center in Gonzales to stay in the emergency management loop. Meanwhile, the HSUS was bringing in millions of dollars in donations to pay for renting and running the Lamar-Dixon operation and keeping it staffed with volunteers and supplied with necessary materials. Laura says, "Everyone has a role to play. When we work together, we achieve positive results."

## Where Will All the Volunteers Stay?

Housing volunteers quickly became an issue. The Red Cross and FEMA erected a tent to hold hundreds of evacuees and volunteers while the HSUS placed fences around the site to protect people and animals. Recreational vehicles and trailers filled the parking lots. Dave Pauli says, "One day 220 volunteers registered and got name tags. We had a FEMA tent that housed 580 people and was filled to overflowing. About 200 people camped out in RVs and cars; 900 people were there. They all had to eat and have places to go to the bathroom and shower. I slept on top of a fiberglass LA/SPCA dog truck, in my rental car, and then in an RV someone donated."

When we spoke with volunteer Patti McKinney, she commented on the living conditions for volunteers:

> In one of the barns, there were showers set up using tarps, heaters, and a great water system. It was very useful for the evacuees. We figured we could use those showers too. Nobody said we couldn't.
>
> One night I went over to take a shower. Military men were sitting outside of it playing video games and guarding. I asked, "Can I use this shower?"

They said, "Are you one of those animal people?"

I said, "Yes, we're caring for the animals."

One said, "Well, you can only use this one shower. You'd better not bring any of those dirty, smelly, poopy clothes in there and rinse them off. This is the only way you can use it."

I said, "Oh, okay. Are you going to sit here, right outside, as I take my shower?"

He said, "Yes, ma'am, this is where we're stationed." It was five feet in front of the shower. And I said, "Well, I'm not comfortable with that."

He said, "That's too bad, ma'am, you're going to have to talk to the Red Cross about that. They're the ones that put us here." He was very condescending. It made me feel like a second-class citizen. I was grateful to have security but wish they had treated us with more respect.

Dave Pauli's expectations about what kind of help he could get from FEMA expanded when Senator John Ensign visited the facility. Dave says, "A FEMA official came on the senator's behalf and asked me what I needed. I was rattled and didn't know what to ask for first." Later Dave called FEMA back and requested five air-conditioned tents, more ice and water, and National Guard to protect the facility. By day 10, a white air-conditioned wedding tent was sent. Dave lay down in it and even though the tent was packed wall-to-wall with people, fell asleep for four hours straight, the longest nap he'd had since he'd arrived. Of Senator Ensign he says, "He's a veterinarian. He toured Lamar-Dixon and Louisiana State University's facilities. He did a rah-rah to compliment the groups for working together. He had the army appoint two military commanders to look into the animal issues we were facing. It was high-level motivation and intelligent insights from a veterinarian who could get a lot of federal resources to us."

## Supplies Poured In

Soon donated supplies began pouring in to Lamar-Dixon faster than they could be unloaded, sorted, and inventoried. One day it was thirty pallets of much-needed dog kennels. Another day it was twelve pallets of ergonomic pillows. Dave gave these to the American Red Cross human shelter.

Laura describes supplies as "air crates, dog food, cat food, leashes, collars, towels, blankets, toothpaste, you name it." Volunteers opened boxes but needed forklifts and trucks and warehouse storage space. The Gonzales Wal-Mart manager donated the use of a hand forklift. He let Dave's staff into the store at 2:00 AM to shop for things they needed. Dave says, "Every time I asked a PetSmart or Wal-Mart manager for something, they helped me." According to PetSmart Charities executive director Susana Della Maddalena, the PetSmart Charities Rescue Waggin', a custom-designed animal transport vehicle, transported one in eight animals to or from the Lamar-Dixon Expo Center.

Sarah Comis, at the HSUS, served as resource management director. She acquired everything the field people needed from corporations or retail businesses. Dave says, "Sarah's work was critical for Lamar-Dixon to continue its operation." This kind of support, from people who weren't at the facility but could be relied upon to somehow get necessary supplies there, proved to be crucial for the survival of Lamar-Dixon and other temporary sheltering and rescue operations all over the Gulf Coast.

## Stolen Animals

Soon problems arose with people trying to steal dogs. Because pit bulls are often used in dogfighting, these dogs are valuable. Until Lamar-Dixon tightened security, some tough-looking characters came through the facility looking for pit bulls. They either stole the dogs outright or conned volunteers into believing the dogs belonged to them. Some men would come in and take a photo of a dog and then say, "This is my dog."

Dave started asking for a photo of the dog on the person's lap at their house. Of course, people would say that all of their photos were gone. Dave and the barn managers had to become judge and jury on the spot. At times Dave had to intervene when volunteers wouldn't return dogs to men they thought might be dogfighters. Then he would have to examine whether the dog had scarring or old injuries or looked happy and friendly.

One thousand pit bulls were rescued and housed at Lamar-Dixon, comprising 25 percent of all the dogs sheltered there. The HSUS had to erect a perimeter fence and hire a private security firm to be present around the clock, increasing safety for both animals and people.

Another "nasty side of animal rescue," as Dave calls it, was the volunteers who wanted a lifelong memento of their experience in the form of a rescued animal. He estimates that rescuers at Lamar-Dixon stole more than one hundred animals. Some volunteers figured they were giving the animals better homes and care than they'd had previously, but Dave says that was not their decision to make, and it impeded reuniting people with their pets.

## Veterinary Medical Assistance

By September 10 the facility had local and visiting veterinarians as well as members of Veterinary Medical Assistance Teams (VMAT), who are deployed by FEMA for animal disaster relief. Public Health Services and FEMA vets worked side by side with Department of Defense army vets, state vets, private vets, and veterinarians from the Louisiana State University vet school.

Faster than floodwaters, rumors spread throughout the facility and on Internet blogs and websites. The most persistent rumors were that the Lamar-Dixon veterinary teams were doing wholesale euthanization of animals and that dogs and feral cats were being assessed as aggressive and put down. Everyone we spoke to denies that this happened. They all say that only sick animals were euthanized. Laura Maloney's LA/SPCA wasn't euthanizing any animals, according to Dave, that were "tame, calm, or had evidence of ownership." Laura says in retrospect that she should have hired a public relations person to balance the rhetoric and rumors. But, she says, "I was focused on the task at hand."

We interviewed Dr. Julie Burge and were surprised to find that even though she is a well-qualified veterinarian, she encountered resistance when trying to volunteer at Lamar-Dixon. We don't know if her experience was unusual. Dr. Burge is a skilled avian vet with a clinic in Grandview, Missouri. She is a sixteen-year member of the Association of Avian Veterinarians, an organization that offers lectures and training on bird medicine and surgery. Nevertheless, Dr. Burge says, "When I arrived at Lamar-Dixon, VMAT turned me away and wouldn't let me work on the birds. One volunteer tech person wanted to have control of who touched the birds and made sure I wasn't able to get in there to do anything. This was her little pond, and I wasn't supposed to swim in it." Dr. Burge blames the lack of response to her expertise on the organizations that were trying, but not always succeeding, in working together. From a volunteer's perspective, she wasn't able to tell who was in charge. Dr. Burge says, "Nobody had ever done anything of this size before. I should have gone to the highest people in each of the organizations and stroked ego. You have to kiss the right behinds to be able to work on the birds." Dr. Burge never was allowed to help with the birds at Lamar-Dixon.

Gold and blue macaws, the sole survivors from a flock of thirty-five.

Another problem we heard from several veterinarians was that they were required to go through an organization's training and that they had to commit to staying at Lamar-Dixon for two weeks. Volunteer turnover made the already difficult job of animal rescue even harder because so much information was lost during transitions and it took a lot of time to fill in the next person. But private vets such as Dr. Burge hadn't attended official disaster training classes and couldn't afford to take two weeks away from their practices or to be out of touch with their clients for such a long period.

Dr. Burge returned to volunteer several times, mostly in Baton Rouge at the home of Donna Powell, the founder of 911 Parrot Alert. Donna was sheltering birds that had been brought to her for safekeeping as well as birds found by animal rescuers. According to Dr. Burge, Donna Powell's home became a major center of bird rescue operations for the New Orleans area. She says, "When I called Donna, I learned that she had more than 60 extra birds in her home; eventually that number grew to 325 birds. Suddenly I found someone who was helping birds and needed me."[3]

## Filled to Overflowing

Lamar-Dixon management had placed a limit on the number of animals the facility could house at any given time. This level was exceeded on September 11. That night, the animal rescue teams bringing in their frightened and sick animals were barred by the military and sheriff's department personnel from entering the facility. Hundreds of animals, many of them deathly ill, sat in the parking lot in cages in the sweltering heat while tempers flared among volunteers who were upset at being turned away from the facility.

Dave Pauli told us, "One crazy night we had to load 770 dogs and cats that came in a five-hour period. We were way over our limit. So we had to reload them onto refrigerated trucks and drive them off-site. They couldn't be humanely held with the heat. We were moving animals as many as three times. We didn't finish until three o'clock in the morning."

The only way animals could continue to be rescued, especially those who were in dire need of medical assistance, was to make room for them. Already, overflow animals were being sent to temporary shelters such as the one Best Friends was running in Tylertown, Mississippi, and that Noah's Wish had established in Slidell, Louisiana.

But it was clear, with more animals coming in, some would have to be transported to other shelters around the country. The ASPCA quickly put together a list of legitimate and regulated animal shelters that would take Katrina dogs and cats. Julie Morris says, "We were up till 1:00 in the morning on the phone to craft a memorandum of understanding for agencies that wanted to take animals. They had to agree to put them on

Petfinder.com, neuter the animals, and return them to owners who claimed them. At first we required the agencies to be recommended. When Hurricane Rita was coming, this higher level of scrutiny went largely by the wayside."

Finally Dave Pauli and everyone else had to get serious about shipping animals to locations all over the country. Animal rescue organizations and shelters lined up for hours, waiting to take their truckload or van load of animals back to their hometowns. Soon airlifts sponsored by T. Boone Pickens and Continental Airlines, Marin Humane, and other organizations began in earnest and continued through October. (Details about airlifts are in chapter 16.)

The Louisiana state veterinarian office was concerned about exporting animals out of the area and imposed restrictions: no fewer than six animals to any organization and only to brick-and-mortar facilities. At first the only animals allowed out of the state were ones who had no collars or identification and who had not been picked up at people's dwellings. These were considered to be strays or unowned.

The state veterinarian office said that after September 30 Lamar-Dixon could accept only critically ill animals. Soon after, another ruling came down that caused quite a stir. The state veterinarian office said that veterinarians from other states shouldn't be allowed to practice in Louisiana anymore. Marie Wheatley, president of American Humane, says, "I've heard conflicting stories about whether at that time they needed outside veterinarians or not. Some people thought there were still a lot of animals to take care of. Others didn't think veterinarians were needed to do for free what local veterinarians would charge for doing."

## Barn 5 Revisited

After seeing volunteers in action, the HSUS hired some of them as permanent staff. When the organization later expanded its Disaster Animal Rescue Teams from three to twelve positions, it hired Lieutenant Randy Covey, formerly of the Oregon Humane Society, as its new director of disaster services. Randy had managed Barn 5 at Lamar-Dixon, and from his Oregon teammates we'd heard great things about how he organized the whirl of activity there. We spoke with Randy only a week and a half after he and his wife, Kathy, formerly the public relations director at Oregon Humane, moved to Washington, DC, for Randy to start his new job.

Randy says, "We set a schedule for animals in Barn 5. They had been walked a lot and never allowed to rest. Lights were on all the time in the facility. The animals needed quiet time. This huge barn had 250 dogs in it. We rigged it up into four sections. We had what we called Organized Chaos in the morning when all the dogs were being walked and having their cages cleaned. Then it was the Barn of Tranquillity in the afternoon while they slept and were left alone. In the evening, we had Organized Chaos again, returning to the Barn of Tranquillity by bedtime."

*Lt. Randy Covey, HSUS/Oregon Humane Society, gives a belly rub to a rescued dog.*

Now Randy has a new goal. He says of his new job for HSUS, "We are going to create the premier animal rescue program in the nation."

Not only in Barn 5, under Randy Covey's supervision, but overall, Lamar-Dixon became more organized as time went on and its contribution to Hurricane Katrina animal rescue was better defined.

## Lamar-Dixon Gets Its Quiet and Clean Expo Center Back

Dave Pauli's impression of the state veterinarian office was that it was in a hurry to get the rescue effort over with and wanted Lamar-Dixon closed by October 15. "To say that we were unwanted clients at Lamar-Dixon would be to minimize how much the facility wanted us off their property. Their management had realistic complaints, such as that one barn was bleaching the kennels and running bleach water into a pond instead of the septic tank." Dave had to travel to Baton Rouge every day for a one-hour meeting with the state veterinarian office to try to solve problems none of them had ever faced before.

However, some animal rescue officials think the haste to close the facility was misplaced. In an HSUS report the president and chief executive, Wayne Pacelle, is quoted as saying, "Given that animals were still being found, and that evacuees were only just returning to New Orleans, the directive to shut down Lamar-Dixon was most regrettable."[4]

Under the supervision of Melissa Seide-Rubin, HSUS vice president of field and disaster services and Lamar-Dixon's last incident commander, the animal rescue operation ended on Monday, October 10, when the last animal, a forty-five-pound pit bull mix, left the shelter as volunteers and staff shed tears of joy and relief. Melissa Seide-Rubin estimated that it would take thousands of person-hours to clean the barns, remove wood shavings in each horse stall, and spray down and disinfect them. Volunteers also had to move and store perishable food, medical supplies, and animal crates for shipping to Louisiana shelters.[5]

## Whatever Happened to Laura Maloney and Dave Pauli?

Laura Maloney's staff and her new hires admire the work she did following Katrina. After the hurricane, Laura was named New Orleans's City-Business Woman of the Year for 2005. She told her staff they were the ones who should be congratulated, and one of the staff replied, "You're the glue, baby. You're the glue."

The ASPCA and the HSUS donated funds for the Louisiana SPCA to rent a temporary shelter in Algiers, Louisiana, and to begin building a new facility. Laura says, "The ASPCA's financial support is allowing us to continue our humane work, such as cruelty investigations statewide, education programs, and behavior/obedience classes. The house that an ASPCA donor bought in St. Amant for our staff to stay in while we worked at Lamar-Dixon is the location for our new animal cruelty division." The ASPCA has also assigned and is paying for a mentor to work with Laura during LA/SPCA's recovery and as it makes the transition to a new building.

Laura's schedule remains full. She is taking a page from the HSUS playbook and hiring public relations help. She hopes in the future to send out accurate information so rumors don't work up animal lovers' emotions unnecessarily. She worked on the passing of a pet evacuation bill sponsored by Senator Huelette "Clo" Fontenot of the Louisiana state senate. United Animal Nations is talking with her about setting up temporary animal shelters near Red Cross shelters for future disasters so people and animals don't have to be separated. Laura is asking for a seat at the table for animal control officials and the LA/SPCA and other local humane agencies to oversee animal rescue efforts at the Emergency Operations Center. She has made it clear to HSUS that she thinks the come-one-come-all approach and credentialing of thousands of volunteers with T-shirts was more detrimental than helpful to her efforts to exercise control over who was authorized to rescue animals and to ensure that volunteers were operating under local and state guidelines. Laura says, "I have always relished the challenges of working in animal welfare in Louisiana, and particularly New Orleans, where the need is great. In spite of Katrina, and in a strange way because of Katrina, I still do."

Dave Pauli is back at his regular job for the HSUS in the Northern Rockies Region doing search and seizure in cases where people are being accused of hoarding and abusing large numbers of animals. He also gets called in on cases that require he trap illegally owned alligators, and he handles emergency and disaster situations in which animals are stuck in traps, running loose, or stranded. He also continues to work on using handheld global positioning system (GPS) units with GPS coordinates to help trapping teams find animals. He says, "For the disaster in Sri Lanka, we sent radio telemetry collars and receivers. This way when we caught a nursing mother dog or cat we could attach the collar, release her, and follow her back to the den to recover all her puppies or kittens." He sent to Laura Maloney remote, motion-activated video and still cameras that she could use to monitor feed stations and animal activities. His favorite saying after Hurricane Katrina is a take-off on a popular credit card commercial: "Animals in disasters: Don't leave home without them."

Dave calls the Lamar-Dixon experience "extremely frustrating and joyous."

## Reunions: The Highlight of Rescue Work

Through all the frustrations at Lamar-Dixon, one highlight kept staff and volunteers going. Everyone agrees that watching joyful, tearful, spontaneous reunions at the facility made all their efforts worthwhile.

American Humane's animal emergency services response team leader, Kerri Burns, says that she had been at Lamar-Dixon for no more than two hours when she was assigned to work in Barn 5. She was told that somebody there needed help. When she arrived at the barn, she found a tall, frail seventy-year-old African American man with his twenty-year-old grandson. They were looking into stalls. The man had lost seven beagles. He called them his "babies."

One cage had five beagles in it. The man said, "Those two are mine," pointing to a pair of dogs. "The other three belong to my neighbor. I don't know where he is." Fortunately, the man was staying with his grandson and could take his babies with him. While Kerri held back tears of joy for this man's reunion and finished up the paperwork, he said, "Thank you. I have another day to live for."

*Kerri Burns, American Humane Association, with a rescued beagle at Lamar–Dixon the night Hurricane Rita was coming.*

While staff at Lamar-Dixon struggled with the influx of thousands of displaced animals, other animal organizations and individuals were sprouting temporary emergency operations all over Louisiana and Mississippi. If you had told some of these people a year, or even a month, earlier that they would be forming new 501(c)3 charities, they wouldn't have believed you.

In the next two chapters their experiences provide a glimpse into the diverse, rough-and-tumble, highly independent, and creative world of animal rescue.

# CHAPTER FOURTEEN

# Animal Rescue Teams and Emergency Shelters

To say that there was a divergence of opinions about how to deal with the Gulf Coast disaster is an understatement equivalent to saying that hurricanes have high winds. Federal agencies and officials stepped on the toes of state and local organizations. National animal groups invaded the territories of state and local agencies. Groups that specialize in rescuing animals in disasters competed over who should be in charge and quickly figured out that they had to put aside their differences and cooperate. Volunteer rescuers arrived by the hundreds, then the thousands. On the PBS show *Katrina's Animal Rescue*, part of the *Nature* series, it was estimated that 250,000 pets had been left in the city.[1]

Hundreds of groups worked in the Gulf Coast, sending staff and volunteers to pick up animals and take them to shelters. A brief introduction to some of these organizations appears in this and the following chapters. You can read more about each of these groups on their websites, listed in the Resources section of this book. Although our descriptions of the animal rescues going on outside of Lamar-Dixon are not comprehensive, since so many organizations operated in the affected areas, we believe they are representative of what went on in the largest disaster-related animal rescue effort in history.

## Disaster Response Animal Rescue, aka the Winn-Dixie Group

Mark and Shannon Martin, Pet Supplies Plus franchise owners, from Athens, Georgia, first went to Slidell, Louisiana, and worked for a while with Noah's Wish to help set up a temporary shelter for animals displaced by Katrina. Noah's Wish helped Slidell Animal Control after its shelter was completely destroyed.

Mark discreetly entered New Orleans on September 7 with a local New Orleans resident who he met in Slidell. They spent the first five days in New Orleans rescuing animals on their own. The task was so daunting that Mark immediately called Shannon, who had returned to Georgia. He told his wife that he couldn't rescue animals alone. So Shannon put out a call via the Internet and on local radio and media, asking for volunteers. Meanwhile, Mark made connections in New Orleans with others who wanted to help rescue animals, but it was the volunteers coming from all over the country who made it possible for him to continue the work. The Oregon National Guard unit gave Mark clearance and support and provided coordinates for where the military had seen stranded animals. They and other federal agencies and officials, such as the Drug Enforcement Agency, the U.S. Marshals, and the Bureau of Alcohol, Tobacco, and Firearms were integral to the success of Mark and Shannon's rescue efforts.

We heard from many rescuers that their first experiences in New Orleans were of emergency medical technicians, police officers, firefighters, and military personnel bringing animals to them or telling them where to find animals. They had found and rescued these animals while trying to save the lives of humans and attempting to keep control of the city.

When Lamar-Dixon filled up and the Jefferson Feed, Pet, and Garden Center in New Orleans, where rescued animals were first being taken, overloaded, Mark and his volunteers set up a rescue operation out of a looted Winn-Dixie, with the permission of corporate manager Keith Cherry. Shannon Martin says, "Winn-Dixie management came through to do damage assessment. Mark and Richard Crook, one of our first volunteers, met with them. Winn-Dixie authorized us to stay at the site. They were fabulous through the entire thing. They gave us permission to use the inventory the looters hadn't carried off after the hurricane. Our rescuers could have soap, shampoo, and canned goods." Winn-Dixie had a backup generator and allowed the animal rescuers to run it for their operations twenty-four hours a day. This gave light and helped to cool down the animals. According to Richard Crook, "The attorneys for Winn-Dixie suggested that the store get something in writing to relieve them of any liability, but the head of Winn-Dixie told them that if some- ` thing happens, something happens."

Most of the time Shannon Martin was busy in Athens, Georgia, set-ting up the nonprofit status for Disaster Response Animal Rescue (DRAR), also known as the Winn-Dixie group, rounding up supplies such as water and fuel, and calling for volunteers. Mark set up discreet routes into the city so that other freelance volunteers would know how to get through military checkpoints.

The Winn-Dixie group started sending animals to Humane Society of Louisiana and Best Friends, both with temporary shelters in Tylertown, Mississippi, and on the airlifts and ground transports to different parts of the country. According to Shannon, DRAR was bringing in 100 to 150 animals a day to Winn-Dixie. At first they didn't have a solid paperwork system, but later they got better at keeping records of where animals were found. Once ground transports and shipping became necessary, they released the animals only to groups that promised to post the lost animals on Petfinder.com. After Hurricane Rita they implemented a tracking sys-tem and established an intake area where people could list animals' tag and identification numbers and detailed descriptions so all this could go into the Petfinder.com database. Shannon estimates that all groups were reunit-ing about 15 to 20 percent of the animals they were rescuing. The Winn-Dixie group had about 80 to 100 volunteers at any given time. Their leads for where to rescue animals were continuing to come from local authori-ties. Vet techs and veterinarians worked at a triage center with donations of medical supplies for providing emergency treatment.

Shannon, still upset over the lack of coordination in the overall animal rescue efforts after Hurricane Katrina, says, "Our group rescued over 8,000 animals after Katrina, and we didn't have millions of dollars in funding. That's frustrating. How many animals were lost because of infighting between national rescue groups? We may never know."

Richard Crook, a firefighter for twenty-two years from New Hudson, Michigan, was invited by the HSUS and volunteered at Lamar-Dixon for a few days but wanted to help in a more direct way. He found Mark Martin at Winn-Dixie and started doing boat rescues while Mark did land rescues. Richard remained in New Orleans for four months and thus got fired from the job he held at the time as the environmental director of a nursing home in Michigan. He says, "The volunteers stayed three to five days or even three weeks, depending on how much vacation time they had. But some volunteers didn't make it more than a day. When they saw the conditions of the animals, they broke down and left within a few hours of arriving. Others would see something that touched them and brought tears to their eyes. So they stayed to do the work. They went on no matter how bad it was." Richard Crook stayed in the area for more than six months and

*Richard Crook leads a meeting of Grassroots Emergency Animal Rescue volunteers.*

formed his own charity, Grassroots Emergency Animal Rescue. He did animal rescue work with the Winn-Dixie parking lot serving as his base of operations the entire time he was in New Orleans. He says, "The city knew I was there and what we were doing." After Hurricane Katrina, Best Friends Animal Society hired Richard to be its rapid response director. He will create and lead a new division of the organization to do future field operations and training for disasters and animal rescue.

## MuttShack

MuttShack Animal Rescue Foundation is located in Los Angeles and was founded and is run by Amanda St. John. For her birthday her husband, Martin, obtained 501(c)3 nonprofit status for the organization. This was his way of showing support for Amanda's stewardship in taking care of animals. The group rescues unwanted animals and finds foster homes ("muttshacks") for them until they can be adopted. It does not run an animal shelter.

Amanda started her Hurricane Katrina rescue efforts by working along with other volunteers at the Winn-Dixie parking lot operation. With Hurricane Rita coming, she set up the MuttShack Animal Triage Center at Lake Castle School in East New Orleans, a private school near the levee at Lake Pontchartrain. There the group offered free emergency veterinary services to animals who were injured in the storm or suffering from lack of food. If the animals had owners and required further services, the owners had to take them to local private vets. After gang members on motorcycles threatened to burn the place down when the center refused to release pit bulls to them, military units were parked outside the school building and offered to protect the volunteers.

Amanda knew how to set up a structure, and she ran one of the tightest ships around. Volunteers had to do rounds of cage cleaning and dog walking before they were allowed to join the rescue teams.

### A Marine Corps Major Takes Charge of Animal Rescue

Amanda St. John clicked with Reserve Marine Corps fighter pilot Marine Major Mike Pagano and asked him to be in charge of field animal rescue for MuttShack. Major Pagano had to cross many hurdles, though, before getting to that point.

He had decided to go to New Orleans after watching the devastation on television from Japan, where his wife was deployed overseas on military duties. Major Pagano first contacted the HSUS about volunteering for its animal rescue teams. He had read on the HSUS website and from other sources that thousands of animals needed to be rescued and had heard the frantic calls all the organizations were sending out for as many volunteers as possible.

To his surprise, when Major Pagano volunteered to be on a HSUS animal rescue team, his request was denied. The explanation given was that he was not credentialed and had not taken the official training that the HSUS required to qualify for animal rescue. He was, however, invited to go to Lamar-Dixon to work with animals who were being housed there.

Major Pagano says that in other disasters or in a perfect world, the regulations of the HSUS and other national animal organizations were sensible, but they didn't work in Katrina. This was catastrophic and not a controlled environment. Being a marine officer, he knew he could both lead and follow as a team member. In excellent physical shape, he could see from watching television that many of the volunteers were not suited for the physicality the job required. He explains, "The conditions were terrible. People were having severe respiratory problems. None of the organizations had enough rescuers. I knew that I needed to go where I could do the most good."

He tried to reason with the person handling volunteer offers at the HSUS that being a marine fighter pilot, trained to work in hazardous and physically demanding conditions, he felt confident that he'd quickly be an asset to an animal rescue team. His skill and experience would not be used to their fullest if he was assigned to cleaning cages or working a desk job at Lamar-Dixon. When the lives of so many animals were at stake, Major Pagano felt that time was of the essence. He believed that the organization should accept the help of someone like him. He was willing to sign whatever form was necessary to release the HSUS from responsibility for him.

Major Pagano told us that he ended the frustrating conversation with the HSUS representative by saying, "You have to be more flexible. You have addresses for over 3,000 homes in one area of New Orleans alone [from people who asked to have their pets rescued]. Give me a fast course, train me on the spot, and credential me, because I'm coming in."

Stymied by the inability to volunteer for the tasks he felt most suited,

Major Pagano was heartened when he watched a man being interviewed on *Anderson Cooper 360°*. Major Pagano says, "The guy was like me, and the same thing had happened to him. He loved animals. He was physically fit, but no organization would take him. He had started rescuing animals by working out of the back of his car. As I watched him, I thought, This is why I'm going."

A friend forwarded Major Pagano an email letter from Sharon Gorski, the Midwest regional coordinator for National Disaster Animal Relief and Supply. Major Pagano calls Sharon a "phenomenal lady who needs to be recognized for her efforts." Behind the scenes, Sharon had helped to form a grassroots operation to organize donations and shipments of supplies to animal rescue groups, to augment supplies for places like the Best Friends temporary shelter, in Tylertown, and to recruit and orient volunteers. Major Pagano wrote to Sharon from Japan and offered to help. She wrote back immediately and told him he could go to work right away at the MuttShack Animal Triage Center.

While heading field animal rescue for MuttShack, Major Pagano worked with screenwriter Karen O'Toole. He gave her the nickname "GI Jane" for her ability to fearlessly rescue animals.

Major Pagano's skirmishes with bureaucracy didn't end when he finally started rescuing animals in New Orleans. He went on to have run-ins with the LA/SPCA and the state veterinarian office. He says, "Even though LA/SPCA was overwhelmed, the Louisiana state veterinarian office was constantly trying to shut us down. So Karen O'Toole and I started going to the Sheraton and talking with Anderson Cooper and reporters for CBS and CNN. After we got media attention on MuttShack and all the animals we were saving, the state veterinarian office backed off. But we were told that we couldn't break into houses anymore without a New Orleans police officer on the premises. So we always had a police officer with us and continued to rescue the animals. We were operating with permissions from various parish sheriff's departments and were getting a lot of support from the New Orleans city police."

We asked Major Pagano about complaints we'd heard from people in the established animal rescue organizations that some untrained rescuers did not fill out proper paperwork, post the found animals on Petfinder.com, or seem overly concerned about reuniting people with their pets. He said something we heard from some volunteers who did animal rescue: "I don't care if the animals ever got back with their owners. They were left to suffer for weeks. They died tied to kitchen chairs and in cages. One man kept telling us how much he loved his dog, a mastiff, and was so worried about what happened to him. He also always added that he hoped the dog had not been neutered. Volunteers spent a lot of time searching for this man's dog. They found that the dog was shipped to San Francisco. When they told the man that his dog was okay, they expected him to be happy. But when the man found out his dog had been neutered — this dog that he loved so much — he said, 'I don't want him.'"

Major Mike Pagano (center) with his fellow animal rescue workers.

Major Pagano concedes that this wasn't the attitude of most people who were desperately looking for their pets, but it justified his feelings that the primary objective had to be to save the animals with the secondary goal being reuniting animals with their families.

## Support Arrives from Unexpected Sources

Captain Stephanie Ostrowski is a veterinary officer for the U.S. Public Health Service (PHS) and works at the Centers for Disease Control in the National Center for Environmental Health and Agency for Toxic Substances Office of Terrorism Preparedness and Emergency Response. Captain Ostrowski was initially deployed to Baton Rouge with the PHS Veterinary Team as part of ESF-8 (Public Health). The PHS Veterinary

Team provided requested support to ESF-11 (Agriculture) Animal Emergency Operations in Louisiana. Because the state veterinarian office needed what is called surge capacity staffing — additional qualified people to do all the jobs — Captain Ostrowski was one of the PHS Veterinary Team members assigned to support emergency response needs. She also performed rapid needs assessments, which meant going to the field to do fact checking and provide same-day reports to headquarters with recommendations for what and where help and resources were most needed throughout the state. She assisted in providing clinical care at Lamar-Dixon and the Louisiana State University animal rescue shelters. After all these mission assignments, in October Captain Ostrowski was appointed to be U.S. Coast Guard Vice Admiral Thad Allen's special liaison for animal issues. He was the principal federal official on the scene assigned to oversee Hurricane Katrina response for the entire Gulf Coast. Captain Ostrowski's job was to provide better coordination between unaffiliated rescue groups and humane organizations with the official emergency response system.

Captain Ostrowski told us, "My staff officers and I regularly traveled out to visit the animal control officials running volunteer-staffed makeshift animal shelters [such as the MuttShack and Winn-Dixie operations] at three of the most heavily impacted New Orleans parishes — St. Bernard, Plaquemines, and Orleans. We took care packages of donated veterinary medicines and animal husbandry supplies from the state warehouse. We brought news from the ESF-11 (Agriculture) Incident Command staff and from their fellow animal control officials in the neighboring parishes. Our presence demonstrated ongoing active concern for their welfare on behalf of the state veterinarian and carried messages of fellowship and support from their counterparts in neighboring parishes. We returned with lists of needed supplies and status reports regarding progress and challenges in each parish, and requests for information and assistance."

Remarking on the level of encouragement for their efforts that came from official sources, Amanda St. John, of MuttShack, says, "FEMA made regular visits, as would the state veterinarian office, fire department, and health department. One of the health department leaders adopted a surrendered dog and wore a MuttShack T-shirt at morning briefings. Volunteers were able to start using FEMA showers and had dinner at the military refectory at the Convention Center in New Orleans. We were their guests, and we cannot thank them enough for their courtesy and hospitality."

Amanda and the MuttShack Animal Triage Center had to face the early frustrations of complete lack of water, electricity, food, waste management, and cell phone or Internet communication for getting help. Eventually she had too many animals to deal with and not enough hours in the day. Her greatest sorrow came when the mayor opened New Orleans for one day before Hurricane Rita, but no residents returned, and the following day a new evacuation order was in place. Amanda says, "People not being allowed back into the city to rescue their animals killed thousands of animals. Many animals were still alive before Rita."

At the height of the frustration, something always happened that let Amanda know she wasn't alone. Her husband, Marty St. John, had been working from California to get supplies to her. As soon as Amanda arrived in New Orleans, Dianne Albers, of the Florida American Kennel Club, responded to Marty's request and sent a 50,000-gallon water truck at a cost of $10,000 a week. Amanda and the volunteers desperately needed the water to wash the burning black toxic sludge off the animals, who Amanda says were burning alive. Amanda told us,

The Florida AKC sent IV fluids, lactated ringers, equipment, centrifuges, lab equipment, crates, leashes, food for animals and people, blankets, clothing, first-aid supplies, inflatable air mattresses, sleeping bags, cameras to photograph and make records for rescued animals, and generators and small refrigerators to keep the vaccines alive. David Levy of Levy and Associates donated a humongous truckload of food.

A woman named Jackie Innuratti drove in from Baton Rouge and took away huge piles of laundry to wash and return to the facility. Locals showed up with food the day before Thanksgiving in gratitude for all the work MuttShack was doing to rescue animals. The principal of Lake

Castle School, Danny McGovern, never wavered in his support. Sandra and Scott Holder and Mary Karr brought in heaters to keep the cats warm at night.

From Amanda St. John's perspective, MuttShack was also being supported by attracting volunteers from all over the world. Amanda says, "We had remarkable veterinarians and vet students to do the emergency work."

We spoke with Chris Robinson, a veterinary technician who manages a small animal hospital in Cambridge, Ontario. Chris volunteered at

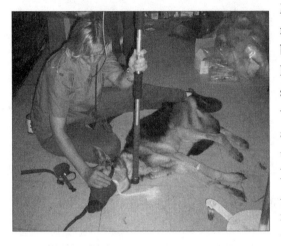

*Dr. Sandra Taylor administers fluid to Miss Cabby at MuttShack Triage.*

MuttShack and told us about a remarkable experience: "A rescuer brought in a German shepherd who had been trapped in a house for seventy-two days! The dog couldn't walk and was completely emaciated and terrified. We got her to trust us so we could feed medicated liquid to her to regain strength. Amazingly, the dog could walk the next day. The vet who worked with the dog, Dr. Sandra Taylor, ended up adopting her. She called her Miss Cabby. The dog was doing well. It is hard to imagine how that dog survived for seventy-two days trapped in a house."

According to Amanda and Marty, MuttShack saved more than 3,000 animals. MuttShack volunteers brought food and water to people who hid in their homes to avoid forced evacuations without their pets. Due to limited resources and the focus on emergency services. MuttShack did not make immediate reuniting a priority but required agencies who took the rescued animals to post them on Petfinder.com. In October 2005, Amanda St. John was honored with special awards from the House of Representatives and the City of Los Angeles for her animal rescue efforts and community service.

# Untrained Volunteers

So many volunteers, many of them untrained in animal rescue and unaffiliated with previously established animal rescue organizations, poured into New Orleans that the state veterinarian office and Laura Maloney, head of LA/SPCA, became worried about losing control over the city's animal rescue efforts. By law and by contract, the LA/SPCA was supposed to be in charge of animal control.

Untrained volunteers sometimes broke into homes searching for abandoned pets and then left the homes unsecured. Laura says, "People without rescue experience took a crowbar and opened up a front door or broke an expensive antique window. Their priority was to save animals at all costs without paying attention to the human side of it. A person who is skilled and trained in animal rescue would not have had this happen as frequently."

After evacuees started returning to the city, some whose homes had been broken into were incensed and threatened lawsuits against the LA/SPCA, thinking it was Laura's volunteers who had left their homes open to looters, raccoons, or anything that wanted to walk in while they were gone. Others emailed or called Laura, outraged that animal rescuers were doing things like breaking into their front doors while they were eating dinner in a back room of the house or rescuing the same animals repeatedly. One man complained that he had to drive ten times to get his dog back from Tylertown, Mississippi, or to Celebration Station, where many of the independent rescuers were taking animals. Outraged pet owners posted signs that said *anyone* trespassing on their property would be shot with no questions asked.

During rescue efforts, spray-painting went wild. Anyone with a bag of dog food and a heart for the animals could paint *LA/SPCA* or just *SPCA* on their vehicle and drive around the city without being harassed by police or military. Looters caught on to this and used it to gain access to homes with impunity and to steal valuable pit bulls for dogfighting rings. Rescuers cluttered the fronts of houses with often-conflicting messages. Sometimes they left what Dave Pauli calls "nasty-grams," berating pet owners for abandoning their animals. Laura and the city officials got the word out that no one would be allowed to break in and enter a home unless a uniformed police officer was on the premises and gave permission to do so.

Some volunteers and groups functioning outside the world of credentialed animal rescue teams occasionally stayed in the city past curfew, risking their lives and risking arrest when they drove into off-limits areas of the city to rescue animals. Some of the Louisiana officials and credentialed animal rescuers were appalled at the unsafe or illegal measures used by such volunteers, and referred to them as rogues, renegades, self-deployed, or cowboys.

Chris Cutter, communications director for the International Fund for Animal Welfare (IFAW), began to invite what are called convergent volunteers and what Marie Wheatley at AHA calls spontaneous volunteers to join his team. He found the self-deployed, for the most part, to be skillful and creative, if underdressed and poorly equipped for the jobs they had undertaken.

We asked Laura Maloney why she didn't shut down the rogue rescuers. In specific reference to the Winn-Dixie operation, she said, "There were so many animals out there. They were trying to get them off the street. At times I would hear great things about what they were doing, that they were caring for the animals well. Sometimes they didn't have enough staff to manage the sheltering. Overall, though, they did a fairly good job."

## Credentialed, Trained, and Well Equipped

Julie Morris from the ASPCA, among others we spoke with, also had concerns over the freelance volunteers, especially in regard to health and safety. Julie told us, "One day, at St. Bernard Parish Animal Control Center, a volunteer showed up with an oxygen tank. This would have been a very bad situation. He was sent home. He meant well."

In contrast to the independent animal rescuers, the teams operated by the IFAW, Code 3 Associates, the American Humane Association, and other groups that offer training and credentialing were prepared to protect themselves and the animals they were to rescue. They were outfitted with the latest equipment, practices, and gear.

Mary Pat Boatfield, executive director of the Nashville Humane Association, sent staff to work in Lafayette, Louisiana, and team members visited Lamar-Dixon. They brought their mobile surgical unit. Mary Pat had received safety training in biohazards while employed at a medical school prior to employment working in humane shelter organizations. She knew that her team did not have the proper equipment and clothing to deal with the toxins and chemicals in the floodwaters and air, and she re-quested that her staff not do animal rescue in New Orleans. Her personnel at Lafayette had a tough time with that decision, although they understood it was for their safety. Mary Pat says that with little protection, volunteers were breathing poisons into their lungs and being exposed to chemical and human waste. Many were returning home with what they were calling Katrina Cough. Mary Pat says, "When you are down there, you can get caught up in it. I wonder what will happen to them a year after they went to New Orleans." Amanda St. John told us, "The early rescuers were getting lung infections, skin rashes, pimples, and boils. We all had husky male voices and sounded like barking dogs."

Drew Moore worked with Jane Garrison and Bruce Earnest as volunteers of the HSUS. Drew is among those official rescuers who have impressive credentials. He is certified in swiftwater rescue; high- and low-angle rescue, where ropes and other specialized gear are used to removed injured people or animals from precarious spots; vertical rope skills; rock climbing; avalanche; canyoneering; wildland firefighting; technical animal rescue; and the Incident Command System, which the Department of Homeland Security uses as its disaster response protocol.

Lieutenant Randy Covey, who led the Oregon Humane Society's Technical Animal Rescue (OHSTAR) team, says, "We had our standard team's Nextel communication system. With most communications down in New Orleans, we were still able to stay in constant contact with each other. We also had laptops and a GPS mapping system — a real plus in a city we didn't know and where street signs were down in many areas and many roads were still closed."

Rene' Pizzo is a Portland fire inspector, firefighter, and paramedic who also served on the OHSTAR team. She says that by using the lists provided by the hotline at Lamar-Dixon, they were able to break into people's homes with their permission and to rescue animals. They broke into homes that were not on their lists only when it was absolutely necessary to save the lives of animals trapped in them, and in such cases they did minimal damage and resecured the homes after they left. For animals they couldn't find, they left a week's worth of food and water. Rene' says, "We painted symbols on the front of each of these homes: F/W (food/water), the date, and LA/SPCA, since Louisiana SPCA was in charge. The positive experiences were when we rescued animals who clearly would not have survived much longer. We would hear their barks or meows or see their faces in windows as we worked in a nearby home."

The San Diego community donated more than $450,000 to the San Diego Humane Society and SPCA's (HS and SPCA) Katrina Animal Relief

Fund. The organization was able to send to Lamar-Dixon several teams of staff and volunteers totaling more than thirty people. Many of those were from the Humane Society's Animal Rescue Reserve programs. Dr. Mark Goldstein, president of the San Diego HS and SPCA, spoke to us about how the organization deployed the San

*Animal Rescue Reserve (San Diego HS and SPCA) team members in full gear save Spike, the cat.*

Diego teams. He says, "Our team used walkie-talkies and cell phones, which worked best for communication while in the field. They wore particle masks and gloves to protect them from possible contaminants. We sent them with explicit instructions not to lead but to be led by the Louisiana SPCA. The Incident Command System model is the only way to function in a disaster so you always know who is in charge. I told our teams, 'You will have a positive impact if you don't let this overwhelm you.'"

American Humane equipped its volunteers for the conditions they would find in the floods. The group's *Standard Operating Guidelines 2005* says, "Our vehicles are loaded with rescue equipment specific to the disaster. We have...swiftwater vests, human and animal harnesses, dry suits, water boots, chest waders, high angle rescue gear, ropes (200 foot one-half inch low stretch lifeline, 150 foot high stretch lifeline), break bars, pulleys, veterinary medical supplies, catchpoles, nets, traps, an Anderson sling for horse lifts, radio communication, kennels, and more."[2]

The way national organizations and trained animal shelter teams, like the ones from Oregon, Nashville, and San Diego, were outfitted demonstrates a big disparity in how the mission to save animals after Hurricane Katrina was carried out. The well-trained groups, prepared with the latest equipment and technology, had "safety first" as their primary consideration. The groups that worked outside of the established animal rescue operations but often had animal control, police, and military officers on their teams, did their best to be safe and careful. Those groups and the individual animal rescuers did not have the funds, equipment, training, or communication systems that would have enabled them to always follow established health and safety protocols.

## At Lamar-Dixon

Jane Garrison was a veteran of animal rescue in several disasters when she came to work as a volunteer for the HSUS animal rescue teams. Dave Pauli, incident commander at Lamar-Dixon, says Jane Garrison has the energy of the Energizer Bunny. He calls her "amazingly articulate and compassionate about animals" and admires her organizational skills and tenacity.

Drew Moore recalls when he and Jane worked as a team and saw some National Guard troops driving by in a construction vehicle that looked like a tank with no gun barrel. Jane told Drew, "I'm going to get us their tank." They needed it to get through impassable areas. Jane waved the guardsmen over and got the tank. Drew comments, "When Jane Garrison says she's going to do something, she does it."

At the 2006 Genesis Awards, Jane was honored for her volunteer work rescuing 1,300 animals in six weeks. During the height of animal rescue Jane, Drew, and Bruce Earnest, three animal rescue teammates volunteering with the HSUS, worked from 5:00 AM until 2:00 AM at Lamar-Dixon and in New Orleans, making the forty-five-minute drive between the two locations every day.

After the first couple of weeks, Jane connected with Dorothy Pizutti, founder of DogDetective.com, and David Meyer, founder of 1-800-Save-A-Pet.com. Dorothy had assembled a database of homes where animals were known to be in need of rescue. With the help of staff at MapQuest, David then linked that database of homes to Map-Quest. The animal rescue teams started taking these lists with mapping features to find animals more effectively.[3]

*Jane Garrison, HSUS volunteer and ARNO cofounder, meets with animal rescuers.*

After dividing the city into sectors, Jane started a food and water program two weeks into the rescue, even though, she says, "At first, I was told by the LA/SPCA that I was not allowed to do this. But after seeing eleven cats dead outside one house and four three-day-old kittens still alive next to their dead mother, I took the matter into my own hands." Jane says that she assigned volunteers to the mapped-off sectors to place food and water at designated locations and monitor and record whether animals were coming to the stations. As a result, countless numbers of animals lived to be rescued later.

In our interview with her, Jane told us about some of her most searing experiences and what she has learned about animal rescue from Katrina.

Thousands of animals died due to the delays in starting animal rescue. When I arrived at Lamar-Dixon, I knew the animals were in a lot of trouble. At other disasters there are camping tents everywhere. I only saw five or six tents on the parking lot and a few people. I started calling volunteers to tell them to get down here.

My first day in the field I experienced gender prejudice for the first time. Local animal control was setting up four teams with four men and no women. I said, "I'm an excellent search-and-rescue person. I've worked in floods and tornadoes." I pushed myself onto one of those teams. No way did I drive thirteen hours from South Carolina to be here and be a transport person. I knew the animals needed me.

We found animals chained to front porches and left in carriers. They died scratching on the front doors of houses; the fear and frustration they must have felt. These were horrible images. We were always pushing. We knew lives were at stake.

It was a smell no one can describe — toxins and chemicals, rotting food from inside refrigerators, mold, death. It was so hot and the smells were compounded by stagnant water. We heard barking dogs everywhere in the beginning. We couldn't get to them because it was too flooded. Then, even worse, was the sound of quietness; the animals were behind closed doors, too weak to bark or already gone.

Rescuers need to get trained. I saw mistakes that cost animals' lives. You have to know where to search. I handle cats well. I'm patient and slow with them. Cats hollow out a box-spring mattress by tearing out the bottom. They crawl up and into couches. You can't just bust into a house with a team of people and expect to find cats. They go invisible.

If you don't find an animal, don't close the house completely. Leave a way for them to escape. Mark the home so people know you have the animals and where you took them. See if there is any mail lying around in the house. Look for a cell phone bill so you can call the person. Always go in the attics, even if the stairs aren't pulled down. Search for clues.

While I was rescuing I stayed emotionally detached. I got into the mode of going as fast and as best as I could, getting from one house to the next. The hard part was when I got out from there on the drive back to Gonzales. I would cry sometimes. So would the other rescuers.

I could hear them talking to their wives on the phone. For me, it wasn't crying over what I saw. It was the magnitude of the disaster, knowing how many animals were there. No way we could rescue all of them. When I went back home for a break, I couldn't watch footage on television. It brought up all the emotions.

No one animal organization had a comprehensive plan on how to deal with a disaster of this size. Everyone had to piece it together on the spot. There were not enough people, not enough boats, not enough vehicles. Lots of supplies and money, but we needed more volunteers.

We were still finding animals alive after five to six weeks and even found some alive as much as nine weeks after the storm. Some had died only a day or two before we got to them.

## Jane and Drew Rescue Luana and Margie's Animals

Jane Garrison and Drew Moore took part in many rescues, at least one of which was televised on the cable TV network Animal Planet.

Luana Maria Rathman and Margie Wilmoth call themselves "humaniacs." They love animals and always end up with the dogs and cats other people don't want. At the time of the hurricane they had three large dogs, Noodle, Kona, and Yetti, a Great Pyrenees; a Chihuahua named Tukie; and ten cats.

Luana and Margie stayed through the storm because they had so many animals to keep safe and they were having problems with their vehicles. They survived six days trapped inside their home with their neighbors, sleeping on the floor at night, staying low for fear of being hit by stray bullets flying through the windows. At the end of six days the National Guard waded through the water to tell them that they could not provide protection and the household had eight minutes to prepare for evacuation. Luana and Margie left out fifty-pound feedbags and water for their dogs and cats, and broke out a portion of the back door so the cats could get out. They carried Tukie and their smallest cat, Chucky Cheese, stuffed together in a soft-sided pet carrier, while a helicopter hauled them up in the scariest ride of their lives. They left hearing the remaining cats in the house screaming in terror.

Luana and Margie were first transported to San Antonio. Margie's sister-in-law in California called Margie to say that she had seen the women's Great Pyrenees, Yetti, on the deck of their New Orleans home when television host Larry King broadcast *Larry King Live* as he flew over the city. From San Antonio, Luana and Margie went to Margie's cousin's home in Houston. After they arrived in Houston, somebody called them to say the women's dogs had just appeared on a preview of an Animal Planet show. Margie and Luana quickly logged on to the Internet and found the Animal Planet website. Sure enough, there were Noodle, Kona, and their cat Bunny Rabbit being hauled off their deck.

The Animal Planet program showed Jane Garrison in a boat with Noodle and Kona and Drew Moore carrying Bunny Rabbit.[4] After Luana and Margie emailed them, Animal Planet staff were able to supply some vital information that assisted the two women in their extensive search for Kona and Bunny Rabbit. Although the dogs had collars and current licenses, the shelter where their records had been kept, the Louisiana SPCA, had been destroyed. Eventually Luana and Margie discovered where Kona, Bunny Rabbit, and Noodle had been transported. Kona was at a shelter in Sorrento, Louisiana, and Bunny Rabbit was at the Virginia SPCA.

Noodle turned up at the Denver Dumb Friends League in the care of Gail Kessler, who had Noodle flown back to Luana and Margie on a commercial airliner. Jane Garrison and Drew Moore filmed for Animal Planet as Luana and Margie were reunited with all of their animals at their home. So Jane and Drew got to experience a full-circle reunion — on national television, no less.

Yetti had escaped capture when Jane and Drew rescued Kona, Noodle, and Bunny Rabbit. After Margie and Luana returned to repair their house, they found Yetti protecting it. She had stayed alive because Jane, Drew, and the Animal Planet crew had left food and water for her every day. Eight out of ten of their cats returned.

## Animal Rescue New Orleans (ARNO)

By the first of October state and local authorities were saying that the animal rescue efforts were coming to a close. After October 1 Jane Garrison decided that the best way to keep the animals alive after the initial rescue efforts was to continue supplying the food and water stations by assigning volunteers to put out twenty-pound bags of food with a basin of two to three gallons of water. The nonprofit organization Jane founded with David Meyer and Pia Salk is Animal Rescue New Orleans (ARNO). It has since been taken over by local residents and after February 15, 2006, was being run by Charlotte Bass Lilly.

The organization works with animal control agencies, shelters, and humane organizations in nine parishes to rescue and humanely trap strays, pets, and ferals and then spay and neuter them and provide medical care through local veterinarians. The organization also picks up as many animals as possible who are scheduled for euthanization and tries to find local foster homes and adoptive homes for them. With the data gathered by volunteers at the food and water stations, some people have been reunited with lost pets. The organization has been able to transport dogs and cats with the help of American Airlines' Airline Ambassadors and Delta Angels, volunteer airline personnel who travel with pets to new homes or to be reunited with their families. Other groups and individuals have also aided in finding new homes and reuniting rescued animals and people. The number of rescued animals still needing homes and facing euthanization at crowded local animal shelters is daunting, though, and ARNO is constantly putting out calls for assistance. Animal Rescue New Orleans supplies more than 4,000 food and water stations throughout the city. The organization is planning for future disasters while reducing the animal overpopulation problems and continuing to rescue animals.[5]

Ramona Billot is a local volunteer who works with ARNO distributing food and water. At times during the early weeks of the disaster no one but a resident could get into an area because security patrols were stopping nonresidents. Ramona, who lives in Plaquemines Parish, says, "I went to a neighborhood I haven't been in before. There are so many spots I haven't hit. I put out food and water in a new spot. A cat came right away to eat. He wasn't feral. He didn't look at me or care that I was there. He ate like he hadn't eaten in a long time. I cried while I watched him. This poor creature had been waiting around the corner. He jumped out the minute I left food for him. If I hadn't done it, how would he have had food?"

## People for the Ethical Treatment of Animals (PETA)

Many people know People for the Ethical Treatment of Animals (PETA) from their media-blitz campaigns featuring animal-loving celebrities like Pamela Anderson and Rue McLanahan and from the organization's controversial billboards. The organization works tirelessly to combat animal cruelty. Representatives from the organization testified before Congress on the dire effects that directives to abandon animals had on the people of the Gulf Coast who were forced to evacuate without their pets.

Laura Brown is the manager of PETA's domestic animal and wildlife rescue department, heading a part of the organization that is not as well known. Laura led PETA's emergency animal rescue team after Katrina and says, "Our team arrived in New Orleans a week after the hurricane hit, when animal rescuers, who had been delayed by red tape and threats of violence, were at last allowed access to the submerged city. We broke down doors, crawled through filth, and waded through noxious floodwaters to rescue animals who, in many cases, were hours away from death. With the help of sympathetic federal, state, and local officials, we rescued more than three hundred dogs, cats, birds, and other animals. We also helped feed, water, walk, and care for thousands more at Lamar-Dixon."

## Code 3 Associates

Code 3 Associates is a remarkable organization that specializes in rescuing animals from disaster. It maintains two offices in Colorado, in the towns of Erie and Longmont. Code 3 Associates partners with qualified organizations to respond to disasters in the United States and Canada. After Katrina the organization sent members of its Emergency Animal Rescue Services team to Louisiana and Mississippi and partnered with the

IFAW, the HSUS, American Humane, and the Houston SPCA, using as a base of operations the mobile command vehicle called BART (Big Animal Rescue Truck). They describe it on their website as "a huge, self-sufficient, disaster-relief tractor and trailer unit capable of responding to disasters as requested."[6] Code 3 Associates certifies and trains men and women in every type of animal rescue, control, and care.

Even organizations like Code 3 Associates encountered delays and challenges on the Gulf Coast. Chris Cutter, communications manager for IFAW, told us, "There were tons of structures and protocols in place. We were down there working for two or three weeks when we were told we had to get permits. This grounded us for a day while we waited to get permission from the state veterinarian office and LA/SPCA. It was comic in a way, to get permission for something we'd already been doing for twenty days. The National Guard, the state of Louisiana, and SPCA all had competing authorities and protocols."

After Hurricane Katrina hundreds of animal groups from around the country worked on the Gulf Coast and sent staff and volunteers to pick up animals and take them back to their shelters. They stretched beyond their usual animal rescue efforts (and funds) to make significant contributions to thousands of stricken animals and the people who love and need them. The substantial achievements and the obstacles and challenges they faced are a testament to their determination to save as many lives as possible.

# CHAPTER FIFTEEN

# More Animal Rescue Teams and Emergency Shelters

Dozens of animal rescue and sanctuary organizations answered the call for courage and sacrifice as they set up emergency shelters along the Gulf Coast. In this chapter we survey several more of the groups whose dedicated staff devote themselves to improving the lives of animals every day, and when the animals needed them most after Hurricane Katrina, they were there.

## Best Friends Animal Society

Best Friends Animal Society has its sanctuary, Angel Canyon, in Kanab, Utah, where it provides a little taste of heaven for the animals sheltered there. President Michael Mountain described the sanctuary to us as a "tax-exempt, nationwide charity providing a no-kill sanctuary." Best Friends is a leader in the effort to bring spay-neuter and adoption programs into the mainstream as an alternative to euthanizing animals due to overpopulation, a practice Michael calls "a significant social evil."

Paul Berry is the director of operations for Best Friends. He is a native of New Orleans but hadn't returned to the city since moving away in 2000 for his position with Best Friends. Prior to Hurricane Katrina, Paul and his staff at Best Friends had developed a Rapid Response Process in case of natural disaster somewhere in the country.

While Hurricane Katrina was ripping through the Gulf Coast, Paul flew to Houston and from there drove to New Orleans to see how he could help the Southern Animal Foundation, a low-cost shelter and clinic he had founded some years before. The staff was shaken and had no electricity, but they and their eighty animals had survived. Paul told us, "I only brought two changes of clothing. I thought I'd be back home within the next couple of days with good photos and a list of supplies so donors could help."

While in New Orleans, Paul got a call from St. Francis Animal Sanctuary, in Tylertown, Mississippi, one hundred miles north of New Orleans. Best Friends had helped Pam Perez and Heidi Krup start the sanctuary, which shelters four hundred dogs and cats. Pam told Paul that the roads to the sanctuary were all blocked with debris, and they had only forty-eight hours' worth of food left.

Before Paul could drive to Tylertown, he witnessed the city flood after the levees broke, a sight that native New Orleanians had always dreaded. Paul says, "I drove toward Baton Rouge and up I-155, trying to get to St. Francis Animal Sanctuary. I also wanted to find my mother and sisters. Turns out, they were okay in Natchez. I lived through [Hurricanes] Camille and Betsy but never saw so much devastation. The trees had snapped like toothpicks and rolled over on houses. It was like this for one hundred miles." Within the next few days Paul got the sheriff's department to clear trees from the road to St. Francis Animal Sanctuary.

Throughout this time he was on the phone frequently with Michael Mountain back home in Utah, and they agreed to set in motion the as-yet-untested Rapid Response team. In accord with their plan, Best Friends sent volunteers, staff, veterinarians, animal rescue teams, supplies, and money to Tylertown. Pam and Heidi, at the St. Francis Animal Sanctuary, made available some space next to their facility for an emergency animal rescue shelter, and Best Friends, with the help of volunteers, transformed several acres of bare, grassy land into a tent-city refuge for more than 3,000 animals arriving from Louisiana and Mississippi.

Paul Berry returned to Jefferson Parish to conduct animal rescue with Best Friends volunteers from Atlanta, leading his tiny brigade of boats through flooded streets. Over the second and third weeks they saw hardly anyone but themselves and the military working to rescue animals and people. The 82nd Airborne, 3rd Battalion, 505th Parachute Infantry Regiment became an invaluable ally, going ahead with Paul and his teams following behind so people and animals could be evacuated side by side.

Paul Berry and his volunteers were being supported by dozens of staff back at Best Friends in Utah. There, staff fielded as many as 100,000 emails and phone calls in the first ten days with requests for help and calls for information. Animals and people were being reunited. Arrangements were being made to pick up pets at bus stops and boat landings where evacuees

*Paul Berry, Best Friends Animal Society, rescues a scared dog.*

were forced to leave them. Michael Mountain says, "We were transporting animals to shelters that promised to place information about them on websites like Petfinder.com, and not to kill them."

Over and over, the people we spoke with talked about seeing the Best Friends' trucks taking rescued animals back to Tylertown from the temporary shelters in the parishes, in Mississippi, and from Lamar-Dixon when the facility overshot its capacity. It was a gargantuan effort. Paul says,

> Hundreds of animals were coming out every day. They were so grateful with loving, sweet kisses, even though their bodies were dehydrated and starving. I was amply rewarded with every single rescue. I met the

most capable, creative, talented, and dedicated people I've ever worked with in my life. This experience reminded me how very good people can be. When we work together, we remove status, false barriers, and official positions and are stripped down to our bare humanity. I had a complete restoration of faith that we can get our social institutions right and make them compassionate and kind. Apathy and cynicism were washed away by the hurricane.

Best Friends continued to work with its volunteers and veterinarians in New Orleans through April of 2006. It teamed up with Animal Rescue New Orleans and opened a facility at Celebration Station, from where volunteers supplied feeding stations throughout the city and surrounding parishes. Best Friends also held a "super-adoption" weekend at Celebration Station and organized a well-publicized adoption-reunion fair at a hotel, which thousands of people attended in hopes of finding their pets.

The organization had collected $4.7 million in donations by the time we talked with Michael Mountain and Paul Berry in December 2005. Michael says, "We are spending every bit of it on rescues and reunions. We are proud to have been out there first rescuing animals and to have stayed there doing rescue work for more than eight months."

## Animal Ark

Animal Ark, in Hastings, Minnesota, has the goal of turning its state into a no-kill community. Under the leadership of executive director Mike Fry, the organization is becoming a leader in the state's animal sheltering community, sponsoring programs to reduce pet overpopulation in feral cats and dogs, organizing adoption events, creating a new no-kill shelter, and producing a radio show and magazine, and an active website. This is a small organization with only ten paid staff. We like to refer to it as "the little animal shelter that could."

When Katrina hit, Mike Fry organized a convoy of nine large moving trucks full of supplies and a mobile surgery suite to take down to Best Friends in Tylertown. Mike says, "When our team saw all the animals, we couldn't just turn around and walk away. We decided to do whatever we could. New teams of Animal Ark volunteers went down every week." These teams took back a total of 250 animals to the shelter in Minnesota. They placed the animals in foster care and held them until March 1, 2006, to give families the greatest possible chance of reuniting.

Mike and his staff held debriefings with his teams every day. He felt it was critical to use the Incident Command System, the nationally recognized protocol for disaster response, and to train volunteers. On the Animal Ark website, Mike and his team started a blog from Tylertown using wireless laptops, typing in their unfiltered accounts of animal rescue in St. Bernard Parish and at Best Friends. Visitors to the site could learn substantive information from people in the trenches. The website received five million hits a month.

## United Animal Nations

Jennifer Fearing is president of United Animal Nations (UAN), a pioneering organization in helping animal victims of disasters; since 1987 it has responded to sixty animal disasters. With its Emergency Animal Rescue Service (EARS), UAN has trained more than 4,000 volunteers, and UAN currently has 2,500 volunteers with the ability to be deployed. After Hurricane Katrina, UAN ran five temporary animal shelters in three states with the help of more than 400 volunteers.

We spoke to Susan McLaughlin, who has taken the EARS volunteer training workshop and volunteers at the organization's national headquarters in Sacramento. Susan says, "I am amazed at what this group does with only nine staff. They put everything into it and devote themselves. Jennifer Fearing is a wonderful, energy-charged person. Animals are so important to her. She inspires everyone."

Kay Mayfield, director of UAN's Emergency Animal Rescue Service, talked with us about her experiences setting up and running UAN temporary shelters in Jackson, Mississippi; Monroe, Louisiana; and Lufkin, Texas. Kay, who is a national responder for Code 3 Associates, sent volunteers to work with that group in New Orleans doing water rescue, and she sent a team of EARS volunteers to rescue six hundred animals in St. Bernard Parish.

Some of our temporary shelters were in the same area as the Red Cross shelter or local hotels. People brought their animals to us to be cared for, and they could be with the animals, clean their kennels, and feed them. They could take their dogs for walks or car rides and bring them back. We had vets on staff. Volunteers walked the dogs, cleaned the cages, and cuddled the animals. They gave them love with treats and toys. All this attention helps animals get through the separation. We are not just helping the animals; we're also helping folks who are displaced by the disasters. They have time and the peace of mind to put their lives back together, to get FEMA help.

Kay Mayfield, UAN-EARS, with puppy guests at shelter in Jackson, Mississippi.

At the second shelter we opened in Monroe, we took 240 animals from Lamar-Dixon who had been rescued from New Orleans. We worked for a month trying to reunite them with their caregivers. Some had chemical burns from the floodwaters and were in terrible shape.

Our paperwork is extensive. All the animals are tagged and have collars on them. We track them by intake number. I know at any given time what kennel a dog or cat is in or where a horse is being kept, if the animal went to a vet off-site, and what medical care has been rendered. I know who the human mom and dad are and where they are staying.

Security is a priority. We don't want somebody walking out with an animal who isn't theirs.

In addition to UAN providing temporary shelter, trained volunteers, and security, Jennifer Fearing says, "UAN organized a national call for thirty-five days with animal organizations and government officials. This is the most collaborative we have ever been with a disaster. I see lots of signs for hope. We can make a greater impact if we work together."

Jennifer feels that UAN was underused in this disaster because it wasn't as well known as the Big Three. That is all changing as the strengths of UAN are being recognized at the national level.

Jennifer helped shed some light on complaints we'd heard from private veterinarians about not being welcomed with open arms if they hadn't gone through official disaster training. She says, "Some vets are used to white-glove, pristine, sanitary environments. They aren't prepared for what disaster medicine is like. It is a MASH style of working where you seek to minimize stress but operate efficiently. Handling and treating animals more than absolutely necessary adds to their stress levels. Some vets aren't comfortable with that style; some vets really thrive in the environment. It's good for them to be trained in advance. With training, they may rule themselves out instead of going to a disaster and having a bad experience."

## One of United Animal Nations' Many Success Stories

United Animal Nations helped people and pets be reunited as well as took measures to ensure that they were never separated in the first place. Felton and Tanzia Prosper and their two children, Kaylynne and John-Michael, benefited from the efforts of the LA/SPCA's animal rescue teams and UAN's shelter when they were reunited with their beagle, Nick, at the Monroe, Louisiana, shelter. After the family was separated from Nick, Felton searched on Petfinder.com every day. In a charming book that the Prosper children wrote and illustrated, seven-year-old Kaylynne writes, "We asked a lot of questions about Nick. 'Where is Nick? When can we get him? Does he have enough to eat and drink? Did he get rescued? Is Nick hurt? Did Nick die?' We really missed Nick and cried for him and prayed for him every day."

On the joyous day that Felton found Nick on Petfinder.com, right before the Prospers were leaving New Orleans for the last time, they called the contact number listed, and Felton spoke with Kay Mayfield. Kaylynne describes it this way: "The nice lady on the phone said that the dog from the computer had a hernia on his belly, a heart mark on his leg, and a rainbow collar! Nick was also still wearing his tag from our vet in New Orleans." Felton says, "We all broke down with tears of joy."

Before leaving Louisiana, the Prospers drove five hours from New Orleans to Monroe. There they met Kay and presented proof that Nick was their dog. But no paperwork could prove the obvious. Kaylynne writes, "When Nick's caretakers came out with him, he ran to us and licked us and jumped on us. . . . This made us very happy. We knew that we had found the real Nick!"

The Prospers drove back with Nick to their new home — and Felton's new job — in New Mexico. A family who attended their church donated a new van to the Prospers. They were overwhelmed by all the support they received.

Now Nick enjoys running in the dog park near the corporate housing where the family stays. An Albuquerque television station did a story about Nick and the Prospers. Felton says,

> Our bond with Nick has gotten stronger. We used to not allow him to sleep in our bed and would crate him up at night. Now we say, "Buddy, we're going to give you a little extra." He gets into bed with us. He's getting a lot more loving. This experience has made me reevaluate my relationship with him. He's probably saying, "We need more hurricanes." To see how much love my kids have for Nick and to have him waiting for me to come home each day is awesome.
>
> I applaud the folks who put their lives in harm's way and the ones who sent me daily updates as they searched for Nick. Words can't explain the amount of gratitude I have for the efforts of these rescuers. The volunteers don't get paid for this. They may take all day to get one cat. They won't leave any pet behind. They go into uncertain environments with mud and mold, and rescue the animals. Before these storms, I didn't know there were groups of people who saved animals like this. My daughter says she wants to work for UAN-EARS when she grows up.

On the day Felton found Nick, Tanzia Prosper said, "It's like God's way of telling us, in the midst of devastation, that we will be okay."

## Noah's Wish

For thirteen years Terri Crisp was the director of the Emergency Animal Rescue Service but left that organization in 2001 to found Noah's Wish. A veteran of seventy disasters, Terri told us, "Noah's Wish is the only organization in the world that focuses *exclusively* on rescuing and sheltering animals in disasters. We exist as much to help the people that are connected to the animals. We have a staff of fifteen and over one thousand trained volunteers throughout the United States and Canada. We are expanding to serve in disasters outside of the United States and Canada." Noah's Wish had the permission of Tammany Parish, according to an agreement made prior to Hurricane Katrina, to set up a temporary shelter in Slidell, Louisiana, on the shore of Lake Pontchartrain.

Noah's Wish has a form that volunteers fill out so coordinators can assess their skills. If convergent volunteers have needed skills, they are mobilized. (Remember Candice King-Palgut from chapter 2? This is the procedure she followed to volunteer with Noah's Wish.) Coordinators schedule their trained volunteers at least three weeks ahead. The minimum length of time volunteers serve is four days. Some volunteers during Katrina returned to Slidell up to four times; on average they returned twice.

Volunteers with Noah's Wish must be at least eighteen years of age and they fill twenty-seven different positions during disasters. The organization has one thousand volunteers and thirty-five coordinators who take more intensive trainings. Terri says, "I see all the volunteers do-ing great things. It is so exciting to witness. The volunteers become my friends. It is an honor to know such incredible people. They work together as a team. What a difference they make."

Noah's Wish and Terri are regularly featured in newspaper articles and on

*Terri Crisp, Noah's Wish.*

CNN. When there is a disaster, Anderson Cooper, of CNN, calls Terri to get her expert opinion and accurate information.

We asked Terri how she came up with the name Noah's Wish for the group. She says, "I wanted a name that would mean the same thing in any country. One morning my cat woke me up early. I started thinking, the name Red Cross doesn't state what they do. Maybe I could go in this direction. My mind wandered. I remembered a T-shirt I saw that said, 'Noah, the original emergency manager.' I sat up in bed instantly and thought, 'We'll call ourselves Noah's Wish. We will carry on what Noah did and make sure in disasters animals won't be forgotten.' If my cat hadn't woke me up, Noah's Wish might be called something else today."

## Louisiana State University

At Louisiana State University in Baton Rouge, the veterinarians and volunteers from Baton Rouge and around the country rallied under the leadership and command of Dr. Paula Drone. Dr. David Senior worked with Dr. Drone and says of her, "She is an exceptionally strong individual and was perfect to fill this role. It was a honor for me to serve with her." Dr. Senior provided vet care at a temporary animal shelter at the John M. Parker Coliseum, part of LSU's AgCenter. The shelter discharged the last animal on October 16 but continued to reunite previous resident animals with their families until January 15, 2006. Evacuees from New Orleans whose homes had been demolished were able to drop off their animals temporarily so they could go start new lives. The School of Veterinary Medicine sheltered and treated 2,000 animals and returned 1,700 to their original families. The others were either adopted in Baton Rouge or sent to shelters that agreed to strict adoption and return policies if the pets were claimed later by their original owners.

Dr. Senior had problems with getting supplies immediately, and the administrators and command team at the shelter had to use their own credit cards to pay for everything. In the first five days, five hundred animals came into the shelter. Representatives from the International Fund for Animal

Welfare (IFAW) soon visited, and Dr. Senior told them the operation needed money, including money to reimburse the vets for their outlays. In less than forty-eight hours, IFAW sent Dr. Senior a check for $25,000.

Dr. Senior and Dr. Drone were on duty when Senator Ensign visited the facility. The only preparation Dr. Senior had time to make was to put on a fresh shirt. He says, "Senator Ensign paid us quite a compliment, coming from a veterinarian. He said, 'I expected it to smell. It doesn't smell.'"

## Humane Society of South Mississippi

When Hurricane Katrina hit, the Humane Society of South Mississippi (HSSM), the second largest animal control provider in the disaster area, was two and a half months away from moving in to a brand-new shelter facility of 41,000 square feet, in a prime seven-acre location on the main thoroughfare in Gulfport. The old shelter sat next to a sewage treatment plant, and the HSSM had been housed in that facility for fifty years, in a building that had been an armory during World War II. Tara High, executive director of the HSSM, calls that building "dank and challenging."

Before the hurricane Tara was serving as president of the HSSM board. She had been in Brazil for two weeks and returned home only two days before the storm hit. All the shelter's plans for evacuating animals fell through. When the shelter filled up with four feet of water, the staff couldn't get animals out, and they lost twenty-three animals. As she recounted the horror of it to us, Tara wept. Tara had to take over running the shelter on the Friday after the hurricane when the executive director gave a notice of resignation.

The HSUS were poised for action in Jackson, Mississippi, when it got a desperate plea from Tara. The HSSM shelter had no power, water, or supplies. The remaining animals needed to get out of the unsanitary shelter conditions. One hundred twenty surviving animals were taken back to Jackson to be triaged by the VMAT teams, and some of the surrendered animals and strays then went to the North Shore Animal League, in New York. The new HSSM facility became a holding area for surrendered animals who would be transported to Project Halo, in North Carolina, for adoption.

Tara feels that the media was so focused on New Orleans after the levees broke that Mississippi and its needs fell off the radar screen. Most of the financial and volunteer help, in both early and later stages of the disaster, went to New Orleans, and the early disparity in services and donations initially hampered rescue efforts in Mississippi.

The ASPCA quickly stepped in and donated money and also paid for a two-year strategic planner to assist Tara in rebuilding. Julie Morris of the ASPCA called Tara regularly to find out what she needed in the way of money and mentoring. Donations from Petfinder.com, Liz Claiborne, and PetSmart Charities arrived to help with new spay–neuter programs. Both the HSUS and the ASPCA made donations to help Tara finish building the new shelter and buy new transport equipment so she'd never again have to rely on others to get her animals out of harm's way. The San Diego Humane Society and SPCA donated money to train Tara's HSSM staff in animal care, husbandry, and sheltering.

Grateful for the support, Tara says that funding remains a priority. "We have a healthy concern for our financial future. I spend my time trying to solicit funds."

## Humane Society of Louisiana

Jeff Dorson, executive director of the Humane Society of Louisiana (HSLA), has been a cruelty investigator for the past twenty years. He wrote an email to tell us that they lost their shelter in Algiers, Lousisiana, and opened Camp Katrina, an emergency shelter in Tylertown, Mississippi, next to the Best Friends facility. There, according to Jeff, they brought more than 100 animals from their sanctuary in New Orleans. Jeff writes, "With few resources, we were able to travel back to the city of New Orleans and rescue another 600 pets."

The HSLA was established in 1988 and since that time has improved the lives of more than 40,000 animals. The HSLA too is trying to rebuild and needs donations.

## Dixon Correctional Institute

With the Lamar-Dixon facility overloaded, the HSUS had to get creative about where to house animals. On September 22 they sent 160 of their animals to a dairy barn at the Dixon Correctional Institute (DCI) to be cared for by twenty-five minimum-security prisoners. The animals included dogs, geese, chickens, and ducks. DCI Warden James LeBlanc, HSUS volunteers, prison staff, and Dr. Eric Davis, veterinary director of Rural Area Veterinary Services for HSUS, supervised the project. The Humane Society of Kalamazoo, Michigan, supplied a mobile veterinary clinic at the facility.[1]

June Towler, a wildlife rescue volunteer from Toronto, spoke to us about her experiences with DCI. "It was so touching to see some of the 'tough guys' walking, cuddling, talking to, and bonding with the dogs. When a favorite dog

*Volunteer June Towler walks dogs at Dixon Correctional Institute shelter.*

would be transferred out, they would shed a tear and give him a good-bye hug. I truly think they got so much out of the program, to have someone to look after who needed them, someone to love. It made me cry to see some of these guys tear up when one of the dogs they bonded with left to go elsewhere. One of the vet techs, Claudia Mattheiss, has gone on to champion the DCI program, working with the prison warden to try to keep the program running indefinitely."

## Pasado's Safe Haven

Pasado's Safe Haven is a sanctuary located about an hour's drive outside Seattle on seventy-six acres of land in the Cascade mountain foothills. The

*Pasado's Safe Haven rescue teams looking for animals.*

organization offers farm animal rescue and provides mobile spay-neuter with public assistance and at low cost to make the surgery available to any pet owner, especially in the rural areas. Pasado's is most well known, though, for its animal cruelty investigations, its support for legislation banning animal cruelty, and the media attention it focuses on violence to animals. Through its work against cruelty to animals it honors its namesake, Pasado, the donkey whose violent death at the hands of three boys in 1992 led to Washington State passing its first felony animal cruelty law.

Before Katrina the organization had never traveled outside its area to do large-scale animal rescue, but like many other people, Pasado's founders, husband-and-wife team Susan Michaels and Mark Steinway, were horrified at the sight of so many suffering animals. Mark took half of his staff of six and asked for volunteers to go to the Gulf Coast. Within forty-eight hours they had fifteen people on a plane flying to Houston. They rented two fifteen-passenger vans and a minivan. The team considered itself to be highly qualified, with a veterinarian, two or three vet techs, a Seattle police officer, an EMT, and physically fit, strong people with diverse skills and search-and-rescue experience. Mark led the team while Susan remained at Pasado's, contacting authorities at Lamar-Dixon to gain clearances and get assignments for the team after it arrived.

At the HSUS registration table, Mark and his team signed in and were told that they could walk dogs and clean cages. Several team members continued working there, not totally wanting to abandon that effort, but most of the team helped out at Lamar-Dixon for one day.

Then Pasado's team connected with the Phoenix SPCA and learned how to get past military checkpoints, even though they didn't have official credentials, and enter the city for search-and-rescue work. They showed officials that Pasado's Safe Haven is a legitimate group, a licensed animal control organization in the state of Washington. After watching the group do search and rescue for a couple of days, the military and police, liking the group's organization, started giving them locations of houses where they heard dogs barking inside.

When Lamar–Dixon filled up and officials started turning rescued animals away, Mark became incensed and from Washington, Susan located a private donor in Raceland, Louisiana, who offered a farm as a temporary animal shelter. (We already read about Carla Dimitriou and her experiences at Raceland farm in the story of Sweetie in chapter 5.) Mark told us, "Raceland was a beautiful facility with a huge cement-floor barn, restrooms, and showers, and we had cages that were donated." From Raceland, Pasado's teams and volunteers rescued 1,200 animals over a six- to seven-week period. They were careful to document where the animals were rescued from, and they enjoyed a high success rate in reuniting pets and their humans.

Toward the end of our interview with Mark, he talked about what he had learned from his experiences in animal rescue after Katrina.

We heard from so many people who said, "I don't care what you do. Break the door down. Do whatever you have to. Just get my dogs out." We weren't trying to destroy property. We were trying to save a life. If you heard a person screaming in a house, nobody would think twice about breaking in to help. Why is a barking dog any different? Is that life less valuable? The lesson for me was that there is no excuse for not doing what is necessary to save the life of an animal. You may have to suffer the consequences. You might get sued by the homeowner. In one day you would collect enough donations to pay for the person's front door.

## Alley Cat Allies

Alley Cat Allies (ACA), out of Bethesda, Maryland, is expert at reducing overpopulation among stray cats by trapping, neutering, and returning the animals to their colonies, and it helps organizations and individuals all over the world with feral cat colonies. Concerned about the desperate need for increased rescue efforts for pet cats and feral cat colonies, the group opened up a temporary shelter in Bogalusa, Louisiana, north of Lake Pontchartrain. There it could take in some of the cats identified as feral by Lamar-Dixon vets as well as rescue many cats from New Orleans.

According to Bonney Brown, campaign director for the organization, many of the cats from Lamar-Dixon were not feral. In some cases their records were mixed up; the paperwork that came with the cats to identify them did not appear to match the cats. If the cats were people's pets, ACA volunteers worked to reunite them with their families.

Bonney says, "At Lamar-Dixon the cats were popped into cages next to strange cats, scary smells and noises, dogs barking. This is terrifying for cats in any shelter setting. Cats are very attached to their homes or territories. They have to be given time to simmer down before anyone tries to handle them."

If a local caregiver was still available to feed the cats, Alley Cat Allies returned the truly feral ones to colonies after they spayed or neutered them. The organization found and carefully screened barn homes in Texas, Arizona, and southern California, and sent the feral cats to those places so the cats wouldn't have to be moved to cold climates.

More than 160 volunteers worked at the base camp with rough accommodations — no phones or electricity. They set up large tents and places for the volunteers to camp. Two of Bonney's former colleagues from Best Friends, Diane Blankenburg and Jim Davis, helped to coordinate the volunteers and rescue operations.

## Farm Sanctuary

Some of the most touching and sad stories we heard in our interviews came from people who rescued farm animals and horses. Kate Walker, placement coordinator and animal caregiver for Farm Sanctuary in Watkins Glen, New York, was sent to Jackson, Mississippi, by her organization to see if she and her team could rescue animals from storm-damaged factory farms. With the HSUS, Farm Sanctuary was researching its locations. Kim Sturla, of Animal Place, accompanied Kate.[2]

Officials of the major companies who own the farms told Kate that no help was needed. But she says it was obvious that they were "cleaning up" after the storms by demolishing buildings with animals still inside of them because it would take too much labor to remove the animals. Kate told about her experiences with saving the farm animals:

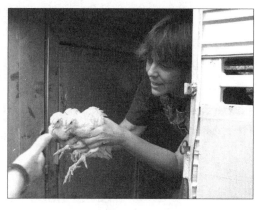

After many dead ends, we were able to rescue over a thousand broiler chicks from a farm that had been devastated by the hurricanes. Two of the huge broiler sheds, where these birds were being raised,

*A Farm Sanctuary worker saves chickens.*

were ripped in half, and the birds had been without food, water, and appropriate shelter for two weeks. The farmer, his family, and staff had caught over 36,000 of the birds and put them into the two remaining sheds, but thousands of the birds remained alive, scattered about the farm.

When I arrived, they had just begun cleaning up. When the farmer realized that we were there to help the animals, he seemed grateful. We caught the living birds and transported a few hundred to California and the rest to our sanctuary.

The reason he let us help is that we established confidentiality with him. He was worried he would get into trouble with the company he worked for. Other farmers we talked with wouldn't hear us out. They couldn't understand why we would have come from New York to save birds. But this farmer said, "I don't want to see these birds suffer, either."

We only had a few people to hold hundreds of birds in pens. We finally loaded them in the trailer when it came. It was so sad. We had worked hard, but there was still almost the same number of birds as when we arrived. Hundreds of birds were still going to die. Some birds were so sick that we had to euthanize them. We had spent a twenty-nine-hour day and night with no rest. We were completely driven by adrenaline.

The farmer had a son. He came over and handed us a chicken. He asked, "Will you bring this one back to New York and make sure it is safe?" He really liked that chicken. Later, he was running out and checking on the chickens and helping us to load them onto our trailer. The son showed compassion toward the animals. It was good to see.

Tricia Ritterbusch, communications director for Farm Sanctuary, wrote to us, "There were millions of farm animals that died as a result of Hurricane Katrina. Kate's story brings to light their plight on factory farms and their struggle through this disaster."

## LSU Veterinary Medical School Does Farm and Horse Rescue

If you lived in the parish of Plaquemines, St. Bernard, or Vermilion or thereabouts, you lived through Hurricane Katrina but were blindsided by Hurricane Rita. Thousands of cattle in the farms of the southern regions of Louisiana were drowned in floods of saltwater during the surge that followed Rita.

Teams from the Veterinary Medical School at Louisiana State University coordinated the rescue of over four hundred horses in the rural areas. They used global positioning systems to locate the animals, and then flew over with a helicopter to communicate to drivers and lead them to the animals. People called the LSU Horse Hurricane Helpline to tell the school where their horses were. The LSU Hurricane Equine Rescue Operations, with teams of vets and volunteers, drove into affected areas and treated injured animals with emergency procedures. They took them to Lamar-Dixon, which had been built as an equine facility and was perfect for horses.

## Rescue Ranch

Lori Wilson, director and president of Rescue Ranch in Belle Chasse, Louisiana, teamed up with Tammy Brentlinger, who came from Scottsdale, Arizona, and Paul Tharp, manager for Best Friends' Horse Haven, to try and save as many horses and farm animals as possible. They brought the animals to Lori's Rescue Ranch. Paul was instrumental in getting hay from a tack store, and the Idaho National Guard delivered it to Lori. Paul Tharp describes his work with farm animals this way: "If you look into the big brown eyes of a calf or watch a young foal or see kids [baby goats] or lambs run and play, you may know how I feel about rescuing large animals."

After the storms Lori spent months caring for the horses on her ranch and rescuing cattle and other animals from neighboring ranches. In addition to the help from Best Friends, the ASPCA and United Animal Nations donated funds to help her buy and get feed delivered. After the hurricanes, Rescue Ranch continues its work of rescuing abused horses, retraining them, and teaming at-risk youths with rescued horses, to the betterment of both.

## Hopeful Haven Equine Rescue

Debra Barlow is president and operates Hopeful Haven Equine Rescue, in Shreveport, Louisiana. After Katrina struck, she supported Lori's work at Rescue Ranch by bringing food for the horses and cattle, and canned goods for Lori and her family. Lori calls Debra her "mama."

Debra regularly rescues abused, unwanted, and neglected horses. By day she is employed as an investigator of animal abuse. Evenings and weekends, though, she is totally devoted to her twenty-seven rescued horses and three of her own horses. She has osteoarthritis and walks with a cane. Yet Debra mobilized ranches all over northeast Louisiana to take in horses that her southern neighbors were trying to evacuate before the storms. She set up convoys of horse trailers and supplies of hay and feed that she delivered to farmers after Rita's surge destroyed their ability to feed their animals.

Debra set up a distribution site where ranchers could meet her convoys on Fridays. She brought in two hundred tons of feed and five eighteen-wheelers of hay to them. She says, "I made a commitment to the ranchers to see them through to spring grass. The land is soaked with salt. They wouldn't have made it through the winter. They have to hold on to the livestock they have left, rebuild fences, and get back on their feet. Our motto is: Rebuilding broken spirits. That means not only for animals but also for people." She calls the horses, cattle, ranchers, and farmers in her area "the forgotten ones."

## Vermilion Animal Aid

Joelle Rupert says that Vermilion Animal Aid, an organization she founded and directs, is a "small, local pet rescue group in rural, far southwestern Louisiana. In normal times we rescue, rehabilitate, investigate cruelty, foster, adopt, educate, spay-neuter, and maintain a sanctuary for old, unadoptable, and abused pets. Since the arrival of Hurricane Rita, we are also running an emergency feeding program for 400 horses and over 2,600 cows, 175 dogs, and more than 55 cats, chickens, goats, and sheep." The HSUS, UAN, ASPCA, and animal organizations and volunteers from around the country answered Joelle's calls for help in the newsletter put out by Brenda Schoss of the Kinship Circle.

Brenda Herbet, who helps Joelle with Vermilion Aid, lost almost everything in Hurricane Rita, yet she works to save the animals who survived and the "tough Cajuns" who are her neighbors. With horror she watched her horses drown in Rita's surge. Brenda says, "I'm going to help everybody as long as I can. But it's really tough. When you lose an animal you've had for years, it's sad. People around here lost 11,000 cows, 800 or 900 horses, and no telling how many dogs and cats. Rita dropped down to a Category 3 but pushed water at a Category 5 level. It wasn't just salt. It came from the Gulf of Mexico where the drilling rigs were. If you walk through the water, the oil in it sticks to your clothes."

For people who lost everything in these terrible storms, finding an animal family member again became one of their only lifelines for hope. In the next chapter you will meet the volunteers and organizations that returned pets to the arms of families who loved them or found new homes for homeless animals who had survived the storms.

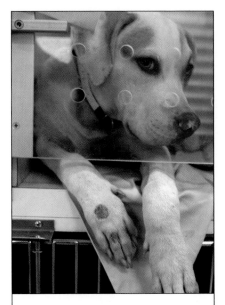

A worn-out rescued dog ready for transport. (Julia Cumes, IFAW)

A lonely dog waits for his family to return home. (Rebecca Brand, IFAW)

April Ball, San Diego Humane, coaxes a dog with treats. (Sabree Hill, San Diego HS and SPCA)

Communication between rescuers: top, date searched; left, group; bottom, number of corpses; right, structural information. (June Towler)

A rescuer comforts scared cats under a porch.
(Julia Cumes, IFAW)

A rescuer bathes toxic sludge off a dog at Lamar-Dixon.
(Julia Cumes, IFAW)

Stephanie Jehle, founder of Operation Underdog Rescue in
Dallas, carries a dog from a house. (Courtesy of Stephanie Jehle)

Lt. Randy Covey, HSUS/Oregon
Humane, rescues a pet from
the second floor of a house.
(Courtesy of Lt. Randy Covey)

Julie Burge, DVM, holds a purple
grenadier finch, one of the
smallest rescued animals.
(Courtesy of Julie Burge, DVM)

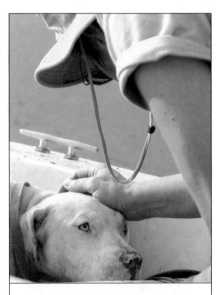

Comfort and compassion from a
friend. (Troy Snow, Best Friends
Animal Society)

Dan Maloney, Audubon Zoo of New
Orleans, hugs Sachmo, a rhino
kept safe during the hurricane.
(Courtesy of Dan Maloney)

Veterinarians perform emergency treatments at Lamar-Dixon. (Julia Cumes, IFAW)

An injured dog in foster care. (Sandi Corrado)

Spray-painted car tells rescuers where to find a dog. (Courtesy of Louisiana SPCA)

Lamar-Dixon's Barn 5. (Rebecca Brand, IFAW)

Rescuers carry animals
to a waiting boat.
(Rebecca Brand, IFAW)

Morgan Bartell, San Diego Humane
(left), and volunteers unload animals
flown from Louisiana to San Diego
Humane. (Simran K. Zilaro, San
Diego HS and SPCA)

A stranded dog needs help right
away. (Mike Fry, Animal Ark)

Rescuers carry crated animals out of
a house. (Rebecca Brand, IFAW)

Laura Brown, PETA's Domestic Animal and Wildlife Rescue, saves a dog's life in New Orleans. (Tal Ronnen, PETA)

Spray-painting gone wild. (Courtesy of Louisiana SPCA)

Soldiers load dogs onto an airlift to animal shelters. (Julia Cumes, IFAW)

Laura Maloney, LA/SPCA, and what
she loves about her work.
(© 2006 by Jackson Hill)

Paul Berry, Best Friends Animal
Society, and a volunteer rescue a
dog. (Troy Snow, Best Friends
Animal Society)

A dog awaits transport to
an unknown place.
(Rebecca Brand, IFAW)

Signs tell the story. (June Towler)

A starving kitty is saved.
(Rebecca Brand, IFAW)

A soldier checks on a rescued bird.
(Captain Scott Shields)

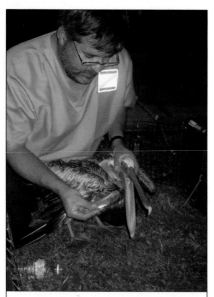

Dave Pauli, HSUS, rescues a pelican
after Hurricane Ivan in Florida.
(Courtesy of Dave Pauli)

Rescued dogs find each other.
(June Towler)

Jeffery Smith, New Orleans resident, and two
of his rescued dogs. (Courtesy of Jeffery Smith)

A dog at the airport awaiting transport. (Chris Cutter, IFAW)

An animal rescuer saves a pot-bellied pig.
(Rebecca Brand, IFAW)

An IFAW rescuer with a dog
on the mend.
(Chris Cutter, IFAW)

Scott and Kyle Radish's dogs,
Corduroy and Bailey, escape the
flood. (Scott Radish)

A San Diego Humane volunteer
leaves food to lure the pets.
(Terry Paik, San Diego HS
and SPCA)

A rescue in 100-degree
heat deserves a kiss.
(Rebecca Brand, IFAW)

Tara High, Humane Society of South Mississippi,
deals with a rescued snake. (Kevin Earley)

A stranded cow at a flooded farm in Plaquemines Parish,
New Orleans. (Sandi Corrado)

IFAW rescuers form a chain to bring animals
to a rescue boat. (Rebecca Brand, IFAW)

Patient animal rescuers use catchpoles and crawl under houses. (Jane Bly)

Animal rescuers sort out donated supplies. (Jane Bly)

Volunteer Diane Walsh with a rescued iguana, Disaster Dan. (Sue Bartski)

A dog eager for transport to a new home. (Chris Cutter, IFAW)

A rescued mother nurses her babies. (Chris Robinson)

Veterinary Technician Chris Robinson replenishes food and water stations. (Courtesy of Chris Robinson)

Why people stayed. (Mike Fry, Animal Ark)

An Animal Ark volunteer comforts
a dog at the Best Friends shelter
in Tylertown, Mississippi.
(Mike Fry, Animal Ark)

They really are best friends at the
shelter of the same name in Tylertown,
Mississippi. (Mike Fry, Animal Ark)

Veterinary medical teams work
through the night at Lamar-Dixon.
(Julia Cumes, IFAW)

Birds at the Lamar-Dixon shelter.
(Dave Pauli)

Animal rescuer June Towler suits up in protective gear. (Courtesy of June Towler)

San Diego Humane employee Lori Biewen comforts a cat at Lamar-Dixon's Barn 5. (Sabree Hill, San Diego HS and SPCA)

Captain Cindy Machado, Marin Humane, with an airlifted dog. (Lt. Steve Hill, Marin Humane Society)

The Prosper family reunite with Nick at the UAN-EARS shelter in Monroe, Louisiana. (Courtesy of UAN-EARS)

Rescuers carry cats to safety.
(Troy Snow, Best Friends Animal Society)

Bonney Brown (right) and Diane Blankenburg, Alley Cat Allies,
rescue a cat from a house. (Jim Davis, Alley Cat Allies)

MuttShack Animal Rescue Foundation founder Amanda
St. John (right) walks rescued dogs with volunteers along the Lake
Pontchartrain levee. (© 2005 by Don Ryan, Associated Press)

# CHAPTER SIXTEEN

# Rescuing and Reuniting

We all love to hear about pets and people finding each other again after the storms. Although these stories are comforting, on December 2, 2005, NBC News correspondent Martin Savidge said, "Despite efforts by hundreds of volunteers, unprecedented cooperation by animal groups, millions of donated dollars, and wide use of the Internet, the reunion rate of owner and pet separated by Katrina is less than 15 percent."[1] There just weren't that many happy endings, at least in terms of reunions. Laura Maloney, executive director of the LA/SPCA, says that while 15,000 animals were rescued in Louisiana, only about 3,000 were reunited with their owners.

The clock was always ticking and time was running out as shelters put their Katrina animals up for adoption. The HSUS, ASPCA, UAN, and Best Friends all asked shelters that had taken Katrina pets to extend their holding period until at least November 15, 2005, and preferably until December 15. It was getting clearer that evacuees were having an extremely difficult time locating displaced pets, and many did not even know that animals had been rescued.

Some shelters, in what was an unbelievably cruel move after all that

the volunteers and animals had been through in the rescue efforts, euthanized Katrina animals when no one claimed or adopted them.

More often than not, when volunteers finally matched humans and
animals for possible reunions, the displaced people could not take back
their pets. Evacuees were staying at families' and friends' homes, in hotels,
in their cars, in FEMA trailers, or in apartments that did not allow
pets. Their lives were in such a state of flux that the last thing they could
manage was responsibility for a pet. They could barely hold themselves
together.

A major factor that complicated the tracing of domestic pets was the
disappearance of records for identifying animals. At temporary shelters
some records were lost or information not recorded at all upon intake.
Most animals brought into the temporary shelters did not have collars or
tags since these had either never existed or were torn off as animals tried
to swim in floodwaters and crawl under houses. Even if an animal did
have a tag with a person's phone number, the phone was no longer in
service or the occupants had evacuated. The records that the tags were
linked to belonged to files that had been damaged or destroyed at local
veterinary offices and animal shelters. Microchipping was not standard
practice in this southern region of the country, so it wasn't usually an
option for finding pets' families. All of these obstacles had to be overcome
to bring pets and their people back together.

## Paradigm Shifts for Reuniting

Two huge shifts occurred as animal rescuers grappled with the immense
problem of how to reunite people and pets. First, the more established
organizations had to revamp their existing strategies and programs to
move more quickly and efficiently in a colossal disaster like Katrina.

Second, rescuers had to trust that perhaps other forces were at work
bringing animals and people back together or moving them in new directions. Call it fate, destiny, divine intervention, good luck, or good karma,
but there was just no other logical explanation for some of the strange
things that happened. Rescuers experienced heartening and startling

instances of synchronicity. Sometimes they would find missing animals just as a person who had been looking for his pets for weeks returned to his house for the last time. Or a neighbor would run out of a nearby home after rescuers captured an animal, shouting for joy because she just happened to be talking on the cell phone with the animal's owner, who had moved hundreds or thousands of miles away. An animal would be found and rescued long after any could have survived or under conditions that no one thought could have sustained life. A person would have done some generous or heroic deed, and it would be his or her animal who was found, against all odds. One clue or event would lead to another to bring a person and pet back together.

Thousands of creative volunteers worked together. Many thought they were being assisted by a higher power to reunite people and pets. Animal rescue was evolving into a new art form.

## Compassionate Foster Homes

Many Katrina animals were either adopted or taken into foster homes. We heard wonderful stories of new homes for abandoned dogs, cats, iguanas, rabbits, snakes — you name it. One story that shines as an example of what happens when a determined rescuer forms a relationship with a special animal is the story of Jennifer Daly, a fourth-grade teacher from Wading River, New York, who volunteered for Animal Rescue New Orleans (ARNO).

As you may recall, Jane Garrison, who cofounded ARNO, divided the city into sections for food and water stations. Jennifer and her teammate were assigned Section 32, with forty food and water stations to refill each day. They took notes on the packs of dogs roaming the area, many of them purebreds who had been pets but now had reverted to wolf-pack instinct for survival. Jennifer says, "This is not the little fluffy pet from six months ago. Now he's a whole other animal. These were mostly pets who had been left alone, were completely frightened, and lay on a front porch, waiting for an owner to return." Jennifer and her teammate left trays under water sources that were accidentally running, cleared glass off paths so cats could walk in and out, and put out food to sustain the animals until they could be caught.

Back at the ARNO facility, Jennifer developed a special fondness for a yellow Lab mix who looked like her childhood pet. The dog, a stray, was picked up and brought to a shelter in Mississippi. A volunteer brought him to ARNO to keep him from being euthanized, as was allegedly happening to other unclaimed animals at the Mississippi shelter.

Wearing gloves as a precaution, Jennifer opened the dog's cage and patiently waited for him to trust her enough to come out. Jennifer says, "Although he was a young dog, his body was stiff with pain. His paws were ripped up, his nails filed down because of the rough time he had spent on the street. He had a film over his left eyeball that surely needed surgery. He wasn't the type to bite or bark. I thought he'd make a great pet for someone. I named him One-Eyed Jack."

Jennifer started calling friends back in New York, but no one was interested in adopting or fostering Jack. Then Markus Vesligaj, a professor at Quinebaug Valley Community College who lives in Norwich, Connecticut, agreed to adopt the orphaned dog. An animal lover with a dog, Rufus, and a cat, Shed, Markus opened his heart to the plight of this hurricane casualty.

Thus began Jennifer's harrowing journey trying to transport Jack to Connecticut. She made arrangements with a major airline and fulfilled all the requirements for transporting an animal. Her troubles began when she arrived for the flight and it turned out to be on the major airline's partner aircraft. The smaller airline's animal transport regulations didn't match the major airline's policies for transporting pets. Exhausted after a week of volunteering, Jennifer had to endure one mix-up and delay after another as well as discourteous service.

The most relaxing moment of Jennifer's tortuous journey was when she found Markus waiting outside for her. He put Jack into the backseat of his car, where he had placed cushions and pads. Jennifer, relieved, says, "Now, One-Eyed Jack would be living in a big old Victorian home with another dog and a cat."

Markus wrote to give us an update on Jack. He says that at first the dog was timid and shaken after the tough airplane journey, and he slept for most of the long drive to Connecticut. But when they arrived at Jack's new home, the dog jumped out of the car on his own and walked on frozen snow, slipping and sliding through his first experience with icy winter ground. When they entered the house, the cat was the first to greet Jack. Markus says, "To my amazement, Jack started wagging his tail incessantly and following Shed everywhere. When my dog, Rufus, came out, Jack was so happy to meet a friendly dog. The two immediately started playing together as if they were long-lost brothers."

Markus had Jack treated for heartworm and scheduled surgery to repair his eye. The dog nobody wanted, who lived through everything nature and human beings could throw at him, is now happy and healthy at home with his new family. It's all because of the love of a very determined couple of educators who could teach us all about persistence and compassion.

## Do-the-Right-Thing Adopters

Sometimes, after adopters had brought a Katrina pet into their fold and fallen in love with the animal, members of the pet's previous home surfaced. This created an emotional, moral, and legal dilemma. Fortunately, most people and shelters did the right thing when Katrina survivors managed to find their pets and wanted the animals back.

Lisa Munsch Smith got an unsettling call one week before Christmas 2005. She was informed that Delta, the black Lab–chow mix she and her husband, Derek, had adopted from a Daytona animal shelter had lived previously with Robin Chelmis, who now wanted her dog, Licorice. Robin's daughter had searched for Licorice on Petfinder.com and had traced the dog to Lisa. Lisa says, "After Robin called, Derek and I went back and forth about which of us would be strong each day. We knew it would be a sad Christmas. We so very much wanted to keep Delta. We loved her." Robin had assured Lisa that Delta/Licorice was indeed her dog, so Lisa set up a rendezvous point in North Florida, at a campsite where Lisa and Derek were staying.

Robin says, "I got Licorice when she was only eight weeks old. She was a stray, in bad shape when I found her, with no hair. I nursed her and took her to the vet. She grew into the beautiful dog she is today. We used to walk on the Mississippi beach together and play. She became my soul mate."

When Robin arrived at the campsite and got out of the car, the dog at first did not jump up or act happy to see Robin. Lisa wondered if she had made a mistake in bringing her to Robin. "But all of a sudden," Lisa says, "Licorice was jumping up with her tail wagging, and she was pulling me toward Robin. Licorice ran and sat in front of Robin. And Robin never stopped smiling. That made it so much easier to see how the dog and Robin loved each other. Licorice did not leave Robin's side the entire time she was there."

"Licorice was on my mind every minute," Robin told us. "I would dream about looking for her. I lost everything, including my family photos from 150 years ago. My people have lived in America since 1630, and our historical memorabilia was gone. My children were grown and had moved away. Licorice was with me through every hardship. I have a liver disease and am going through chemotherapy. Licorice used to stare into my eyes and lie on my knee while I was recovering. She'd throw my arms in the air to make me pet her. She used to like to take a nap under a bush with my three-year-old granddaughter. I think I will be all right now."

## Do-the-Wrong-Thing Rescuers, Adopters, and Shelters

There were reports circulating that some volunteers, rescue operations, and animal shelters became judge and jury over whether an animal should be returned to what they decided had been negligent or abusive families. If a rescuer grew attached to an animal, or a temporary shelter didn't keep good records, or the animal shelters had hurriedly adopted Katrina pets out to new homes, it was difficult, if not impossible, to return animals to original owners. Newspaper reporters tried to lay guilt trips by writing stories of desperate evacuees pleading with shelters and adopters to return their pets. Lawyers took on the cases for dogs and cats, as the pets' previous families challenged new families or organizations in court.

On January 26, 2006, Judge R. Ruggiero Williams, presiding judge of the Superior Court of New Jersey Chancery Division, in Somerset, Hunterdon, and Warren Counties, ruled that the Great Dane named Chopper had to be returned to Annabelle Arguello after he had been adopted by a woman who had gotten the dog from People for Animals, in Hillside, New Jersey. The judge ruled that because Annabelle had clearly given the dog up at Lamar-Dixon for temporary sheltering only and had unsuccessfully tried to find the dog after he was transported to New Jersey, the dog belonged to her. This ruling was expected to set a precedent for similar court cases and disputes to follow.

## The Animal Airlifts and T. Boone Pickens

As Lamar-Dixon filled up and hit a crisis point, T. Boone and Madeleine Pickens, along with Continental Airlines, came to the rescue. Lisa Schoppa is the airlines manager of product development and specialty sales and runs Continental's PetSafe service, a quality-controlled program for shipping pets in climate-controlled vans at all major airports and an alert system for planning resources in advance when animals are traveling. On September 7 Lisa got a call from PetRelocation.com, out of Austin, Texas. Oil- and businessman T. Boone Pickens and his wife, Madeleine, had contacted this organization saying they wanted to pay for an air shipment of animals out of Lamar-Dixon to the Marin Humane Society, in Novato, California.

The first flight took place on September 13. Continental named subsequent flights Operation Pet Lift and ran the program at only the cost of the flight with volunteer flight personnel and with approval from the highest levels of the company. In addition, Continental raised the limit for the number of pets who could travel in cargo, coach, and first class to enable people who were trying to evacuate from the Gulf Coast to bring their animals with them.

Fourteen Continental flights flew from September 7 to October 2. Animals were transported to Helen Woodward Animal Center in Rancho Santa Fe, California, and humane societies and SPCAs in Los Angeles, Marin County, Palm Springs, Phoenix, San Diego, and West Palm Beach.

Continental employees donated more than 800 pet crates, and the HSUS donated another 1,200 for the project.[2]

Lisa Schoppa says, "It was strange in New Orleans. Our terminal had turned into the medevac area. The gates were empty. The deserted airport was eerie. Usually there are lots of planes. It looked like the military had taken over with buses and jeeps. An Apache attack helicopter flew in and around our plane. Military guards were everywhere. It was so quiet. I felt sad for what used to be a thriving metropolis. I wondered how long it would take to rebuild."

In New Orleans Lisa and the volunteer flight crew waited while government officials made decisions about letting animals out of the state. Madeleine and T. Boone parked behind the Continental plane, but when Lisa invited them onboard for a cool drink, T. Boone was gone. He and a couple of his ranch hands had driven to Lamar-Dixon to physically get the animals. Lisa asked, "Are they packing?" Madeleine replied, "He brought cash. That works better."

*Madeleine Pickens loading dog crates onto a Continental flight as Court TV films.*

Soon T. Boone and the ranch hands returned to the airport with the trailer load of animals. Each animal was accompanied by information about the address where he or she had been found and the date picked up. All of this plus vet records went to the Marin Humane Society.

Lisa says, "There were six to eight guys from Court TV at the airport with their mikes and cameras. Most of them put down their equipment and started grabbing kennels to help us get the animals onto the plane. There were 150 animals with 110 in coach cabin. We had never carried a full plane of animals. We wrapped the entire coach section in plastic. We took straps from the cargo bin that are used to hold dog kennels. Those straps fit around the seats and into the tracks on the floor. The odor was pretty bad. Many of the dogs had diarrhea, and a lot were ill and emaciated. When we reached the West Coast, there was press and publicity. People came out in droves. Vets came onboard with stretchers, and we pointed out the sickest dogs. On the plane we had given them water and dog treats. The dogs licked the food off our hands and looked at us. This was the only way we knew some of them were still alive. None of them died, but it was heartbreaking to see them so ill."

Lisa made sure a vet assistant rode with the rest of the Operation Pet Lift flights. Vets volunteered for the duty, and others sent supplies. Lisa says, "In all, we flew 2,000 animals with about half of them pit bull mixes. Not one dog growled or snapped at us. We had to check and recheck, open and close their cages. They must have felt stressed. Yet they were calm, didn't bark, and showed no aggression. It was almost as if they were say-ing, 'Thank God you're here to help us.'"

After each flight took off, Lisa and the flight crew bathed some of the dogs in the galley behind the cockpit. The crew allowed ten dogs at a time to walk up and down the aisle, to play, stretch, roll over, and sleep. One dog walked into the cockpit and put his feet up on the console. He vis-ited with the pilots for a while and then went to sleep.

Operation Just Paws was a charter flight to the Santa Cruz, Califor-nia, SPCA, paid for by the Doris Day Animal Foundation. That airlift occurred on October 10 and involved one hundred volunteers, who unloaded the more than one hundred animals at the airport. Doris Day greeted and kissed every dog that was taken to the Parkview Veterinary Hospital for Treatment.[3]

The North Shore Animal League, in New York, airlifted 219 animals on two flights from Louisiana and Mississippi. And the American Board-ing Kennels Association, a national pet care service trade association in Philadelphia, airlifted animals to their locations for adoption and reunion.[4]

## Marin Humane Society and Bill McLaughlin

The Marin Humane Society (MHS), in Novato, California, under the direction of Captain Cindy Machado, drove the shelter's staff to Houston after Hurricane Rita to help with two DC-9 cargo plane airlifts that MHS staff loaded for transporting animals to shelters.

Continuing the airlifts after the MHS staff returned to Marin, Captain Machado and Bill McLaughlin, a real estate developer in Marin, coordinated a total of twenty-two flights from the Gulf Coast to California. They called the MHS airlifts Orphans of the Storm. Patti Mercer, president of the Houston SPCA, organized the process of preparing animals for flights and transferring guardianship to the Marin Humane Society. Patti had to make decisions about which animals would take this journey, depending on their adoptability, age, health, and temperament. Other animals would stay in Houston. Fourteen of the flights were on Continental 737 passenger jets.

After Continental ended its participation in the airlifts, Bill McLaughlin found private companies to charter flights. A woman with a private

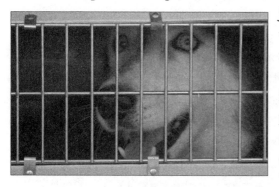

*A dog from the Marin Humane Society's Orphans of the Storm airlift awaits transport.*

jet let Bill use it for two flights. Bill was on the phone continually, communicating with airports and local and federal security, and coordinating ground transportation and suppliers to deliver the correct size of cages (donated by PETCO and other companies) to the right places. The Pickens family, Solomon Family Trust, private donors, and the humane societies where the animals were sent picked up the tabs for the flights. Bill says, "This was a full-time job. I was dealing with three different time zones. My phone rang from 4:00 in the morning on. There were delays and heat issues. The animals had multiple health problems. It seemed like we were getting them out of harm's way."

Bill, who became an expert on airlifting animals out of a disaster zone, says, "I would hate to lose the organization and format we worked out. Even the phone numbers we pulled together could be used in the next disaster. I learned later that Wells Fargo had the capacity to haul animals in their forty-foot rigs. I would have used them if I had known."

Orphans of the Storm transported 130 to 150 animals per plane at a cost of $46,000 to $50,000 per flight. Captain Machado told us,

Bill didn't think of himself as an "animal person," but there were tears in his eyes at times when he looked at these animals. He is a professional who had the resources and knowledge. He made contacts with the airport and the bigwigs who oversaw it. He coordinated airlifts for the animals to other parts of the country. Because of Bill, we only needed to contact the ground crew for each flight. We had to make sure the shelters that we sent the airlifted animals to signed agreements to care for, adopt out, or reunite the animals if owners came forward by the end of 2005. We had dogs with heartworm treated by University of California at Davis vets. We knew how to handle the animal part of the program. Although we named the project Orphans of the Storm, these really weren't orphans. They were potentially someone's valued family member. They had just been in the wrong place at the wrong time.

## Delta's Angels

Barb Peterson is a Delta flight attendant who now lives in Sandy, Utah. She grew up with rabbits, chickens, cats, and dogs on a Kona coffee farm, on the Big Island of Hawaii. Her love of animals caused Barb to feel empathy when she watched Anderson Cooper on CNN talk about the plight of the animals and the people who were forced to leave without them. She told us, "I thought, How can I help? Can one person like me make a difference, make life better for these people and their animals?"

The answer to those questions turned out to be a resounding yes.

Barb feels that God answered her prayers when on a flight she was working, she met Teresa Dockery, who is the director of Spay Virginia. Barb told Teresa that she wanted to get involved in any way to help the Katrina animals. Teresa said that Barb could help by spreading the word that New Orleans would need many volunteers to help the animals who had

*Barb Peterson (Delta Angel), Angela Badie, and little Adam with rescued dogs in crates at Portland airport.*

been left behind. After that flight Barb made a poster with information about the needs of Katrina animals and put it up at work.

Soon after meeting Teresa, Barb came up with the idea of using her flight benefits and flying to reunite displaced pets with their families. She reunited her first pet and person on September 28, 2005. After that delivery she thought, If I could get more people to help, we could have more reunions. She teamed up with Rebecca Compton, an airline administrative assistant in Salt Lake City, and the two women emailed employees systemwide and recruited volunteers to help with this cause. Volunteers from Salt Lake City reservations as well as ramp and flight attendants came to the aid of the animals. Some flew to get the animals; some donated their buddy passes (standby status on flights that Delta employees can give to friends and family) so others could use them for the animals.

Barb worked on her days off and during vacation time. She and those who came to be known as Delta Angels brought out animals who had been rescued from the Gulf Coast and sent to shelters in Atlanta, where the shelters were now threatening to euthanize them. Barb linked up with Angela Badie, a pregnant marketing manager, who received the animals in Portland, Oregon. Angela loaded in her van as many as six to eight animals each trip, hoisting them in fifty-pound crates. Then Angela brought the animals to no-kill shelters in Portland, Oregon, for adoption and fostering.

Barb says, "Passengers on the plane would see that I had a Katrina pet and want to know the story. I'd tell them what I was doing. One gentleman waited in the terminal and asked, 'Mind if I give you a hug? You're a hero.' I just said, 'Somebody has to do it. These poor animals need to be back with their families. They weren't asked to be left behind, and they have no voice. We are their voices.' Truly, the accolades don't mean that much. I just wish I had more volunteers. Lots of animals still need to be rescued."

Delta Angels brought small animals in carriers onto the plane with them. Barb says that when the larger dogs they were transporting had to go into the cargo area, the reservation desk and flight attendants at Delta made sure the pilots knew they had "precious cargo" on board. The pilots then immediately adjusted the temperature and pressurization so the animals were comfortable.

Usually Delta allows only a limited number of animals onboard. To help accommodate displaced families and their pets and to allow the Delta Angels to transport more animals, the airline has been making an exception to allow more pets onboard and in the cargo area.

## A Delta Angels Reunion

One of the grateful people who benefited from Delta Angels' compassion is Julia Hager. Her Pomeranian, Solomon (Solie), was her devoted companion as she went through a divorce, becoming like the child she had always wanted. She had adopted him from a couple she met at a pet store, and she thinks that Solie must have been abused earlier in his life because he gets aggressive when the lights go out at night. Shadows on the wall drive him crazy. She worried about what would happen to Solie if they were separated and he was later rescued: Would he be put down as an aggressive dog?

Solie and Julia did become separated, and the dog ended up in Aspen, Colorado, being fostered by a businesswoman named Melinda. After much searching, Julia found that her other pets had been taken to Lamar-Dixon. Her cat, Shelby, had been transported to Kittico Cat Rescue, in Dallas, and was returned to Julia by a retired Continental Airlines flight attendant. Her parakeet, Romeo, was returned to Julia's mother when she moved back to New Orleans. It was Barb Peterson who delivered Solie back into Julia's arms after ten different people had relayed the dog to various sites.

Barb says, "I was amazed when I met this little Pomeranian in Aspen. Becky Compton had him overnight until I could fly him to Jacksonville, Florida, the next day. Becky said that the dog was a little high-strung and didn't know that he had a name, so she called him Cujo because he was so tiny but had the bark of a huge dog. We laughed and I asked Becky, 'How could a tiny precious thing like him have such a fierce growl?'"

When Barb got Solie to Florida, she met Julia and hurriedly unzipped the kennel. She was in complete shock when the fierce, loud barking dog jumped out of the bag and into the arms of his mommy, licking and kissing her teary face. Barb couldn't believe that after all this time and so many different homes, he still remembered his one and true mom. She says, "Julia and Solomon were kissing and hugging each other. This was truly my favorite reunion. They're all special, but this one really touched my heart."

Julia says that Solie clung to her in the car on the way back to her new apartment with his head and whole body pressed against her heart. She says, "He would not move. He was glued to me. It was a good feeling." Now Solie enjoys playing in the sand and catching a football on the beach in Jacksonville, Florida, where they live.

By the time we spoke with Barb near Christmas 2005, she had delivered more than forty dogs and twenty cats either to their families or to safe no-kill shelters. She says, "Now that I know I can do something, I am going to be more active in changing laws about how animals are treated. I can't sit back and be complacent anymore. This has been the most gratifying, rewarding thing I've ever done in my entire life. I would say to anyone who wants to make a difference: saving even one animal is saving one life. Don't sit there and do nothing. Just do it."

## Petfinder.com

Petfinder.com, a company started in 1995, helped facilitate many pet-people reunions. Jared and Betsy Saul founded Petfinder.com with the mission of ending euthanasia of adoptable pets by using the power of the Internet. Their website links 22,000 animal welfare professionals from more than 10,000 groups with people who are looking for a pet to adopt. The service is free to both animal shelters and adopters. Normally the website has over a half million visitors each day, making it the 124th largest website on the Internet. Although Petfinder.com is a for-profit organization, the Petfinder.com Foundation is a nonprofit charity.[5]

On September 27, Petfinder.com issued a news release saying that the company had established the Animal Emergency Response Network (AERN) to help reunite companion animals with their caretakers. The new database would allow displaced hurricane victims to post information on where their pets had been left so rescuers could find them. Rescuers could also post descriptions and photos of animals they had found, and volunteers could sign up to offer foster care for displaced animals. The organizations that participated in AERN were listed as Maddie's Fund, American Humane Association, HSUS, ASPCA, Best Friends Animal Society, LSU School of Veterinary Medicine, UAN-EARS, IFAW, Code 3 Associates, and Alley Cat Allies. With AERN in operation, evacuees no longer had to call as many as five different hotlines to get help rescuing pets. All the information was brought together in one set of data with records and reporting generated from one source.[6]

We interviewed Ed Powers, director of shelter outreach and business development for Petfinder.com. He used to be the director of operations for the Animal Rescue League of Boston, a position that gave him knowledge and insight into the needs of animal shelters. Ed talked with us about the process of setting up AERN:

> We designed, built, and launched AERN in the midst of the largest national disaster in the United States. That was a challenge. Our first priority was to get into the system requests for animals needing to be rescued. Then we focused on tracking animals through the over two hundred sheltering systems where animals were being taken. Our third priority, in regard to getting the programs working well, was to match pets with owners.

When we started AERN, the disaster relief had already been going on for ten days. We had to merge into our system and make workable data from eight separate databases. One of the biggest problems we had was that the data the emergency shelters were inputting was atrocious. Our first thousand records consisted of Polaroid-scanned photos with the word *dog* — no breed, sex, color, or age. Initially we couldn't let the public do a search based on breed. We didn't want people to go in the database and look for a beagle when we had thousands of records with no breed attached to them. The person might not realize that he had to search the entire system, not just the beagle or breed category.

It took hiring a lot of new staff and volunteers and having national groups combine efforts to get the data cleaned up. Animals were listed on several databases. Rather than updating records, many of the sheltering groups were entering new records for animals that already had entries. We had to try to find all the duplications.

In version 2 of the AERN system, we incorporated all we learned from the feedback we got. Version 2 has an emergency plan for how to respond in the event of a disaster. The general public will be able to put in a request to have an animal evacuated and then continue to monitor where the animal went. Our goal is to expand upon the level of collaboration with other agencies like the National Animal Control Association, State Animal Response Teams, and state veterinarians. After we got AERN going, the HSUS and AHA hotlines started promoting our database.

When you think about everything involved, the number of reunions is phenomenal. Animals were sent all over the United States, and so many humans were displaced.

## PETS 911

PETS 911 is a for-profit company funded 100 percent by corporations, which means that all of its services to the public and animal welfare community are free. It offers a website, a toll-free bilingual phone hotline and works to consolidate information about shelter pet adoption, fostering and volunteering resources, lost-and-found searches, emergency clinics and veterinarian listings, health, and training so the public has access to all the information it needs to decrease euthanasia of animals.

We asked Kate Donlon, director of PETS 911, what the organization does for animal rescue. She explained that PETS 911 is part of a national, award-winning network of Web portals that includes the AMBER Alert portal and Earth 911. Kate says, "After Hurricane Katrina, PETS 911 provided its automated toll-free telephone system for people to input their lost pets' information any time, day or night. We assisted with over 3,000 inquiries from the Louisiana area and provided technology to help major animal welfare organizations communicate information to the community and the nation. Our goal for the future is to create one solution that integrates a seamless online and telephone system that is drawn from the best practices and lessons learned post-Katrina."

## Stealth Volunteers

Some animal rescue volunteers started out helping people and then put their skills to work on behalf of the animals directly. Marilyn Knapp Litt is one such volunteer. Her Internet skills allowed her to provide a critical service — and start a new group in the process. Marilyn volunteered doing intake at a Red Cross shelter, in San Antonio, Texas, where evacuees from Hurricane Katrina were coming in to the system. In the course of helping them, she came across the Petfinder.com database for the first time and realized that people who had been separated from their pets could use this website to find them. Marilyn told us her story:

> Two hundred fifty thousand people came from New Orleans to Texas. The people I was meeting while I volunteered at the Red Cross had lost absolutely everything — their homes, jobs, friends, and some of their families. Many of them had never left New Orleans in their lives or had never been in Texas. They were looking for jobs, trying to start a new life. I couldn't fathom the kind of gutsiness and courage I was seeing in these people. I wanted to help them.
>
> Most of these people didn't know anything about computers or

Petfinder.com. If they left an animal behind, they thought it had drowned, gotten chemical burns, or starved. I saw on Petfinder.com that many pets had been rescued. I thought it would be a relief for evacuees to know what had happened to their pets.

I'm Internet savvy and have worked with computers since the eighties. I'm in my fifties and a retired federal webmaster. I run an online discussion group for women Vietnam veterans, so I know how to tap in to communities. I'm not a longtime animal activist. I didn't know anybody in the animal welfare community. I'd never heard of Petfinder.com before this. All of my background and experience came together when I decided to find the owners of animals.

I asked for volunteers on NOLA.com [the New Orleans–area website] to help find pets that were listed on AERN. I called the group that we formed Stealth Volunteers because we had the philosophy of not waiting for permission, just go out and "git 'er done." At its peak, we had over a thousand volunteers.

Petfinder.com gave me a thousand email addresses of people who had signed up with them to do administrative work. Gradually I created a buddy system so the more experienced volunteers could teach the new ones. It was like a multilevel marketing operation with sets of instructions. The HSUS also gave me the recognition I needed to keep things going.

I think we identified a gap in the system. Rescuers and shelters who put information about animals on the Internet expected owners to come to them. I realized we had to be more proactive. We had to find the owners. We made efforts to leave messages, but nobody was picking them up. We did the research and figured out where people had lived, who might know them, and where they had evacuated.

Stealth Volunteers' future in local animal rescue now lies in the hands of Sheryl Hogg. She is calling the organization Home Safe with Stealth. But Marilyn says that the Stealth Volunteers are not standing down. They will stay on call in case there is ever another displaced animal disaster on the scale of Hurricane Katrina. By February 2006 when we interviewed Marilyn, Stealth Volunteers had reunited 800 pets with their families, and she says, "This is more than any other group."

# No Animal Left Behind

Anita Wollison is another entrepreneur who jumped into the fray to help people and pets reunite. Working from her home in Wilmington, Delaware, she first specialized in sending rescuers to addresses where pets were left and in getting supplies to staging areas and temporary shelters in Louisiana and Mississippi. By the end of September she had started an Internet blog and recruited volunteers for facilitating reunions.

Anita says, "By October 1, I was intervening in what we call problem reunites, where a pet is at a shelter or rescue organization that refuses to return the pet to the owner. Most of the people I work with have lost everything, yet all they want is to get their pets back."

Anita has been able to get results and cooperation in the quest to have pets returned because she adopts an agreeable tone and maintains a professional stance. She has many years of experience as a counselor, trainer, event organizer, and volunteer coordinator. Anita has a master's degree in counseling and completed a great deal of work toward her PhD. She tries to use negotiating skills with the people and shelters that are keeping pets. However, at times she has had to recruit pro bono lawyers to file lawsuits to get pets returned to their original families. On an evening in November, the first night that Anita had taken off since the hurricane, she received a call that a special dog named Candy, an Akita, had finally been located in a warehouse:

> This poor dog lived through a horrible hurricane and the subsequent flood. She must have floated across the canal. She lived for over two months in the warehouse. A man who worked at the warehouse started putting food and water out for her and did this every day for two and one-half months.
>
> Candy was so traumatized that the man couldn't get close to her, but he saw that she had on a collar with tags. He eventually gained her trust, was able to find the rabies ID on her collar, made some phone calls, and contacted the owner. Candy turned out to be the best friend and constant companion of a quadriplegic young man named Jason, who had evacuated to Dallas with his mother.

Jason called Nancy, another volunteer who was helping to look for Candy. Nancy called me. I called Jane Garrison, who answered her cell phone right away — not something that happened all the time due to the number of calls she received and her responsibilities with the animals. It was almost curfew, but Jane went to the warehouse immediately with a rescue partner. They weren't able to get to Candy that night, so they went back first thing the next morning and got her.

The man who had been feeding Candy handed over the dog's collar and tags. When Jane brought Candy to the animal clinic on Magazine Street, unbelievably, she landed in the arms of her very own veterinarian, who was volunteering there that day. He had all of Candy's records and observed, "She's overdue for her shots." She was relatively healthy. It was amazing. After what this dog went through, the worst her vet could say was that her shots were out of date! That made me shed tears of relief and happiness.

I then called Caroline, a volunteer who lives in Shreveport, Louisiana. Caroline got up at four o'clock the next morning and drove to New Orleans to pick up Candy, and then drove her to Dallas. Caroline wanted to make sure Candy was personally delivered to a grateful Jason and that there would be no chance of her getting lost in the system.

I received a beautiful card from Jason and his mother, with Candy's old New Orleans heart-shaped rabies tag enclosed. I cherish this very much. It binds us. Candy and Jason's story and her rabies tag remind me that all of us are links in a chain.

## Best Friends Pet Reunion Fair

Best Friends lived up to its name on the weekend of December 16–18, 2005, when, in conjunction with LA/SPCA, HSUS, St. Bernard Parish Animal Control, Grassroots Emergency Rescue, Pasado's Safe Haven, Petfinder.com, Stealth Volunteers, and No Animal Left Behind, Best Friends hosted the "Locate Your Lost Katrina Pet Event" at the Garden District Hotel, in New Orleans. At that time thousands of families were still searching for their pets. It had been difficult for them to gain access to or even locate all the places where they could search. Best Friends set up banks of computers and invited families to work with "reunion specialists" to help them search. The event was publicized on New Orleans's area radio station, WWL Radio, and in other media. Thousands of people came to look for their pets.

Nikki Morris, a Wacho-via bank systems analyst from Charlotte, North Carolina, volunteered at the event. This is how she described it for us:

Francis Battista, outreach director for Best Friends, spread flyers everywhere asking for volunteers for this event. Volunteers from Tylertown set up laptop computers at the hotel ballroom. Two sweet, upbeat elderly women helped people fill out forms that listed their pets' distinguishing features. Then the people would go to a room with a big movie screen and look at photos of the animals with their Best Friends ID number posted in the photos. The animals were not in cages, so the people could see them well.

The volunteers strongly encouraged people not to be ashamed to write down the IDs for as many animals as might be theirs. They explained that the animals may not look the same as they did before the storms and that Best Friends and ARNO had put collars on all of them. The gentleness and kindness of the volunteers and Best Friends staff were wonderful.

I could see that the people had their hopes up high. Forty volunteers sat with laptops and waited for people to come with the ID numbers of animals they might have recognized.

My work was serving coffee to people who were in the room where the movie-screen images of animals were being shown. The people had tears in their eyes. They didn't want to leave the screen to get coffee. They were so afraid they might miss seeing their pet. So I started bringing coffee, water, and cookies to them. They were writing furiously. I saw broken people, saddened people. Leaving their animals was not what they meant to do. This is not what they were told would happen when they evacuated.

I watched a man go to Francis at the computer. Francis pulled up more information about a dog the man thought was his. Francis found out that this dog was already spayed at the time she was found. The man said, "No, my Katie wasn't spayed."

It was such a patient process. I was sobbing by the time the man looked at one of the Petfinder.com entries and said, "That really looks like my Katie. She had puppies three months before. I still don't have a place to live. I'm in a shelter."

Francis said, "It's okay. We'll hold Katie for you. When you find a home, your pet will be delivered to your front door."

"But I don't know how long it will take before I have a place to live," the man said. "I can't afford to pay for her boarding and food."

Francis said, "Your Katie will be safe and sound. You can come to visit her. You have no reason to worry about money."

It was so uplifting to watch this man walk around the room, crying and hugging people and saying, "They found my Katie."

So, what does the future hold for animal rescue? What lessons have rescuers, disaster survivors, organizations, and governments learned?

# PART FOUR

# THE FUTURE OF ANIMAL RESCUE

*Photos on previous page, left to right:*

An American Humane Association
volunteer with a rescued dog.

Tanya Andrews reunites with her dog,
Sandy, at San Diego HS and SPCA.

Best Friends Animal Society volunteer
provides a shoulder to lean on.

# CHAPTER SEVENTEEN

# Today's Sanctuaries, Breed and Horse Rescues, and Animal Shelters

We turn now from rescuing domestic pets to exploring how individuals and organizations provide sanctuaries for domestic as well as wild, exotic, and farm animals and horses. These are areas of animal rescue most of us know little about.

A highlight of researching and writing this book was interviewing Tippi Hedren. Okay, we admit, we were starstruck while talking with such a movie legend and effective animal activist as Tippi Hedren. Mother to actress Melanie Griffith and mother-in-law to Antonio Banderas, Tippi is a native Minnesotan of Scandinavian heritage. A former New York fashion model, she appeared in her first movie as the star of Alfred Hitchcock's classic film *The Birds* and later appeared in another Hitchcock classic, *Marnie*.

In the hour that we spent talking with Tippi, she didn't mention her illustrious movie career, the many celebrities she knows, or the long list of awards she has been honored with for her humanitarian work and animal activism. Instead she focused on the animals who had inspired her to devote thirty years to saving as many of their lives as possible.

## The Shambala Preserve and the Roar Foundation

In the forefront of today's wildlife caretaking, the Shambala Preserve is an eight-acre sanctuary located in the high Mojave Desert northeast of Los Angeles, California. It's one of a kind in the United States and is maintained by the nonprofit Roar Foundation, a charitable organization established in 1983 by actress and conservationist Tippi Hedren. She serves as the Roar Foundation's president, guiding the organization's efforts to increase the public's knowledge about wildlife.

Tippi's devotion to wild animals began in 1969 while filming a movie in Africa. She described for us how her acting career and love of animals intertwined. "In Mozambique we saw an abandoned house that had been taken over by a pride of African lions of all sizes. The lions were sitting on the house's verandas and windows, napping, going in and out the doors. It was an amazing sight. I was fascinated by them. This was the genesis of the idea for our movie *Roar*."

*Actress Tippi Hedren with her cat, John Saxon. (Copyright © 2006 by Bill Dow)*

Tippi and her then-husband returned to California determined to coproduce the movie that would depict African wildlife in all its glory. A script for the movie *Roar* was written, involving twenty-eight to twenty-nine big cats. It would star Tippi and her daughter, Melanie Griffith. Tippi says, "We were going to use Hollywood acting animals and shoot the film. Over and out. Trainers read the script and laughed. They said that it couldn't be done. They told us that these animals have the instinct to fight. We would have to acquire our own animals to do the movie."

Tippi started the animal preserve Shambala with plans for it to serve as a home for rescuing big cats and as an African-type set for *Roar*. Tippi says,

> We began accepting animals that had been confiscated by California Fish and Game. Then the U.S. Department of Agriculture called to ask if we could take animals, as did other agencies and humane societies. Our little pride of exotic cats grew and grew. When we shot the first scene of the film, my then-husband was bitten on the hand. We had to stop filming. During the course of the film I was hurt, my daughter was hurt, my two stepsons were hurt. We also had a flood in the area. A lot of people who were very dedicated to this film and the animals helped us through that. The movie that we thought we would film in nine months wound up taking five years. In 1981 we released the movie all over the world except for in the United States, where we didn't accept a distributor. They wanted the lion's share of the profit, but we wanted the money to go to the animals. In 1983 we formed the Roar Foundation and started accepting donations as a 501(c)3 charity.

We asked Tippi what *Shambala* means. She said that a woman who helped her with the tedious job of putting the nonprofit foundation together gave Tippi a gift by telling her the name of the preserve could be a Sanskrit word, *Shambala*, meaning "a meeting place of peace and harmony for all beings, animal and human." She said, "Wouldn't it be wonderful if our world were like that?"

Many of Shambala's residents are cast-offs from private owners, zoos, and circuses. The animals could not be introduced back into the wild. Tippi says, "When we take an animal, it is a twenty-year commitment. They have a long life here, twice or three times what their life span would be in the wild."

Tippi says she awakens each morning to the roar of lions. It must be quite a symphony with more than seventy animals: African lions, Siberian and Bengal tigers, leopards, cougars, bobcats, servals, mountain lions, a lynx, a Florida panther, a snow leopard, and a cheetah. Tippi says, "We have eleven species of exotic animals here." She also emphasizes that none of Shambala's animals are used for breeding, buying, selling, trading, or any commercial purpose.

*Cyprus, the lion, a Shambala resident.*
*(Copyright © 2006 by Bill Dow)*

Tippi talked with us about the philosophies behind Shambala and its daily operations.

I feel such empathy for these animals born in captivity. They should not be here. If I could beam them up over to the countries where they are supposed to be living, I'd do it in a New York minute. They should be in the African savannah with their prides, living in the wild, being the predators they are born to be.

We give the animals here the best healthy food and human and veterinary care. We don't use volunteers for the animals. Our staff of twelve professionals has been with me for years, and we share the same philosophies about how these animals should be treated. The tigers have pools of water or the river or lake that they can splash in, with plenty of space to play, along with trees for them to climb. To keep them from being bored, we move them periodically from one compound to another. We let them be who they are. It's very simple. We give them a good life. The adult wild ones are so beautiful, magnificent, and unique. It's fascinating to observe their different personality traits.

As director of the preserve, I am on constant watch over what's going on, which entails conferring with the Shambala staff as to what needs to be repaired and whether all the animals are healthy and content. Each animal is checked every day.

Each day is different. I'm not only keeping up with the administration of the Roar Foundation in the office, but I'm working on fundraising events with the executive board to provide the Roar Foundation with enough funds to take care of these animals. We have to raise more than one million dollars a year, and we are now over thirty years old.

I live on the preserve, so when I hear a cat fight I find out which compound it's in and alert the staff. The animals do have arguments, and their teeth and claws can hurt. If any animals are injured, we immediately give them antibiotics and contact one of the veterinarians. Our vet bills are quite minimal, though. The animals are in excellent shape. They have shots and are wormed every year.

Zeus is adjacent to Delilah. One day Zeus became aggressive and said something that made Delilah very angry. She started digging and dug a three-foot hole in the ground. She digs huge holes in the sand when she gets angry. Once the big cats start arguments, it carries over to the other animals. They listen to what each other are saying and start fighting among themselves. It's like listening to two people who are in an argument, saying who said what to whom and having all their friends take sides. After a fight between two of the animals, there is a cacophony around the preserve. Then we have to strategically move the animals to different compounds. Then peace and harmony reigns again at Shambala Preserve. Things are constantly changing here. It is always profoundly fascinating.

We lost our bull elephant, Timbo, in June 2005. He came to live with us in 1972. His death had a devastating impact on me and Chris Gallucci, who took care of Timbo since 1981. What power these elephants have! What an honor it is to be their friend!

Elephants have only a certain number of humans to whom they will listen. Cora, a circus elephant, lived with us from 1978 until 2000. It is amazing to get to know these animals. I used to go with their human guardian, Chris Gallucci, and with Cora and Timbo on long walks up the river, out into the desert. Sometimes Timbo would put his trunk around my wrist. He would then put the tip of his trunk on top of my head and give me a massage. I've had an extraordinary life.

Even though Tippi says she has had some amazing friendships with animals at the preserve, she and her staff are clear that the big cats are predators, not pets, and they treat them as such. She says, "It took a long time for us to get it that these aren't animals who can be tamed. I'm a perfect example, with the injuries my family and I have had. We don't have those relationships with the animals anymore." Although she and her staff have personal domestic pets, no dogs are allowed on the preserve. A cat can climb up a tree; a dog can't. Tippi has a philosophy of no longer allowing her photo to be taken with wild animals in order never to portray the image that wild or exotic animals should be pets.

Because of her experience with and commitment to the animals, Tippi has become an advocate for national legislation to protect exotic and wild animals held in captivity. She says, "I have been very concerned that most states do not have laws to protect wild animals. Why aren't there laws protecting big cats and the humans who are injured or killed by these so-called pets?"

She is especially concerned about what happens to children when they are exposed to wild animals in unsafe settings. She told us, as an example, "In 2005, a ten-year-old boy went to visit a friend of his father's. The man had ten to twelve big cats. One of the tigers and a lion were released from their cages and subsequently jumped on the boy. He is now a quadriplegic on life support in a Minneapolis hospital. Just because you raise a wild animal does not mean the animal will be a good pet."

In 2000, with Representative Tom Lantos of California, Tippi worked on a failed attempt to get a bill passed that would regulate the sale of exotic cats. Next she worked with Representative Buck McKeon, of California, who sponsored the Captive Wildlife Safety Act. It prohibits crossing state lines to sell exotic felines as pets. About the legislation Tippi says:

I testified on behalf of the bill. The final bill was much watered down from the first bill I coauthored, but it passed unanimously in the House and Senate, and President Bush signed it into law December 19, 2003. We are now authoring another very short bill, the Shambala Wild Animal Protection Act, which will stop the breeding of wild and exotic animals for sale or trade as pets.

It's not for the faint of heart to go into these issues. I look back and think that the powers that be moved my life around so that I would attain some celebrity. For some strange reason people listen to celebrities. So I believe that if you're going to be involved with talking to the public, you have to really know what you're talking about. I have over thirty years behind me of working with problems of wild animals in captivity and a continuing litany of horror stories to tell how these animals are treated. How much space does a lion or tiger need? We can't give them enough space in captivity!

Tippi and others who fight for laws to protect wildlife have their work cut out for them. Wildlife trafficking is the second largest illegal trade in the world, outmatched only by the drug trade. The estimated annual value of the market for wildlife trafficking is $10 billion.[1]

Shambala is open to the public one weekend a month with a three-hour planned program, provided you make a reservation and offer a modest donation. The Roar Foundation has a membership program, and people can sponsor an animal through the Adopt a Wild One program. The Partners in Education program operates in conjunction with various unified school districts. The staff helps visitors understand the species and personalities of the animals.

Tippi says that she especially enjoys teaching students about the preserve and explaining that no wild animal should be a pet. When two Asian leopards came to Shambala, she asked local schools to name them in a contest and suggested high school students write essays about the animals. She says, "Many of these essays are fabulous. It gave the students a real purpose for learning about the needs of the animals and what the animals' purpose is for being on this planet."

*The Cats of Shambala*, a book that Tippi wrote in 1985, is available on the Shambala website, on eBay, and on Amazon.com. When the Shambala Wild Animal Protection Act secures a Senate and House number, it will also be posted on the website with information on writing letters to Congress in support of it. Tippi says, "We don't want one more child, adult, or animal hurt by wild animals in captivity or have any more animals being held in deplorable conditions. Unfortunately, even after this bill is passed, it will take another twenty years to phase out the tens of thousands of exotic animals living in homes as pets."

At the end of the interview, Tippi reminded us that people can go to the Shambala website or call the organization for more information about the issues she cares so deeply about. She closed by saying, "Never forget to tell your friends, relatives, and family the urgent reasons to spay-neuter your pets, and never acquire a wild animal as a pet."

## Other Caring Sanctuaries

Millions of wild animals are kept privately, yet they never adjust to captivity. People who thought it would be great to have a monkey or tiger find out that they are living with a predator who has grown too big and dangerous to handle. These animals were taken (often stolen) from their natural habitats, and after contact with humans they can't be returned to the wild. They need a safe refuge to avoid being disposed of inhumanely. In addition, circus or zoo animals who age or become ill and animals who have spent their lives in research institutions need a place of safety. (Fortunately, animal-free circuses are becoming more popular.) Thus the need for animal sanctuaries.

The Association of Sanctuaries (TAOS) is a group that assists and accredits superior sanctuaries for wild, farmed, and companion animals and has established standards for animal care. Through on-site visitations by staff and volunteers, TAOS assures that its members adhere to a code of ethical obligations. These include, "To strive to keep animals in a natural, spacious, and enriched a setting as possible and that will exceed minimum conceptions of their needs."[2]

The American Sanctuary Association is another group that sets standards for care and offers accreditation for sanctuaries that accept homeless and nonnative wild and domestic animals. The member sanctuaries do not breed, buy, sell, trade, or use animals commercially. The American Sanctuary Association provides an efficient way to find and identify quality facilities. Its president is (guess who?) Tippi Hedren.

Before donating money to a United States sanctuary, it's a good idea to visit TAOS and American Sanctuary Association websites to see if the sanctuary is an accredited member of these associations.

Below are snapshots of some sanctuaries that we believe do an outstanding job of rescuing and saving the lives of animals. You've already met a few of them in our stories of rescuing animals from Hurricane Katrina. Websites of all organizations can be found in the Resources section.

*Best Friends Animal Society*, in Kanab, Utah, provides the largest sanctuary for abused and abandoned animals — dogs, cats, horses, farm animals, and a host of wildlife find refuge there.

*Pasado's Safe Haven*, in the foothills of the Cascade mountains in Washington State, offers twenty-four-hour rescue and rehabilitation for dogs, cats, and farm animals, on seventy-six wooded acres. The group presses for legislation and court convictions that end animal cruelty.

*Home for Life*, in Star Prairie, Wisconsin, has created a prototype sanctuary facility for as many as 250 animals who are unadoptable. Often people make a bequest in their wills or establish a trust fund so their animals will go to Home for Life and have a quality life without the threat of being euthanized or placed somewhere else.

*Chimps Inc.* is a private sanctuary dedicated to furthering chimpanzee conservation through education. It offers recuperation and retirement for chimpanzees to live out their lives in dignity after they have been used in biomedical research or the entertainment field or have been kept at parks or zoos. Dr. Jane Goodall is on the sanctuary's advisory board.

*Farm Sanctuary* is a rescue, education, and advocacy organization that runs two shelters where visitors are free to roam and visit animals who were rescued from factory farms. The group has a 300-acre sanctuary in the coastal mountains near Orland, California, and a 175-acre sanctuary in the Finger Lakes region of New York.

*Humane Farming Association* operates Suwanna Ranch on more than seven square miles of land, offering hands-on emergency care, rehabilitation, and refuge for abused farm animals. It never turns away farm animals seized as a result of a cruelty case. It also runs a wildlife sanctuary with protected habitats for deer, coyote, bear, bobcat, wild pigs, quail, wild turkeys, and other wildlife.

*The Elephant Sanctuary* in Hohenwald, Tennessee, is the country's largest natural habitat refuge for endangered African and Asian elephants. It sits on twenty-five acres of land eighty-five miles southwest of Nashville. The sanctuary provides a haven for old, sick, or needy elephants.

*Cleveland Amory's Black Beauty Ranch*, in Murchison, Texas, is run by the Fund for Animals. This 1,620-acre refuge is a sanctuary for chimps, burros, elephants, horses, calves, and two hundred rescued Katrina chickens.

*The Donkey Sanctuary* was founded by Dr. Elisabeth Svendsen in 1969 and is the largest sanctuary for donkeys in the world. The sanctuary also educates people around the world on donkey care and follows up on reports of cruelty to donkeys.

## Horse Rescue

Horse rescue presents its own unique challenges and rewards for those hardy and industrious souls who are willing to spend the time, effort, and money it takes to rescue and rehabilitate horses. Although cruelty is rampant in all aspects of animal welfare, cruelty abounds especially in the horse industry, where horses face tortuous deaths to be rendered as horse meat or for other purposes. Although many organizations, including the HSUS, are working to end the sale of horse meat to countries where it is eaten, the battle rages on, especially with the Department of Agriculture protecting this lucrative business.

### Front Range Equine Rescue

Front Range Equine Rescue, established in 1997 by Hilary T. Wood, is a nonprofit organization, in Colorado Springs, Colorado, dedicated to stopping the abuse and neglect of horses. Hilary serves as president of the organization, overseeing the day-to-day operation of horse rescue in her region and reaching out nationally in educational and fund-raising efforts. She implements programs such as Stop the Backyard Breeder and Save the Wild Horses.

Dancer, Hilary's first rescue horse, became her inspiration. She says that her dream of having a horse came true when she found Dancer. "It was as if I had found the magic lamp and rubbed it and there was Dancer, a very thin, overworked horse with hooves in bad shape. My fondest experience with horse rescue happens over and over. It is the first time a new horse's eyes brighten up and he whinnies in recognition that I am going to take care of him."

Hilary says the work of horse rescue is not glamorous. "Everyone starts out with cleaning stalls, pens, and water troughs. There is no riding of the horses due to liability and safety reasons. I believe the hands-on experiences with horses give the volunteers a great feeling of satisfaction."

Early support for Hilary's horse rescue trickled in to keep the organization in operation — a box of apples from a grocery store, supplies from local people, and money to help the horses. Then the organization got a big break when in 1998 Hilary received a call that *Parade* magazine wanted to do a story on her work. The article was published in December 1998 and gave Front Range Equine Rescue national exposure so Hilary could educate people across the country about how to better care for horses.

Hilary believes that most people don't realize that horses need rescuing. She advises those who love horses not to let anyone suppress their dream of working with horses, especially if their dream involves saving horses' lives.

## Heart of the Redwoods Horse Rescue

Heart of the Redwoods Horse Rescue is a local organization, based in Eureka, California, that was established as a nonprofit in 2003. The organization originally served Humboldt County but has recently branched out to encompass northern California and southern Oregon.

Duane Isaacson serves as president and is responsible for overseeing the entire rescue operation. As is true of many small rescue organizations, all the board members work as volunteers. Duane serves as horse trainer, rehabilitating and retraining rescued horses, and he teaches people how to better get along with their equine companions. He also does demonstrations at animal health fairs and equine clinics, plus he works as a stable boy, cleaning stalls and grooming horses.

During our interview with Duane he talked about why he and his wife, Sara, have been doing horse rescue for nearly a decade.

Every success is great, but my deepest and most profound experience has been with my saddle horse, Sonny, the horse that started our involvement in horse rescue. He was sold at auction [to a local man who frequently sells horses for slaughter] because he was considered dangerous and untrainable. The man had labeled Sonny a "psycho horse." He had been to several "trainers" who beat him severely in their efforts to make him submit.

To Sonny's credit, he never lost heart or let them break his spirit. He simply bucked them off more violently than ever. I bought Sonny from the meat-market man. The rest is a long story of helping Sonny get over all his old history and the two of us learning about each other. I taught him about humans, and he taught me about horses. To be honest, I am lucky to have survived the experience, but somehow the two of us managed to get through. Today he is my best saddle horse.

It seemed that in the long run it was really Sonny who rescued me. What horses have brought into my life and what they have done for me personally I don't think I can ever repay. The horse rescue is my effort to make some installments on that debt.

My greatest frustration continues to be the attitudes and ignorance of people. Humans so easily dispose of living creatures when they no longer serve the purpose of the human. People rarely feel or exercise compassion for animals, horses in particular. Horses are expected to do what we say, or else. We create slaves rather than nurture partners.

When I am helping the horses, I am helping people. If I can get humans to change their relationship with their horses, their whole life improves.

# Breed Rescue

Breed rescue groups are growing, and in our opinion this is one of the best trends to hit animal rescue since Noah built his ark. Because breed rescue groups specialize, they understand the unique needs and characteristics of that breed and can place the animals in homes that are suited to them. Diane Walsh is a manager at AT&T by day, but outside of work she and others in Barrington, Illinois, volunteer for Illinois Doberman Rescue Plus. Diane talked with us about her devotion to this breed.

Dobermans get abused as guard and fighting dogs. They get pretty banged up. We have a volunteer who goes to the Chicago shelters. We get calls from the shelters and animal control about purebred Dobermans who come in. When we pick them up, we also look through the euthanasia list and pick up dogs of other breeds who have little time left and whom we know we can adopt out easily. That's why we are called Doberman Rescue Plus.

I transport dogs from the owner who is giving them up or from animal control facilities to foster homes or the veterinarian's office for medical attention — neutering, heartworm preventative, vaccinations. I love every aspect of saving the dogs. I organize adoptathons, where we bring all of our foster animals to a central location so people with preapproved applications can see several dogs at once. We do not adopt without a home visit. A number of us do a monthly stint at PETCO to educate the public on the Doberman breed and rescue.

One of my favorite memories is my first volunteer experience. We had a Doberman named Corazon, Cora for short. She was not pretty. She was six years old, all red with a long tail, natural ears, a horrible case of dandruff, and she had Wobblers disease, which is eventually fatal and affects the neck and spine. In short, Cora was a mess. We had little hope of finding her a home.

I was going to PETCO to do public education about Dobermans and asked our president, Pam Abare-Newton, if I could bring Cora with me. Pam didn't think anybody would look at Cora. So I asked if I could bring our mascot, Melvin, who is a beautiful Dobe, *and* Cora. I thought a little old lady might drop by and just love Cora unconditionally. So Cora and Melvin came to PETCO with me that day.

While another volunteer, Kim Smith, and I were at PETCO, a couple came over to talk with us. They had adopted a Dobe from us the previous year and wanted to tell us how much they loved their dog, Gino. [At the end of the day] my cell phone rang. Pam was calling to tell me that Cora had been adopted. Gino's parents went home, picked up their mom (a little old lady), and brought her to meet sweet Cora. The mom took Cora home that minute.

But this isn't the end of the story.

Cora needed a lot of medical attention. The little old lady couldn't afford the vet bills. So this gave birth to our Guardian Angel program. Our board of directors devised it to provide dogs with rich, full, and rewarding lives for whatever time they had left.

Cora eventually went to live with Gino's parents, as the mom could no longer take care of the dog's special needs. Cora died as a well-loved member of a family.

Breed rescue groups do the best they can to educate the public on their breed. Since pit bulls are not recognized as a breed by the American Kennel Club and have such a terrible reputation (many people say undeservedly so), there are very few pit bull rescue groups. These dogs, mostly sweet and loving toward humans, can be hard to place in good homes. Pit bulls are descended from dogs bred to be aggressive toward other dogs, and their lowered inhibition to attacking makes them valuable in dogfighting. With so many pit bulls rescued on the Gulf Coast, the breed's reputation made it difficult to find shelters in other parts of the country that would take them or people who would adopt them.

## Greyhound Rescue

Greyhound rescue is probably the largest and most organized of all the rescue groups. Rory S. Goree has served since 2002 as president of Greyhound Pets of America (GPA), a nationwide nonprofit organization with more than 10,000 members who are dedicated to finding homes for retired racing greyhounds. The group finds homes for 5,000 greyhounds each year, and its volunteers have adopted out more than 65,000 greyhounds since they started the organization in 1987.

Rory told us he had always enjoyed dogs but didn't have an affinity for greyhounds until a dog named Anna Marie stole his heart. He said, "Anna Marie was my idea of the perfect greyhound. The volunteers of GPA California put in much time and effort to make sure my adoption was right for both the dog and me. I was extremely impressed with the entire process and felt that I too wanted to be involved in bringing together other people and greyhounds to give them the happiness I had found with Anna Marie."

*Rory Goree, Greyhound Pets of America, with rescued greyhounds.*

Rory believes that many people working for better animal welfare also care deeply about humans. Many greyhound people, for in-stance, "take their greyhounds to retirement homes, schools, and libraries. Their visits to the schools and libraries with the dogs are reaching the generation of tomorrow. Just a touch today can make tomorrow better not only for mankind but for the animals that grace our lives."

According to Rory, 99 percent of retired racing greyhounds have a great temperament. "Other dogs are being yanked away from their mothers at six weeks. Racing greyhounds are with their mothers and littermates until they are eighteen months old. They play and learn with other dogs. This makes greyhounds different, more socialized and calm. They had what nature meant for dogs — to be raised with their dog families."

## Rescue Groups Abound

Lest you think that dog breed rescue is the only game in town, a simple search on the Internet will help you locate individuals and groups that rescue just about every kind of animal you can imagine. In the Resources list at the back of this book you can find the websites for groups that rescue cats, hedgehogs, wolves and wolf-dogs, ferrets, bats, chickens, iguanas, snakes, turtles, and birds — just for starters.

If you have fallen in love with a certain kind of animal, you can find like-minded people by searching the Internet. Who knows, maybe you will be the one to start a branch of a rescue organization in your own hometown.

## Today's Animal Shelters

Today's animal shelters and sanctuaries are not the dog pounds of the past. They are no longer dingy, sad courts of last resort for throwaway animals. Today's animal shelters are vibrant organizations offering educational and recreational programs, people-friendly environments, and expertise that makes them vital members of their communities. In many areas they are private, nonprofit charities with hundreds of volunteers dedicated to the welfare of humans and animals.

While the quality of care given by animal shelters across the country continues to increase, some trouble spots remain. On its website, People for the Ethical Treatment of Animals (PETA) explains that shelters in America vary widely in their practices. "Some animal shelters are wonderful places; others are hideous dumps." Some are funded by local groups, others by government agencies, some with tax dollars. "Sometimes tax money comes with a stipulation that some animals must be turned over to experimenters. Every effort should be made to eliminate this policy, which is known as "pound seizure," the group explains.[3]

Animal shelters located in less affluent areas face their own unique set of obstacles. Niki Dawson is the shelter manager for the Liberty Humane Society, in Jersey City, in an inner-city area. Her proudest achievement is helping indigent and needy people with the kind of proper food and care for their pets that they would not be able to afford with their own resources. Her shelter's Pet It, Don't Sweat It program does free neutering for dogs and low-cost spay-neuter for cats. The shelter works with human food banks and social service agencies to get pet supplies to people who need them and to counsel those who have problems with their pets. Niki says, "We don't only help animals, we help people with animals."

## The Changing Roles of Animal Control Officers

Animal control officers today are not yesteryear's dogcatchers, known for their cold indifference. Today's animal control officers exhibit the sophistication, integrity, and intent to stop cruelty. They are sworn police officials who investigate and build cases against people who are cruel to animals or who hoard them by "rescuing" them without giving them proper care (see chapter 21 for more information on animal hoarding). Today's animal control officers work with district attorneys to prosecute offenders.

Sandi Corrado is an example of the new kind of animal control officer. She volunteered for about seven weeks after Hurricane Katrina, making three trips to New Orleans to help at the Winn-Dixie group. Before her volunteer stint in New Orleans, Sandi was the chief animal control warden and supervisor for a city shelter in the Chicago area. In that capacity she supervised all the shelter operations, from adoptions to facility maintenance to keeping medical and financial records and statistics. She answered calls from police dispatch for stray dogs and injured or rescued animals, and she fielded citizen complaints. She was on call twenty-four hours a day, year-round, for emergencies involving animals. In addition to all those duties she educated residents on animal laws, helped with cruelty investigations by joining in on raids, testified in court on animal cases, and rewrote the police department's strategic operating procedures manual.

Captain Cindy Machado, animal services director for the Marin Humane Society, just north of San Francisco, oversees all animal services in the entire county and its twelve cities. She talked about the new directions for animal control:

Most animal control now is done through both nonprofit and governmental organizations. That combination helps more. We have law enforcement and peace officer oversight of investigative field officers. We're the animal cops.

Marin Humane is the home of the California Animal Law Enforcement Academy. We offer an eighty-hour two-week course to train folks in animal law. Animal control and police officers and another classification, humane officers, take the course. . . . We do training all over the world.

Captain Machado says she sees many people who want to get into the field. "There are a lot of people I get calls from who are stuck in jobs but their true passion is wanting to help animals. They realize that they could get into the field through animal control. It's one of the most exciting things I've seen."

Heidi Brasher, community outreach manager for the Houston SPCA, talked to us about the success of the television series *Houston Animal Cops*. The cable network Animal Planet funds this series, which is broadcast nationwide. It has done much to show the daily life and responsibilities of animal cruelty investigators. Heidi says, "Our animal cruelty department investigates 10,000 cases of animal cruelty and neglect yearly. *Houston Animal Cops* has been a good source of funding. It's a great educational tool to help people understand how to be part of the solution by reporting suspected abuse."

Kerri Burns, American Humane's Animal Emergency Services Response team leader and a former police officer, trains police officers how to safely approach an animal and recognize aggression in dogs. She shows a series of slides, and the officers learn how to read a dog's body language. Kerri says that the need for this training became more apparent after the Patton Case in Tennessee in 2003. A highway patrol officer pulled over a vehicle with a family inside, and the officer told the driver to get out with his hands up. The driver asked if he could shut the car door. The officer said no. The family's dog, Patton, jumped out of the car, and the officer shot the dog, who later died. It turned out that the officer had pulled over the wrong vehicle.

Kerri trained some of the two hundred Tennessee Highway Patrol officers at an animal shelter in their community where she did most of the videotaping for future training classes. Kerri taught the officers how to protect themselves and animals. At the end of the training the Tennessee police chief adopted from the shelter a dog Kerri had used in the training sessions to help her demonstrate techniques.

Captain Machado told us, "Marin started a program in the eighties to train police in dog behavior after a number of serious issues. We also train park rangers, meter agents, anybody who is going onto somebody's property where animals might be present."

Volunteer whistle-blowers become eyes, ears, and loving hearts for animal control officers. An example is a relatively new organization that seems to be making an impact. Dogs Deserve Better (DDB) was founded by Tammy Sneath Grimes, of Tipton, Pennsylvania, to stop the practice of keeping dogs chained or in pens. In 2003 the organization was the first-place winner of the ASPCA/Chase Pet Protector Award. Volunteers can start a branch of DDB in their areas and use the posters, video, T-shirts, and other resources in English and Spanish that the organization provides to help animal control end this inhumane way of treating dogs. The group's educational efforts help children as well as dogs. Every year many children who wander close to chained dogs are bitten by them because the dogs aren't socialized and have never known human companionship.

## Shelters of the Future

The animal shelters of the future, as well as the more progressive and well-funded ones today, will enhance their communities in addition to rescuing and saving animals from disaster. They will be educational hubs offering classes that teach people about animal behavior, show children compassionate animal care, and help those bereaved through pet loss.

The animal shelters that show the greatest promise for the future provide positive exposure to animals. Their trained volunteers take animals to hospitals, nursing homes, assisted living facilities, and schools. Their staff and volunteers, as those at the humane societies of Arizone, Nashville,

Oregon, and San Diego, receive extensive training so rescue teams can evacuate animals safely after disasters.

Animal Humane Society, in Golden Valley and Coon Rapids, Minnesota, an open-admissions facility where no animal is turned away, was established in 1891 and is one of the largest humane operations in the nation. The organization provides temporary boarding for household pets in connection with local Red Cross agencies. According to its website, "Disaster victims are required to have a referral from the responding Red Cross agency. The Society provides housing and food for the pet up to two weeks at no charge. The Animal Humane Society is also a member of a MN-ADC (Minnesota-Animal Disaster Coalition) and has been instrumental in the creation of an animal disaster response model for the state of Minnesota."4

Today's futuristic animal shelters are integral to their communities. They provide a variety of services, including cruelty investigations and disaster preparedness, and use innovative programs to reduce animal overpopulation for domestic and feral animals and to foster wildlife protection.

Their fund-raising activities often feature local or national celebrities who adopt pets from their facilities. They have informative and well-designed websites. Some, like the websites of the San Diego HS and SPCA and Marin Humane, offer virtual tours of their facilities. Skilled public relation staff produce press releases and four-color publications and forge relationships with local and national media.

Some high-end facilities have received bequests that allow them to hire architects to design aesthetically pleasing buildings on acres of property. The animals in some state-of-the-art shelters do not live, stressed out, in kennels around the clock. Instead, as with San Diego HS and SPCA and the San Francisco SPCA, dogs and cats rotate into homelike apartments with nice furniture and paintings on the walls. Visitors can envision the animals in their own homes, curled up on their sofas. The staff can observe and correct behavior, such as scratching (or worse) in the wrong places. Cats live in habitats, not cages, where they roam freely. Everybody gets spayed and neutered so that they do not contribute to the overpopulation. Filtered air and state-of-the-art sanitation systems cut down on the allergens and animal smell, while carpet cuts the noise.

In essence, these facilities are comfortable, inviting places to visit.

They are designed to facilitate adoptions, maximize resources, and make their communities proud.

To help shelters improve and enter the twenty-first century in style, the Big Three animal welfare organizations all offer animal sheltering conferences and support for their members. The Society of Animal Welfare Administrators provides professional development for administrators of animal shelters in the United States and Canada and has formed a new Disaster Committee under the leadership of board member Dr. Becky Rhoades.

In the future, not all animal rescue will be done by shelters. Already today, in every city and town, there are individuals who rescue animals. Some of them start nonprofit charitable organizations while others don't have the time, money, or resources to do more than find foster and adoptive homes for the animals people dump onto them. Comic Elayne Boosler is one such individual; she founded the nonprofit organization, Tails of Joy. Its goal is to help make the world a better place for animals and their people by raising funds for the smallest, neediest rescues all across the country.

## No-kill Shelters

Perhaps no other issue divides today's animal shelters and organizations more than the conflict over how to solve pet overpopulation. The most hotly debated subtopic in the overpopulation issue is what is termed the no-kill movement, or solution.

Various figures are offered as to the number of cats and dogs surrendered to shelters and euthanized annually. According to PETA, six to eight million dogs and cats go to shelters each year and it costs $2 billion to capture, care for, or euthanize animals in shelters.[5]

*Bottom line: Nobody wants to kill companion animals, but nobody actually is able to stop the killing completely.* No-kill shelters, which do not have open-door policies, stop accepting animals when they fill up, or they are part of communities that are not completely no-kill, thus sending the killing elsewhere.

Euthanasia of healthy and adoptable animals is the dirty little secret of the animal sheltering industry. People go into animal welfare and sheltering because they love animals and want to help them. In a September

2005 article in the *Washington Post*, Karin Bruilliard writes, "Many shelter workers adore animals but must bear the emotional brunt of animal over-population while putting up with a public that often derides their work and treats animals callously. The job can be so traumatic, shelter direc-tors and psychologists say, that workers are often afflicted with night-mares, depression, suicidal thoughts and fears of going to hell."[6]

If animal shelters in your community say that they would love to end the practice of euthanizing healthy and adoptable animals, refer them to Maddie's Fund, a family foundation established in 1999. Richard Avanzino is currently the president of Maddie's Fund, the Pet Rescue Foundation. Shelters, rescue groups, and animal control agencies can apply for grants and assistance to help them become more effective at saving animals' lives.

Nathan Winograd, a leader in the no-kill movement, offers what he calls a no-kill blueprint. He consults with shelters, providing an on-site assessment that includes making recommendations for improving opera-tions, covering everything from landscaping to creating a more favorable adoption program. He is the current president of the No Kill Advocacy Center, in San Clemente, California.

For more on the no-kill philosophy, go to the Resources section.

## Asilomar Accords

In August 2004, twenty-one animal welfare industry leaders from around the country, including representatives of the Big Three, met at Asilomar, in Pacific Grove, California, for the National Animal Welfare Summit. Their goals for the meeting were to meld their philosophies and to sig-nificantly reduce euthanasia of healthy and treatable companion animals in America. Over the course of the summit and subsequent meetings, the group drafted what became known as the Asilomar Accords.

The Asilomar Accords defined terms and proposed how shelters could consistently and publicly report statistics regarding the euthaniza-tion of healthy and treatable animals. They called this the "Annual Live Release Rate" and devised a formula shelters can use to calculate it uni-formly. The accords also defined terms such as *healthy* and *treatable*. The accords are available online, and reading them is an eye-opener. If all animal shelters abided by them, there would be full disclosure, and the public would know exactly how many animals are being euthanized nationwide, and the figures would be calculated consistently.

## Solutions Abound

Pet overpopulation is being treated in a number of effective ways that any compassionate community would be proud to support. Below we discuss the practical and effective strategies that progressive leaders in animal welfare use to decrease the number of animals without killing them.

### Adoption, Adoption, Adoption

Bringing animals to the people — shopping malls, churches, any public places where people congregate — instead of expecting people to go to shelters increases adoption rates. Also, locating the animal shelter in a familiar and safe place draws adopters. Ed Boks, general manager of Los Angeles Animal Services, is a leader in the movement to have entire communities become no-kill. He told us that he established Maricopa County Animal Care and Control, in Phoenix, the first municipal no-kill shelter in the United States. He contends that when he let the community know he had moved the shelter to what used to be the old Department of Motor Vehicles building, the adoption rate went from 12,000 to 22,000. Ed says, "When you make animals available in a location that is free of killing and guilt, people make the right choice to save a life."

The North Shore Animal League of America (NSAL) in Port Washington, New York, has a National Shelter Rescue Team that offers a mobile adoption program and other outreach services. Each year the league sponsors a Pet Adoptathon. According to Heather Hunter, director of public relations for NSAL, "The Pet Adoptathon is a thirty-six-hour weekend where thousands of participating animal shelters worldwide all have highly visible adoption events and over 20,000 animals find new homes."

Corporations jump in to help with adoptions. Helen Woodward Animal Center, in Rancho Santa Fe, California, partners with Iams for the

Iams Home 4 the Holidays campaign, in which 2,000 animal shelters across the country encourage prospective families to bring a shelter pet home for the holidays. Actress Diane Keaton is a spokesperson for the project. When a family adopts a shelter animal, they receive an Iams Friends for Life starter kit containing food samples, coupons, and important tips on pet care and training.

Not to be outdone, Pedigree also has started sponsoring an adoption drive. Purina funds Pets for Seniors, a program that matches aging animals with senior citizens.

### Spay-Neuter

Estimates are that in six years an unspayed female cat can generate 420,000 descendants and a female dog 67,000 dogs. Spaying or neutering animals increases their longevity and makes them less aggressive. The most effective spay-neuter programs involve mobile clinics in vans that are equipped to do surgery on the spot. Animal shelters, such as Pasado's Safe Haven, in Washington State, and PETA, take these surgery vehicles into communities where people don't usually get veterinary care for their pets. They offer the procedures at low cost or even for free. Some shelters get results by using a voucher system. When a person adopts from participating veterinarians and have their pets spayed or neutered, they get a discount or money back from the shelter.

### Trap-Neuter-Return

Trap-Neuter-Return (TNR) is a program for feral cats and dogs that is promoted especially for the treatment of overpopulation in feral cat colonies. A TNR program keeps feral cats out of animal shelters and euthanasia chambers. It also makes the cats less inclined to kill wildlife for food because sterilizing cats helps to take away their predatory drive.

Alley Cat Allies includes lots of information about TNR on its website. Bonney Brown, campaign director, says, "People call us with questions like how to tell the difference between a feral and a runaway cat and how to care for ferals. If someone needs help getting started, we try to pair them up with an experienced member of our Feral Friends Network. Vets who spay feral cats are also part of the network."

## Fostering

Most animal shelters these days have volunteers who keep animals in their homes before they are ready for adoption. Kittens and puppies get socialization and attention in these loving homes. Animals who are recovering from surgeries receive extra medical attention. Marin Humane, in northern California, adds the element of an individualized evaluation that the foster home fills out to share with potential adopters.

Amanda St. John, founder of MuttShack Animal Rescue, whose work we glimpsed in chapter 14, explained to us that her entire organization is composed of foster homes, or "muttshacks."

> We don't spend our money on buildings, staff, and infrastructures. We don't maintain a workforce to feed and walk animals. I guess you could say that we are the antishelter. Since no city, community, or organization could ever build a shelter large enough to house every lost or displaced animal, why even try?
>
> Besides, animals don't belong in shelters. With few exceptions, people hate going there. It's depressing. Animals need to be in a loving, nurtured environment. It's so much healthier for them physically, psychologically, and emotionally, and they get adopted much easier.
>
> Bottom line: MuttShack animals are fostered first, and then they always get adopted into loving homes. They go from loving foster homes to people and homes we have screened and checked out. What could be better than that?

## Internet Adoption Sites

Petfinder.com, PETS 911, and PetHarbor.com all came to the public's attention after Hurricane Katrina when they expanded their systems for reuniting people and pets. But in their regular operations these organizations are leaders in helping to match people with animals for them to adopt. They are changing the face of adoption because animal shelters of any size, foster homes, veterinarians, and individuals can post information about their services and adoptable animals. Prospective adopters can search by zip code and breed to find suitable animals.

### Shelter Pet Adoption Insurance

Petfinder.com has introduced ShelterCare insurance for homeless pets in a collaboration between Petfinder.com and PetCare Pet Insurance. Shelters that are members of Petfinder.com and in states that approve the insurance (most states do) are eligible. Petfinder.com makes a gift of prepaying the first month when someone adopts a pet from the shelter. Ed Powers, director of shelter outreach and business development for Petfinder.com, told us, "ShelterCare covers eleven common incidences of illnesses that a dog or cat who has come from a home or the street to an animal shelter might have. It also covers accidents that might occur in a new home that isn't pet-proofed yet. The insurance bridges the gap from an animal going from the sheltering world into a new home. One of the most common reasons given for an owner taking an animal back to a shelter is medical or traumatic injury and the unexpected financial costs associated with treatment."

As you can see, the state of animal welfare and care varies widely from community to community within this country. Saving animals from disaster is becoming integral to the daily life of communities. Animal shelters are taking better care of animals as well as becoming friendlier to humans. Animal shelters, foster care operations, and sanctuaries are using sophisticated, high-tech means and media attention to end overpopulation, keep animals alive and healthy, and place them into new homes.

Animal control has some teeth in it (pun intended). Most judges are still way too lenient in their sentencing of animal hoarders, owners of puppy mills, and animal abusers. Many lawmakers are still too out of touch to pass tough enough legislation to stop animal cruelty. But animal-loving people and organizations mobilize quickly through email and telephone campaigns to right wrongs.

We have a long way to go before all animals will be saved from needless suffering, but as a society we're moving in the right direction.

# CHAPTER EIGHTEEN

# Training and Careers in Animal Rescue

The other day we called our daughter to tell her we had signed up for a training course in saving animals from disaster. There was silence on the other end of the line while she digested this latest news. After all, we are middle-aged, not very athletic, and don't exactly enjoy roughing it in the great outdoors. We are not the kind of people anyone would envision slogging through mud while clutching frightened sixty-pound animals in our arms. At last she fought back whatever she might have wanted to say and murmured sweetly, "That's nice."

We loved her for it.

We were as apprehensive about taking the training as she must have been to see us go off on such an uncharacteristic adventure. But we knew that to write this book we had to immerse ourselves in the world of animal rescue. Besides, we hoped that someday we would be able to volunteer in a disaster and help animals and people through the fearful experiences of separation and loss. We also figured that training would enable us to prepare our own animal and human family for emergency situations.

The American Humane Association's three-day Animal Emergency

Services Volunteer Training Program, with animal rescuers Kerri Burns and Ginger Bross, scored high on all those counts. We finished it feeling much more confident, holding certificates of completion that will serve as credentials when the next call goes out for volunteers after a disaster. Plus, we formed some great new friendships with people who love animals as much as we do.

Do our skills equal those of people we saw on television doing rough-and-tumble animal rescue? No. One of the benefits of the training was finding out all the things we don't know and still need to learn. But we are now armed with an awareness of the basics, and we know where to sign up to become more proficient if we want to volunteer in the more skilled and physically demanding activities, or to continue our training with online courses such as the ones offered by FEMA. We also were heartened to learn about the many volunteer positions that don't require a lot of physicality.

## Why an Animal Lover Needs Training to Rescue Animals

People with the best of intentions want to help during a disaster. They ask, "How complicated could it be to save a dog or cat? I know dogs. I've had them all my life. I know cats. I'm owned by a cat."

As you will learn in an animal rescue training course, it can be very complicated indeed.

Susan McLaughlin took United Animal Nations' Emergency Animal Rescue Services (EARS) volunteer training workshop in 1998. Later she also took the three-day training offered by Noah's Wish founder Terri Crisp, veteran of seventy disasters. Susan told us that in addition to classroom training in the basics of animal rescue, volunteers for EARS Crisis Response Teams (CRT) are also encouraged to take online FEMA courses. After passing these courses, the CRT volunteers and leaders would be the first to be called up and sent out (deployed) on animal rescue missions to evaluate the situation, make connections with the proper authorities, and determine how EARS can provide assistance.

What being deployed typically means for the organizations that provide training is that officially deployed volunteers have their airfare paid or reimbursed, their living accommodations (primitive though they may be) taken care of, and some food and meals supplied.

There is a bonus for those who volunteer through a nonprofit animal rescue organization: tax deductions. Dick Schneider, a tax adviser at Winona State University, is quoted in the *Minneapolis StarTribune* as saying, "While the motivation of none of the volunteers we met [in New Orleans] was to create a tax deduction, the deduction may be an additional thank-you for giving of self to others."[1]

## Katrina Animal Rescue Volunteers Saw the Value of Training

Dr. James Gardner volunteered at the Lamar-Dixon, Pasado's, ARNO, and MuttShack operations. He set up a dog park for MuttShack and acquired the nickname Bark Park Man. Even though he went to New Orleans as a freelance volunteer, he quickly figured out the value of training. He says, "You can hurt as well as help. You handle a dog wrong and he bites you; because you're incompetent, the dog has to live with the label of being aggressive" — a label, we might add, that can be a death sentence for an animal.

We heard from many volunteers like Angela Smith, from Eustace, Texas. She volunteered several times for various organizations and came back determined to go for training. Angela says, "Animal rescue after Hurricane Katrina was the most rewarding and the most devastating experience in both the lives of my husband, Ronny, and me. We are working on getting secure credentials and education so we may be called in first response with another disaster and make a difference again in animals' and owners' lives."

## Training Teaches Safety First

Stephanie Houfek, originally from New Orleans but now from California, volunteered twice with Best Friends in Tylertown. She filled a van and, with two other volunteers, drove across the country to bring supplies. She advises,

Work with a reputable group. Do not work with renegades. The system needs to be a system and not just a free-for-all. Get trained. Know it will be hard and it will be one of the most difficult things you will experience. There is no way to explain what it was like. You had to experience it. Get all the shots — hepatitis, rabies. Protect your entire body, including having breathing equipment. Do not follow others who think they are too tough to wear safety gear. Most everyone I worked with who refused to wear gear got sick.

Kerri Burns was our AHA trainer. She is a volunteer team leader for the AHA's Emergency Services Response team. Kerry explained how her animal rescue teams operate:

We do the right thing. We work in teams. The safety officer on the team is in charge and can stop a rescue at any time if human safety is at risk.

We take the cage to the animal rather than bring the animal to the cage. We don't just grab a catchpole out of the vehicle and run into the home. Two people go inside, calling softly, "Here kitty, kitty." This reduces injury, bites, and stress on the animals. If you run into a house, the animals panic. You lose them. We take the extra minutes to look at the house first. Is there an open window? We push in an air conditioner or break into a back door carefully and if there is an animal still inside, we secure the house when we leave.

Training will teach you what clothing, protective gear, inoculations, equipment, and skills you need to rescue animals without risking the safety of animals, other people, and yourself.

## Training Provides a System

We repeatedly heard from volunteers that the stressful situations in disaster rescue are made more stressful by disorganization. Each animal rescue training program explains the National Incident Management System (NIMS) and the Incident Command System (ICS) that NIMS uses.

Offering a unified approach to disaster management, ICS has worked for years for firefighters.

The White House report on the federal response to Hurricane Katrina says, "NIMS provides a common, flexible framework within which government and private entities at all levels can work together to manage domestic incidents of any magnitude. In March 2004, the Secretary of Homeland Security approved the NIMS and sent a memorandum to officials at all levels of government asking for continued cooperation and assistance in further developing and implementing the NIMS."[2]

Unfortunately, NIMS did not seem to have been fully implemented by the time of Hurricane Katrina, so rescue and relief efforts were not as well coordinated as they could have been. But the concept of unified command remains a good idea. In the ICS model, each person within an organization reports to only one person. Organizing through NIMS enables agencies to work together during a disaster, designating senior members or qualified people from each discipline to develop a single plan of action. Dr. Mark Goldstein, president of the San Diego Humane Society and SPCA, says, "When we started the process of helping three days after the hurricane, we sent in trained people. At a disaster, well-meaning but not capable volunteers become a liability. They want to help but can get injured. The Incident Command System model is the only way to function in a disaster so you always know who is in charge."

Dr. Mary Lou Randour, a clinical psychologist who is director of education for the Doris Day Animal Foundation, went to Lamar-Dixon at the request of the HSUS to give support to the volunteers and first responders there. She says,

Most groups, including groups in animal protection, aren't oriented to the command and control structure. It is like a military operation with clear roles and functions. My fantasy is that the groups each bring in somebody who knows this structure and how to impose it. It needs to be fine and tight. ASPCA, American Humane, and HSUS have to completely work this out ahead of time, including having software to keep track of pets and ways to communicate when cell phones don't work. A lot of groups are getting together to have debriefing and reviews after their experiences with Hurricane Katrina.

Lt. Randy Covey, director of the HSUS Disaster Response Team, said that if more volunteers had been trained in ICS in addition to understanding the basics of handling stressed animals during and after a disaster, the work at Lamar-Dixon would have been much easier. "Having a trained, knowledgeable person responsible for an area with people willing to follow direction and trust the experience of the person in charge would make it run better."

## The Effects of Post-traumatic Stress Disorder in Animal Rescue Work

Post-traumatic Stress Disorder (PTSD) ran rampant among volunteers after they returned from the Gulf Coast. They suffered from the effects of working long hours, seeing animals suffer, feeling hopeless over the enormity of the task, being deprived of sleep, and suppressing their emotions so as not to be viewed as wimps by the more macho or experienced types.

Anna Rising, an executive recruiter, went four times from her home in Kirkland, Washington, to Louisiana to volunteer first at Pasado's and then three times with ARNO. She says,

> The post-traumatic stress that I and everyone I know who was involved [has suffered] has been much more extreme than any of us expected. It depends on what people saw. People are still having nightmares. There's a real sense of unfinished business because there is still so much to do.
>
> I connected with people on the Internet who live in this area. When I came home I wanted to talk about it with people who had shared the same experiences. Nobody understands what it's like, so much devastation. You see it on television, but to be there — to actually see it, to smell it, to hear it — is totally different, even surreal.

On my fourth trip, in January 2006, I felt a terrible sadness. Everything still looked the same. I would drive down streets that were covered in horrible, gray ash. The cars were covered with white mold. The plants were dead. Only one in thirty houses had people in them. There was garbage everywhere. There were animals everywhere. One evening I left out food and watched as ten cats came for it, like some kind of weird movie. Before, they were all hidden.

Healthy stress management was the exception, not the norm, after Hurricane Katrina. Dave Pauli, running Lamar–Dixon, had to send home some volunteers and to take away phone privileges from one of the HSUS's volunteers. He says he watched people burn out, explode, and lose their grip on reality. We heard stories from reliable sources of volunteers who were off their medications or succumbing to their drug or alcohol addictions and becoming dangerous to themselves and others.

PTSD occurs with animal shelter workers too. Jan Herzog, who managed a humane society in a small Texas town for thirteen years, was run off the road by some farmers she had to investigate for starving their cows. She wound up getting out of the sheltering business because she was having severe nightmares and emotional stress due to having to euthanize animals rather than allowing them to be disposed of cruelly by their owners. Jan told us, "I'd be interested in the impact of working in a shelter. I'd like to see studies about the tragic effects on people's families, marriages, lives, and mental health. I know from my experiences that it is enormous."

Signs of PTSD are a sense of numbness and unreality after reentering daily life, losing your temper or crying easily and frequently, sleeplessness, nightmares, and a compulsive feeling of needing to return or to do more to help. If you are suffering from symptoms of PTSD, get qualified help so you can process the dreadful images and experiences, and assimilate the joy of doing so much to help animals and people.

## Training Lessens PTSD

Dr. Melissa Hunt, clinical psychologist at the University of Pennsylvania and researcher on PTSD and pet loss, told us that there is a great deal of evidence showing that training makes a huge difference in PTSD. She says, "One of the symptoms of PTSD is that the person experiences helplessness during traumatic events. Training allows people to feel that they are not helpless. This makes a big difference. Training prepares you psychologically and mentally for what to expect. Training equips you with a very specific set of skills. You know what to do. You have a job. You know exactly what the parameters are. You are equipped to do it."

Kathleen Regan Figley is the corporate executive officer of Green Cross Foundation, an organization that certifies professionals and laypersons to help people after catastrophic events. Through the Green Cross assistance program, crisis intervention and compassion stress management services are offered to first responders and the general public after a disaster. The HSUS asked Green Cross for its services after Hurricane Katrina.

Kathleen Figley trains laypersons, counselors, and therapists to assist with compassion stress management or secondary traumatic stress, which comes from experiencing or witnessing the pain of others. The Green Cross defines compassion fatigue as "the combined effects of previous personal trauma in the life of the caregiver, secondary traumatic stress, and burnout. Increased anxiety, depression, nightmares, recurrent thoughts of clients (or clients' stories), relationship problems, and loss of hope can all be symptoms of secondary traumatic stress and/or compassion fatigue."[3]

She is a veteran of more than thirty disasters, including the December 2004 Asian tsunami, the 9/11 terrorist attacks, the Northridge earthquake in southern California, and Hurricane Andrew. She believes animal care work is harder than working with people. "You don't have the dialogue. You can ask questions of humans and satisfy your need for information. With animals, you only have their eyes speaking to you. Everything has to come from your intuition and training."

Emotionally, the work takes a toll:

As an animal care rescuer, you bring animals in from a disaster and turn them over to somebody else. You don't usually know what happens to them. Yet you have developed attachments to the animals in very intense environments.

Rescue work gives animal care workers a sense of purpose. You are devoting yourself to a greater good. You are making a difference, an impact. The work takes a heavy toll on the emotions, though, and may delay grief over your own losses. You may also have felt a lot of joy at being able to help. To fulfill a purpose amidst all of the chaos is very positive.

Kathleen Figley says that self-care is both "the most important and hardest thing for people to do in a disaster environment. Self-care doesn't totally prevent compassion fatigue and PTSD, but it mitigates them." She emphasizes, "You need to take breaks and have good stress management. Animal rescue workers have an intense desire to relieve the pain of others. But you are looking at the insurmountable and wondering how you will get through it. The answer is rotating shifts. Limit your exposure to traumatic stimuli. After Hurricane Katrina, some rescuers stayed way too long. This leads to accidents and poor judgment."

She adds, "It's unethical not to practice good self-care. The first rule is to do no harm" — including, and first of all, to yourself!

Often attention to self-care is denied out of guilt, dedication, or pressure from others. The workload is so intense that people have a hard time stepping back. Instead, they absorb more. The common thinking is that what people do during nondisasters is what they are likely to do during a disaster. If they tend to overcommit and overwork, it is easiest for them to keep doing that. In day-to-day life, what is your resilience factor? Do you take care of yourself? Do you bounce back fast? Are you likely to minimize emotional impact? This is how you will play out in a disaster.

Kathleen Figley says that there are many helpful ways to release and work through the trauma:

Animal rescue workers need strategies for dealing with intrusive thoughts and images. Some rescuers release by talking. Others need to write or draw. It's important to get what's inside of you out. Sometimes there is too much emphasis on talk when any way of processing the pain is good. In a catastrophic environment, people who cry are sometimes viewed with a slanted eye. Crying needs to be okay, accepted, even embraced, not viewed as a weakness or something to be pushed away. It makes sense to cry.

Don't judge people for the way they cope. Sit down with someone who is in distress. Help them process so they can go back to work. They just need to let it out.

To take care of yourself during animal rescue work, she recommends bringing two very simple aids: "I suggest that those who deploy to disasters bring earplugs and face masks for two reasons. First, thousands of animals are in cages, and there is the smell from animal waste. Second, you need to sleep at night and get some relief in what is the worst kind of camping."

Her other recommendations for self-care and soothing include visualizations, music, protein bars, exercise, and finding support people:

Learning how to use guided visualization helps a responder have a mental place to go. When I worked [after] September 11, I would pop an image of my favorite beach into my mind. You can train your brain to give you a minivacation. This is a self-soothing method that brings down the anxiety level and can be used to calm yourself.

Bring a cassette player with batteries and earphones so you can listen to music and don't have to constantly hear the sound of animals in distress. Take three days of healthy food with you — protein bars, whatever keeps up your nutrition. Build exercise into your disaster deployment. Keep your body moving so stress can be processed.

Have two supports — inside the disaster and at home. The inside person knows what you're going through and recognizes firsthand what you are feeling and when you need to stop and take care of yourself.

The one at home keeps you connected to your roots and your life. Then when you go home, the transition will be easier because your family has some sense of what you experienced.

And after you return home, Kathleen Figley advises, "Go on a news diet. Watching news reports keeps the pain alive. It retraumatizes you." When you get home, "You need to be kind and gentle to yourself. Know that you did the best you could under horrible circumstances. Support is critical to handling your feelings."

She emphasizes the importance of training. Before heading to any disaster, she says, be sure to get training because training helps to mitigate stress:

When people know what to expect, it reduces their stress levels. This is the value of training. Training also helps you learn how to operate like you are in a field hospital. You patch the wound and move on to the next one. It's not like a typical day at a veterinarian's office. It's constant high pressure. There's a difference between day-to-day and catastrophic animal care giving.

People go into this field due to compassion and empathy. They are the kind who like to make connections. They care about animals and people. It makes them feel good. It is unrealistic to expect these people to stay emotionally detached. Good boundaries are different from emotional detachment. You can have good boundaries and make the connections too.

The emergency management community wears people down to a nub. They are putting people at risk. It will take lawsuits and penalties before a shift is made. If organizations put their staff and volunteers at risk, knowing things can be done to prevent injuries, there is liability. Not training people before disasters creates liability.

At the Green Cross website you can take a look at the protocols, and you will also find lists of things people who deploy to a disaster need to do and know before going. Kathleen Figley also offers training through Figley Institute.

## Training Helps You Not Be Judgmental

One of the major issues, especially among early volunteers in the disaster zone, was that they were understandably disturbed and upset by finding animals left behind in such dire straights while their human families had evacuated. Not knowing all, or even any, of the individual reasons residents made their decisions, some volunteers jumped to conclusions. They condemned and harassed people for saving themselves while leaving their pets behind. Later, as the weeks and months wore on, it was even harder for volunteers to handle the sights of animals who had wasted away or were found barely surviving inside crates, locked in houses, or chained to whatever would hold them in death's grip.

Kerri Burns, American Humane trainer and former police officer, offers advice that is hard to follow but that other trainers we spoke with echoed. She says, "Be nonjudgmental. In police work I saw so many things. It's not my place to be judge and jury. I don't know the circumstances. My focus is simply to do the job. I have to walk into a house or backyard and know that the only thing that matters is saving the animal. Nothing else matters at that moment. Stay in the moment."

## Training and the Future

Look in the Resources section at the end of this book for places you can get training in rescue for future disasters and in the daily operations of animal shelters. The FEMA courses can be done at home and will help you take care of your own pets even if you aren't going to volunteer in a disaster. Drew Moore, who volunteered on the HSUS animal rescue teams, says that in addition to the FEMA animal rescue courses, the American Red Cross offers courses in first aid and CPR and sheltering operations. The HSUS offers the Emergency Animal Sheltering and Disaster Animal Response Training. Also, check with your local animal shelter to see if it will be offering volunteer disaster or emergency rescue training.

The organizations that offer training and have the largest number of volunteers are strategizing with federal, state, and local officials to create disaster plans that prevent volunteers with no officially recognized training credentials from entering disaster zones. Spontaneous volunteers who haven't been through organizations' training will be given jobs that don't require the intensive skill level, gear, and knowledge that teams like Oregon Humane Society's OHSTAR have. The animal rescue volunteers of future disasters won't be able to post spray-painted or shoe polish signs on their vehicles and sail through checkpoints. Official animal rescue vehicles will be laminated and affixed with signage of the animal rescue organizations they represent.

In an article posted online at the Best Friends website, Claire Davis reported on a meeting that took place in April 2006 between animal rescuers and Dr. Renee Poirrer, DVM, head of the Louisiana Veterinary Medical Association's State Animal Response Team. According to Davis, Dr. Poirrer told local animal shelters and rescue groups to forge memorandums of understanding with Louisiana's parishes. Dr. Poirrer announced that out-of-state veterinarians would not be allowed to practice in a disaster without a Louisiana license. The article says that Dr. Poirrer claims that in the future animal rescuers must be certified or they won't be allowed in a disaster zone and if found there, would be asked to leave. She is quoted as saying, "Required training includes taking ICS 100 and 200 courses as well as NIMS 700 and 800 courses."[4] These are the FEMA courses that are available online.

To discourage the self-deployed, animal rescue organizations that have memorandums of understanding with cities, counties, and states will work closely with military and law enforcement. They will also have systems (most do already) for gratefully accepting the help of noncredentialed volunteers and placing them in positions that don't require extensive training. The groups are working together to agree on what training they can all accept so organizations can securely and easily work with one another's volunteers.

We encourage everyone who is reading this book to do what so many thousands of others have done since Hurricane Katrina: sign up for training. If you have the stamina and interest to become a more highly skilled rescuer, Code 3 Associates, in Erie and Longmont, Colorado, provides technical search-and-rescue training, rough water training, and large-animal rescue programs. Felton Fire Department, in Felton, California, trains firefighters and other emergency responders to do large and small animal rescue. More fire departments across the country are now learning emergency techniques and equipping themselves with Best Friends Pet Care's pet oxygen masks to save pets' lives in home fire rescues. (This company is in Norwalk, Connecticut, and is not related to the Best Friends Animal Society.)[5] Check to see if your local fire department is availing itself of these new training techniques. It may be your pet whose life they save.

## Jobs and Careers in Animal Rescue and Welfare

If you're interested in making animal rescue and welfare the focus of your career, the doors are wide open. Julie Morris, of the ASPCA, says, "Virtually every job or career a person is currently doing can be transferred to doing animal rescue. You may not touch an animal day to day, but you'll be saving animals through the work you do." She offers an example: "Jennifer Fearing, president of United Animal Nations, has a master's of economics from Harvard and puts it to good use in her current position. You would be surprised at the wide variety of skills people bring to their work in animal rescue and welfare."

Julie gave examples of what large organizations are looking for in staff and volunteers. She said that every group needs legal expertise, accountants, staff who are educated in marketing, management, or any of the professional skills. Doing public relations for an animal organization entails writing letters to legislators, producing newsletters and publications, designing direct-mail campaigns, forging positive relationships with the media, and overseeing website construction and updates.

While being a veterinarian or a vet tech is rewarding, work in animal rescue is not limited to those choices. A person could become a meeting planner for special events or an expert at hosting fund-raisers or applying for grants.

Several people we interviewed commented on the fact that people skills are essential in animal welfare work. Julie Morris says, "If you work in an animal shelter, you have to not only be able to love the animals in your care, each of the shelter staff members has to love people too. In the seventies, frontline staff were often rude to people but loved animals. It doesn't work that way [anymore]."

You may need to be creative to see how your job skills cross over to rescue work. Public safety, law enforcement, education, intervention, counseling, ministerial, medical, legal, and communication job experiences translate well into animal rescue.

Dr. Mark Goldstein told us that working in animal rescue and welfare is "incredibly rewarding, but you often have to put yourself in difficult situations. Don't think you can be self-trained for these jobs." He added that those who are looking at animal rescue as a career should not expect to get rich. The riches are not financial but emotional. "The work will pay back to you as much as you give to the people and animals you help."

Rewards come in the gratification that is derived from saving lives, having work that is meaningful, and bringing more joy and love into the world. Also, we were touched by how often staff members of animal rescue organizations were talking to us on the phone with a small dog or cat curled up on their laps. What great jobs to have with animals as your office mates and coworkers!

Each of the major organizations lists job openings on its website. The HSUS offers a degree in humane education that can be earned online in conjunction with Humane Society University and Webster University. The American Humane Association is collaborating with Regis University in developing a unique academic program for humane-focused nonprofit professionals. It is a graduate certification in Humane Management and Administration and can be applied toward a master's degree in nonprofit management. This program is available online and is ideal for those who are changing careers and for volunteers or board members of humane societies, as well as for employees in animal care organizations who want to become managers. The HSUS keeps a list of universities that offer coursework in animal ethics, animal rights, and animal welfare. Keep in mind that it's a good idea to volunteer first before launching into a career in animal welfare. (See the Resources section for websites to visit for more information.)

Rene' Pizzo, the Portland firefighter who served on the OHSTAR team, explained how she moved into animal rescue: "I read Terri Crisp's book about her experiences, and our previous OHSTAR members had an online journal that they kept when they responded to other disasters. I knew I had a number of skills with my firefighter/paramedic background as well as my animal-handling background and former USAR K-9 [Urban Search and Rescue canine] training experience that lent themselves well to animal rescue. And I love animals." Rene' also said, "Train, train, train. We do tons more training than we do animal rescuing, so volunteer with a group of people that you like a lot. We have fun together and trust in each other."

Are you interested in becoming an animal control officer, humane officer, cruelty investigator, livestock officer, field supervisor, rabies control officer, or site investigator? From clerks to data processors, dispatchers to animal groomers, the variety of choices is endless. (See the National Animal Control Association's website for job opportunities in animal control.)

If you are looking at the possibility of working at an animal organization in your local area, Tammy Masters, a nurse who works on the sets of Hollywood studios and does independent animal rescue, has some good advice. Tammy says, "Animal rescue is a very rewarding career. But not all rescue groups are reputable. Most are, but there are those who do not give good care and just warehouse. I would strongly encourage anyone who wants a career to be prepared for a lot of frustration but to keep on going because helping one animal makes it all worth it."

Some volunteers we spoke with decided, after working the Katrina disaster, to get into the field of animal rescue and welfare. Meri Pinelli, from New Orleans, says, "Katrina was a lightbulb moment for me. While I always volunteered for animal organizations, this is now where I want to do my life's work. Whatever I want to pursue from now on has to have something to do with animals. Even the work I do for animals on the computer has helped me to realize what my vocation is going to be."

Animal rescue, welfare, and advocacy can combine the best of both worlds — employment and your love for animals.

# CHAPTER NINETEEN

# Preparing Animals for Disaster and Evacuation

Nadia Sutton is a lifelong animal lover who introduced herself to us as "slave to MacDuff, the Diva cat." She is the founder of PAWS/LA, an organization in Los Angeles, California. It provides pet food, veterinary care, and in-home services at no cost to companion animals of seniors and people living with life-threatening illnesses. Nadia started the organization in 1989, in response to a friend who was hospitalized with complications from AIDS. His parents had taken his cat away, and it had demoralized him. Nadia took care of the man's cats so he could continue to be with them, and he lived another six months. She says of her volunteer work, "We receive so much more than we give."

Nadia told us that her life was saved by one of her cats ten years ago. She had moved into a new apartment, and one morning at five o'clock her black cat, Chat Noir, woke her by screaming and clawing. When Nadia got up she saw flames shooting from the apartment below up to her window. Barely able to breathe from the smoke, Nadia called the fire department. She got her cats into carriers, managed to throw on some clothes, and ran downstairs with the cats. In less then two minutes, the firefighters arrived.

Nadia says, "Some careless people had left their rug on top of a heater. Another minute and we would all have died. Because Chat Noir woke me, my cats and I were saved. I know that God came through Chat Noir. I was feeling very grateful. It was pouring rain. The man who lived next to me invited me inside. I said, 'Look, I'm sorry. I don't have my bra on.' He said, 'Don't worry, sweetie, neither do I.'"

Accidents and disasters happen quickly. What if Nadia had not had the cat carriers ready and easily accessible? Could she have saved the lives of the cats, even after one of them had warned her, and kept the building from burning down?

## What Would You Do?

What if the worst happens to you and your animal and human family? Maybe it is the police or the National Guard pounding on your front door at 3:00 AM, telling you that the nearby chemical plant is leaking deadly fumes and you have to leave *now*. Or that there is an out-of-control wildfire or a train derailment with hazardous fumes spreading or a river rising and spilling over its banks. At the most, you might have five minutes to escape.

What if you aren't home when disaster strikes? How will your animals survive?

When we took the animal disaster-training course offered by the AHA, our instructor, Kerri, said that everyone needs to plan. "Those who are prepared are the ones who will survive a disaster."

Planning means you made a choice. You chose to be smart, to be aware, and to know that disasters are possible, even in the illusory safety of your home. Planning means that you are proactive and working to beat the odds.

In researching this chapter, we found at least fifty articles and disaster-preparedness checklists in print and on websites. After Hurricane Katrina, every newspaper, magazine, and animal organization cranked out checklists with item after item to add to our already overflowing to-do lists.

We've provided the addresses of many websites in the Resources section of this book. You can visit the websites and read more about what to do to save your pets from disaster. But if you're like us and get overwhelmed easily, you might appreciate knowing the top five things you can do to prepare your pets for disaster. The following are five simple points to consider as a way of assessing your preparedness. Much of the information was adapted from material developed by the HSUS and American Red Cross. The questions below each point will give you ideas for actions to take.

## Pet Disaster-preparedness Quiz

1. Take your pets with you and get out fast.

- Can you gather all your pets quickly and put them into pet carriers?

- Can you grab leashes, muzzles, and water bowls and pack a couple days' supply of water bottles and food in waterproof containers for each pet?

- Can you get your pets out of the house in less than five minutes?

- If you have a bird, do you have a blanket in your car that you can wrap over the carrier to keep the bird warm if necessary?

- If you have a snake or reptile, do you have a large pillowcase handy so you can secure the animal until you reach the evacuation site?

- If you have small mammals (hamsters, gerbils, and so forth), do you have carriers suitable to keep the animals in while you evacuate? Do you have bedding materials, food bowls, and water bottles nearby?

2. Make sure your pets can be identified even if their collars come off.

- Are your pets wearing securely fastened collars and ID tags with their names and identifying information either laminated or written with indelible ink?

- Are your pets microchipped? (For microchips, contact 24PetWatch, HomeAgain, and Avid.)

- If you have a bird, do you have a leg band for him or her with identification?

- Do you have identification and emergency phone numbers securely fastened to your pets' carriers?

- Does the collar ID tag and microchip have the pet's name, your name, and *two* emergency telephone numbers, including one that is *not* your home?

3. Keep photographs and descriptions of distinguishing features and medical conditions of your pets in the glove compartment of your car and/or in a safe deposit box. Include a photo of you with your pet so you can claim the pet at a rescue site.

- If your pet escapes from the carrier or runs off from the house when a firefighter busts open the door, do you or does someone else have photographs and descriptions somewhere, other than at your home, so you can make a flyer and post the information on PETS911.com?

4. Keep in your car or away from your home a list of places to evacuate.

- Do you know where you can go with your pets in the event of an emergency evacuation?

- Do you have a list of nearby pet-friendly motels along a fifty-mile evacuation route?

5. Make sure your pets are taken care of even if you can't do it yourself.

- Have you posted on your front door a Rescue Alert sticker listing the type and number of pets in your home?

- Have you made prior arrangements with people you can trust who will help you and your pets in an emergency?

- Have you made arrangements with a friend or relative (someone not allergic to pets) who will allow you to spend the night or a few days and bring your pets?

- Does a friend, family member, or neighbor have access to photographs of and veterinarian information about your pets in case you are too sick, injured, or far away to save and find them?

Did you discover holes in your readiness? If so, you are not alone.

We, like many others, were shocked to find how many times we answered no to the quiz questions.

So now is the time to become the doer, the smart one, and prepare for an event that you hope never arrives. Look at the questions again and do whatever you need to do, immediately, to answer each question with a yes.

Jeffery Smith, a New Orleans resident who had to leave without five of his pets — two large dogs, two cats, and one bird — after the levees broke, added a practical bit of advice to the quiz above, something that should be obvious but is often overlooked. Jeffery told us, "Never own more pets than you can evacuate with!"

## It Could Happen to You

Unfortunately, the odds are that most people will experience a disaster in their lifetime. Earthquakes, home fires, accidents, wildfires, floods, tornadoes, hurricanes, and mud slides affect millions each year. Human-made disasters, such as hazardous material spills or terrorist attacks, dramatically increase the odds against your safety.

The ASPCA in its publications and on its website lists the steps you can take to be prepared, with the idea that each type of disaster requires different measures to keep your pet safe.

The ASPCA's Julie Morris told us that the importance of preparation was reinforced for her when she was forced to evacuate her home early one morning.

When I was the executive director of the Humane Society of Ann Arbor, Michigan, I experienced an immediate evacuation call from local police.

At 3:00 AM I heard police loudspeakers outside on the neighborhood streets, telling everyone, "Get out of your homes immediately!"

I was disoriented with it being so early, especially since Ann Arbor is not exactly a big area for disasters. The first thing I did was to round up my dog and two cats. The loudspeakers continued, and I heard that explosions were expected from the local oil refinery. It looked bad at the time, so I didn't want to leave the animals behind.

I did not know when we would be able to get back, so I drove my dog and cats away from the evacuation area to a friend's house. I knocked on the door, and the tired, half-asleep husband let me in. Keeping the cats in their cage, I went to sleep on my friends' couch. I woke up in the morning hearing the husband say to his wife, "I'm not sure if it was a dream, but I think I let Julie Morris in the house last night." I yelled from the couch, "I'm here!"

That morning I learned that the authorities had let everybody back into their homes in the evacuated area at 5:00 AM, so the evacuation had been for only two hours. But had the oil refinery actually blown up, we could have been gone from our homes for weeks.

Julie stresses, "As soon as the police or local authorities tell you to leave the area, there is obviously a reason, so protect yourself and your animals. You just don't know what will happen." And if you have to evacuate, she says, "Leave with your animals! If you don't, a rescuer has to try to save your pets. Or if you return to the disaster area for your pets, you could place yourself or other people at risk."

A great idea is to have a Rescue Alert sticker on the front door of your house. You can get this for free at the ASPCA website. It alerts emergency personnel that there are animals in the house and tells the number and types. The Oregon Humane Society also offers a free pet Rescue Alert sticker on its website. Code 3 Associates has a downloadable emergency release form, which allows anyone who needs to offer emergency medical care to your pets to have permission to do so. Fill it out ahead of time so you don't have to try to remember all the information when you are in a panic.

## A Pet Disaster-supplies Kit

If you are away from your home for a day, a week, or longer (some people from the Gulf Coast have not returned more than six months after Hurricane Katrina), you will need supplies for your pets. On its website the HSUS, working with the American Red Cross, recommends that your pet disaster-supplies kit should include:

- Medications, a first-aid kit, and medical records (stored in a waterproof container)
- Sturdy leashes, harnesses, and/or carriers to transport pets safely and ensure that your animals can't escape
- Current photos of your pets in case they get lost
- Food, potable water, bowls, cat litter/pan, and can opener
- Information on feeding schedules, medical conditions, behavior problems, and the name and number of your veterinarian in case you have to foster or board your pets
- Pet beds and toys, if easily transportable

None of these preparations is hard to accomplish. Creating your pet disaster-supplies kit is a one-time task, and then it will be ready for use in the months and years ahead.

Also, we think that businesses are missing an opportunity. They could manufacture and sell affordable portable animal disaster-preparedness kits containing everything people and pets need to quickly evacuate in an emergency, with a place for pets' identifying information in each kit.

## Plan for Safe Havens and Designated Caregivers

Plan ahead by designating a caregiver in case you aren't available, and know the places where you or they can evacuate with your pets. Animal rescuer Eric Rice brought up an excellent point. He said, "My home is in the Annapolis, Maryland, area. My work is in Baltimore, which is forty-five minutes north. What happens if I go to work in Baltimore and a dirty bomb is dropped on Annapolis or the Washington, DC, area? I can't go back to get my pets. How do I prepare for that?"

Ask yourself the same "what if" question, and look at the list below for things you can do to make it safer for your pets if you aren't there to protect them.

- Ask friends, relatives, and others who are not affected by the disaster if they will get your pets for you. Make sure these friends or relatives won't be evacuating in vehicles that are too crowded or to places that won't let them bring pets.

- Prepare a list of veterinarians and boarding facilities within one hundred miles of your location for possible boarding. Find out if the facility where a friend might take your pets has an evacuation plan in place for the animals in its care.

- Find out if a trusted neighbor would be willing to take your pets and meet you at a prearranged location. This person should be comfortable with your pets, know where your animals are likely to be and where your pet disaster-supplies kit is kept, and have a key to your home. If you use a pet-sitting service, it may be available to help, but discuss the possibility well in advance. Always be prepared for any possibility.

- Check with local animal shelters to see if they provide emergency sheltering or foster care for pets in a disaster. This should be the last resort for your designated caregiver to use because local shelters will likely be overburdened during and after the disaster and possibly affected by it themselves. Find out what the animal shelter's euthanasia policies are should you not be able to get in contact with the facility to reclaim your pets right away.

## Use the Warning Time Well

If you are lucky enough to be warned ahead of time that a disaster is approaching, you can better prepare to protect your pets. You can call ahead to confirm emergency shelter arrangements and make reservations at pet-friendly hotels. (Remember, many hotels waive their no-pets policies in a disaster evacuation.) With warning time, you can check to be sure your pet disaster supplies are ready. Keep all pets in the house so that you won't have to search for them if you have to leave in a hurry.

Be sure all dogs and cats are wearing securely fastened collars and have up-to-date identification. Also, attach the phone number and address of the place where you will evacuate or of a friend or relative outside the disaster area. You can buy temporary tags or put adhesive tape on the back of your pets' ID tags, adding the temporary information with an indelible pen.

Keep informed about where pet-friendly evacuation shelters will be located in your area. In case you can't get into a pet-friendly hotel, a pet shelter next to a people shelter may be your last resort. Many of these animal shelters will require that you bring your own crates, pet food, supplies, medications, and veterinarian records showing vaccinations. Of course, there will probably be exceptions made for people who had to flee hurriedly. But being able to get into the relatively few spaces that would be available in one of these shelters is another good reason to have a pet disaster kit in your car.

The Humane Society of South Mississippi, Harrison County schools, and the civil defense are going to have pet-friendly evacuation sheltering for future hurricanes. According to an article by Karen Nelson, posted on the *Biloxi Sun Herald* website, the shelter will be "near the masonry shop on the grounds of Harrison Central High School."[1]

In contrast, Dr. Renee Poirrier, in a Best Friends online article about a meeting with animal rescuers that took place in April 2006, is quoted as saying that Louisiana will have pet shelters in future disasters but won't announce their locations in advance because they don't want to encourage people to rely on them. She stressed individual responsibility in preparing to evacuate with your pets and says, "For the most part, we're going to expect people to take care of themselves."[2]

As each state and local area throughout the country devises preparedness plans for evacuating pets in a disaster, each resident will have to adjust accordingly.

## Preparations and Planning for Horses

It is important to take extra care with large animals. Horses are especially vulnerable during and after a disaster because just transporting them requires planning and considerable resources. Horses' lives depend on you and the work you have done prior to a disaster to ensure their safety.

The following is from the HSUS website about why people with horses need to be prepared: "If you think disasters happen only if you live in a flood plain, near an earthquake fault line, or in a coastal area, you may be tragically mistaken. Disasters can happen anywhere and can take many different forms, from barn fires to hazardous material spills to propane line explosions, and train derailments — all of which may necessitate evacuations. It is imperative that you are prepared to move your horses to a safe area."[3]

Without preparation and planning, your horses could be on their own for days after a disaster. We recommend you visit "Disaster Preparedness for Horses" on the HSUS website for detailed information and suggestions to help you plan for emergencies.

If you are lucky enough to know ahead of time that you need to evacuate, you can make arrangements in advance for where to take your horses, and you can prepare the necessary trailers and equipment.

On the MyHorseMatters.com website, veterinarian Dana N. Zimmel writes, "Hurricanes, tornadoes, flooding, and fire are the most common natural disasters in the state of Florida. The leading cause of death in large animals during Hurricane Andrew in 1992 included animals killed in collapsed barns, electrocution, kidney failure secondary to dehydration, and animals hit and killed on roadways or tangled in barbed wire after escaping from their pasture. Each farm should have a written disaster plan to optimize safety and survival of all animals."[4]

Dr. Zimmel's excellent and comprehensive article includes a list of things to do prior to a storm or other disaster, including outfitting each horse with at least one, if not all, of the following:

- A leather halter with name/farm information in a ziplock bag secured to the halter with duct tape

- A luggage tag with the horse/farm name and phone number braided into the tail (make sure this is waterproof)

- Photos of each horse as proof of ownership highlighting obvious identifying marks

And don't forget to have your horse microchipped.

## Preparing Livestock for Disaster

Because of the size of livestock, special consideration must be given to transporting them during an emergency evacuation. But even if you are sheltering them in place, being prepared calls for a written, proven plan of action before, during, and after a natural disaster.

Collapsed barns, dehydration, electrocution, and accidents due to destroyed fences are the most common causes of livestock deaths in hurricanes or severe storms. Having a farm animal disaster kit, accessing safe transportation — trucks and trailers — and writing a complete plan to protect livestock from hazards are all steps toward keeping them safe. For detailed information on disaster preparedness for livestock, visit the HSUS website.[5]

We interviewed Kate Walker, from Farm Sanctuary, about what farmers and ranchers need to do in order to prepare for a disaster. She said, "I think it is very important that every business and organization dealing with farm animals has a written emergency disaster plan prepared ahead of time. The one thing that struck me as I did my work in farm animal rescue was the lack of generators. Many farms are mostly automated, yet there was no backup power. Having generators would be a basic way farms could prepare for disasters."

## What Animal Rescuers Want to Tell You about Preparing Your Pets for Disasters

Since we were interviewing two hundred people who rescued animals after Hurricane Katrina, we thought it would be a good idea to ask them, from their firsthand experience, how they suggest people prepare for disasters. Many of them said that they went right home after volunteering and made sure they had followed their own advice.

*Melissa McGehee Smith:* "If it is potentially too dangerous for you, and you are being asked to evacuate, it certainly is too dangerous for your pets. Don't leave pets behind, even if you try to create a safer place for them in one of your home's rooms. If left, your pets are likely to be injured, lost, or worse."

*Karen O'Toole:* "Leave enough food and water for one month, even if you think you will only be gone a few days. Don't risk it. I found a pit bull on the brink of death. He had dragged four water jugs to his bed. Each jug's top was chewed up — he was on the right track — but he was

*Melissa McGehee Smith with rescued cat.*

unable to open them and get to the water.

"Also, don't assume pets could drink water from the toilet bowl or a dripping faucet. In a catastrophe pipes break and toilets back up. Many pets died from dehydration, even though their loving families thought the animals would be okay. We found them on bathroom floors, where they may have been trying to find water.

"Record your animals with local police, fire department, and your security company. Again, please just take your animals with you! If you must leave animals behind, you can help rescuers save them by marking your house on a stable structure, not a window or glass door that might break. For example, '2 Dogs Inside.

1 Cat.' Let us know what you have. If there are no animals left, mark that too: 'No Pets.' After Katrina we had no sure way of knowing where pets were left. It was a coastalwide guessing game. By marking your house, you'll help us find your animals. Give them the chance to be rescued quickly."

*Tammy Masters*: "If you have to go without your pets, leave lots of food and water. Contact an animal rescue group and immediately let them know where your pet is. Never tie up animals. They don't have any chance then. I personally would never leave my animals, no matter what."

*Jan Mitchell*: "Make sure that you get the cats first and that you always know where your kennels are if you have animals that need to be in them. If you can stay calm, your animals will reflect that. If you might have to evacuate quickly, check on your cats often to know where they are so you don't take a long time to locate them when you are panicked. During fire threats in my hometown, I wrote to my pet sitter and said, 'There is nothing more important in my house than my animals. If you can only have enough time to get them out, that is enough.'"

*Kathleen Pantaze*: "Always take pets with you. Police and people in government are just focused on people and politics, not animals. I know; I work for the government. They do not have the ability to understand the emotional reality of people's needs. They are interested in protecting their interests and avoiding criticism. Do what needs to be done for your pets. Microchip, microchip, microchip!"

*June Towler*: "Keep a collar with ID tag on your pet at all times. Have the ID include your pet's name, address, and phone number. Provide another emergency contact person who is outside your area on the pet's microchip information form. Taking a muzzle with you may make the difference in whether or not your dog will be allowed on an evacuation vehicle."

*Melissa McGehee Smith*: "Know exactly where your animals are kept in the temporary shelters, and have accurate descriptions and photos of them. Bear in mind the animal may lose significant amounts of weight, depending on the time it took to be rescued, and may generally look just like five hundred other such pets in the vicinity. If you list your cat for rescue or on Petfinder.com as a fat black-and-white cat named Slinky,

it isn't going to get you far. Think of distinguishing marks and traits of the animal, such as neuter-spay information, scars, odd markings (black-and-white with a white spot on left front paw), etc. In a major disaster this animal most likely will not look like the pet you left behind. He could be starving, dehydrated, dirty, matted, injured, sick, too scared or weak to respond to his name. In a lot of cases, bandannas and collars have come off as well."

*Stephanie Jehle, Operation Underdog Rescue, goes under a house to rescue an animal.*

*Stephanie Jehle*: "Don't board your pet within the city that is being evacuated. We saw animals in cages of facilities that didn't remove the animals before the humans left. If you have nowhere to take your animals, then bring them with you and board them in a safe facility outside the danger area."

The procedures in this chapter are relatively easy to carry out, but few of us, until now, thought about them. But after hearing about the disastrous consequences that befell animals and people who weren't prepared for disasters, we're making new resolutions.

What can you do *today* to make sure that the pets who depend on you are safe?

# CHAPTER TWENTY

# Media, Celebrities, and the Internet Bring Attention to Animal Rescue

In the news coverage of Hurricane Katrina, two related images in particular galvanized animal lovers around the world. The first was Snowball, a fluffy white miniature poodle trying to get onto a bus, and the other was the boy who cried so hard he vomited when forced to leave Snowball behind in New Orleans. Such is the power of the media.

*Anderson Cooper 360°*, a news magazine show on CNN, kept images of animals and their suffering in front of viewers just about every day that Anderson reported from the Gulf Coast. Anderson's father was born near Meridian, Mississippi, so the journalist has deep roots in the devastated region. When Anderson was driving to Gulfport with his CNN crew, some people cleared the road for them. Anderson found out later that one of the men who did the good deed was his cousin.[1]

On Monday, September 9, 2005, Anderson led in to a piece about animal rescue by showing the tragedy of abandoned animals. He said,

The first days after Katrina we found dogs stranded in trees, dogs on walls, pacing, surrounded by water. This is what helpless feels like. Motoring in a boat, we found animals everywhere, adrift, abandoned by their owners, alive or dead. There are so many dogs . . . that are just starving. And you try to feed them as much as you can. But there's too many of them roaming around. It's going to become a health hazard. Since then, teams of animal rescuers from all over the country have waded into dirty, diseased water trying to coax stranded pets into crates and onto boats.[2]

In our conversations with people from all over the country, we found that many of those who volunteered had watched Anderson's segments about the animals as well as ones on *Dateline NBC*, Wolf Blitzer's *The Situation Room*, MSNBC's *Rita Cosby Live & Direct*, and *Scarborough Country*, as well as on *Oprah*, *The Tyra Banks Show*, PBS's *Nature*, Animal Planet, National Geographic specials, and national nightly news reports. *USA Today*, the *Washington Post*, and the *New York Times* were only some of the newspapers that focused a national spotlight on the forgotten ones, the animals.

All this coverage was a far cry from most of the previous images we have seen of animals in the media. In a *New York Times* article from November 2005, Roy Peter Clark, vice president of the Poynter Institute for Media Studies, is quoted as saying that journalists gravitate toward three types of pet stories: "One is the cynical story that satirizes humans' over-attachment to their pets. Then, there are the outrage stories, usually written when human beings cause intentional harm to animals. And then there's the heroic dog, sort of the Lassie paradigm." But after Katrina and the news reports of heartrending human-pet separations and reunions, "There's a renewed understanding of how much pets mean to certain people, and how hard it is for some people to take lifesaving actions if it requires them to abandon their pets."[3]

With twenty-four-hour news channels, newspapers, and national publications focused on the Gulf Coast story, for the first time in history millions of people were experiencing what the media can do to save the lives of animals.

By showing the horror of Katrina and the need to rescue the thousands of animals left behind, Anderson Cooper's insightful questions and a determination to help spurred a movement toward animal rescue that continues to reverberate. Bonney Brown of Alley Cat Allies says, "CNN correspondent Jeff Koinange in particular was incredible — a male role model helping animals in the media. His beautiful voice is usually heard covering international events for CNN, and when he went to New Orleans, he got involved. On camera he went to a family home where cats were stranded. Koinange and the husband and wife walked through waist-deep water. Finally they hitched a ride with army guys on a vehicle that could drive through water. He and the other fellow climbed upstairs and found most of the cats. They carried the cat carriers out over their heads because of the floodwater. Koinange is an articulate man who worries about world events, and he cares about cats."

Michael Mountain, president of the Best Friends Animal Society, had high praise for many media outlets, especially Fox News and CNN, which covered the work of Best Friends repeatedly, and for the team from *Dateline NBC*, which went out of its way to help the animals. "Many of the reporters ended up taking animals to foster and then adopt themselves and were very helpful with many of the reunions."

Bonney Brown adds, "The media has been generally good on animal issues except for the early reporting, when there was hardly any coverage. People who were concerned for animal welfare called and wrote letters complaining about the lack of coverage."

Chris Cutter, communications director for the International Fund for Animal Welfare, said the media photographers and videographers continued to cover the work of animal rescue workers after Hurricane Katrina. He says, "We think it's important for reporters and photographers to capture what we're doing and provide it to media. I met a guy who works for the [New Orleans] *Times-Picayune* as an arts and entertainment writer, reviewing movies. On a personal level he lost everything, but on the professional level, covering the disaster oddly caused him to write a series of compelling articles. Professionally it was the best thing that's ever happened for him to have stayed in the city. He and his colleagues found a house with a working landline and turned the house into a newsroom. They walked around and found stories every day."

Chris had his own brush with media fame when he was able to bring a dog back to a Los Angeles woman on *The Tyra Banks Show*.

All the major animal organizations use the media to get their messages out. Most of them have communications directors or hire the services of public relations firms. They know it is money well spent. According to Kate Donlon, director of PETS 911, that organization's support from media partners allows articles about lost and adoptable animals to be sent to more than two hundred World Now affiliates.

We cannot overemphasize how important it is for animal shelters and animal welfare organizations to have volunteers or staff who specialize in focusing media attention onto pet adoption and publicizing the many ways these organizations serve their communities. Repeatedly we spoke to good-hearted people with their noses to the grindstone, overwhelmed by the demands of their jobs and oblivious to the need for good relationships with the press. The organizations that invest time and money in writing press kits and presenting themselves as class acts attract volunteers, donations, and resources.

## The Power of Celebrity Animal Lovers

Who can doubt the power of celebrities in our starstruck culture? When those celebrities love animals and embrace animal causes, the public and their fans pay attention and follow their example. Untold numbers of animals' lives are saved as a result of celebrity participation in animal welfare causes.

PETS 911 provides animal welfare groups with celebrity-based public service announcements that include a tagline personalized for their organization. This means that if an organization is a PETS 911 member (which is free), it can draw attention to its services and the pets needing adoption with the help of donated talent from celebrities such as Jay Mohr, Melanie Griffith, Bill Maher, Edie Falco, Wendie Malick, and Stockard Channing.

While writing this book, we asked celebrities to tell us about their experiences with animal rescue and to share with readers their thoughts on the Hurricane Katrina disaster response with regard to animals. We were heartened by the number of celebrities who took the time to share how much their hearts are touched by animals. Most interviewers never ask celebrities about the special pets in their lives, so they seemed to relish the opportunity to support animal rescue and to thank all those volunteers and organizations who gave of themselves to save animals after the hurricanes and who also provide services to animals and people every day.

## Celebrity-studded HSUS

With a country moved by the plight of pets and farm animals during the disaster caused by Hurricane Katrina, the Hollywood community used its celebrity power to shine a spotlight on what people could to do help. Sean Astin, Bill Maher, Wendie Malick, Joe Mantegna, Persia White, and Carrie Underwood, all friends of the HSUS, created television and radio public service announcements in support of the HSUS's animal rescue efforts in the Gulf Coast.

Gretchen Wyler, from the Hollywood office of the HSUS, worked with celebrities to film the spots requesting donations and support for animal rescue on the Gulf Coast. On the HSUS website, Gretchen wrote, "The outpouring of support from the Hollywood community was just incredible. Stars are always there to use their voices for these important causes."[4] These celebrities and many more were honored in March 2006 at the HSUS's Genesis Awards program for the work they do to help animals.

## Celebrities Actively Contributing to Animal Welfare

Linda Blair is a celebrity who does much more than lend her name to support animal welfare and rescue. The actress, most widely known for her starring role in *The Exorcist*, is founder and president of the Linda Blair WorldHeart Foundation and calls herself a "hands-on animal advocate." In 2005 she traveled many times to Houston and New Mexico to help with the rescue efforts, which included assisting in saving animals and reuniting Hurricane Katrina pets with their people. Among the animal causes she works for are the elimination of dog fighting, puppy mills, and animal cruelty.[5]

Some celebrities bear special mention because they have so consistently over the years supported animal welfare and rescue. Betty White, Mary Tyler Moore, Bernadette Peters, and Valerie Harper are leading actresses who write about and actively participate in finding adoptive homes for animals who are in shelters. On her daily television talk show Ellen DeGeneres promotes rescuing animals. Oprah Winfrey often does shows involving outstanding animals who have contributed much love and devotion to people's lives. Bob Barker, host of *The Price Is Right*, has long been an advocate for spay-neuter initiatives. Shirley MacLaine's book *Out on a Leash*, which she coauthored with her dog, Terry, brought positive attention to animals as sentient beings and to the joyful possibilities for raising human awareness through animal communication.

We were especially gratified when Montel Williams, a vocal animal lover, featured a story on his show in February 2005 from our book *Angel Dogs: Divine Messengers of Love*. By inviting the author of the story, her daughter, and the dog who saved her daughter's life to appear on his show, Montel helped to increase gratitude for the gifts that animals bring into the lives of people every day.

Many celebrities lend their names and support to PETA in its efforts to educate the public to save animals. Actress Pamela Anderson often helps PETA lead crusades, as do Edie Falco, Simon Cowell, Paul McCartney, Russell Simmons, and Bill Maher. But long before Pamela and others stars helped out, the organization was graced with the support of one of America's most beloved actresses, Rue McLanahan.

## Golden Girl, Rue McLanahan

Rue McLanahan, one of the "Golden Girls," is loved by audiences all over the world for her work in the long-running television show of the same name. But Rue is also golden when it comes to saving the lives of animals. Rue is the aunt of our friend and fellow author Amelia Kinkade, who wrote the wonderful book *Straight from the Horse's Mouth*. We chatted with Rue one afternoon about the work she does to help animals and were inspired by her single-minded devotion.

Rue developed a love for animals when she was a child. "I was always feeding strays and started adopting them. I would take home a stray dog or cat and then find them a home or else keep them. I've always done that. Just can't go and leave them." Growing up in Manhattan, she brought home dozens of dogs and cats, showing an early devotion that helped her mature into a powerhouse for animal welfare.

Rue shared an experience she had while taking tap dancing lessons in New Jersey. "Just before we moved to California, I found a stray female dog. She was brown, middle size, just standing there eight feet from my black VW Beetle. I was driving from dancing class, and I told the dog, 'I am going home. You'd better go with me because I'm your best bet.' She looked at me with indecision and then jumped straight up in the air with all four legs and got into the backseat of my car. That dog found a happy home with my sister, Gretel."

When Rue moved to California in 1973, she found out she was not the only actor who loves animals. She became active in the organization Actors and Others for Animals and has joined twenty other groups around the country, including Friends of Animals and PETA, an organization for which she has done advertisements and public service announcements. Rue told us, "I think everybody should be personally involved in rescuing animals. It says about any country what they are like. If you don't care for animals, you are not going to take care of people either."

## Dee Wallace, ET's Mom and Friend to Animals

As we write this book, actress Dee Wallace, best remembered as ET's mom in the 1982 film *E.T. the Extra-Terrestrial*, is starring in a new sitcom, *Sons & Daughters*. It is filmed in a studio where Tammy Masters, one of the animal rescue volunteers we interviewed, works as the set nurse. At Tammy's request, Dee graciously shared her thoughts about the important work of saving animals. "Animal rescue is an expression of our own souls and hearts. When our love rushes forward to help those who can't help themselves, we advance exponentially in our soul work. Animals are our children."

Regarding the Gulf Coast catastrophe, Dee says, "We all know it needed to be handled better and more humanely. Obviously it was heart-wrenching. I think in future plans, there need to be more funds and a network of information to make it expedient for finding and relocating pets."

We asked Dee why animal rescue is important, and she responded, "It's who we are, and compassion is the foundation of the very country we live in. Whenever we help those less fortunate, we help ourselves. Animals are our soul mates and healers."

## Joe Mantegna, *Joan of Arcadia*'s Dad and Italian Animal Lover

Writer, producer, director, and actor Joe Mantegna has taken just about every creative role in the television and movie business and done exceedingly well at each of them. You may remember him most from his acting in the *Godfather* trilogy. But our favorite is when he played Amber Tamblyn's father and Mary Steenburgen's husband in the television series with heart and soul, *Joan of Arcadia*.

Joe explained that his daughter's love for animals influenced him greatly and that their family has rescued many cats. He was glad to see that caring people and groups stepped in to help rescue animals after Hurricane Katrina. "It's tragic, especially for those in our society for whom their pets are their only family. There needs to be an established, coordinated plan for such incidents that takes into account animal rescue and welfare. It's a reflection on ourselves as the dominant species on the planet and on us as a society and a country."

## Molly Sims, *Las Vegas*'s Model Animal Lover

If you have ever watched the dazzling television series *Las Vegas*, you have seen the gorgeous supermodel and actress Molly Sims playing James Caan's daughter, Delinda. Molly told us, "The attention placed on animals in need after Hurricane Katrina was a large outpouring of love and concern that helped to save countless animals' lives. It shows respect for life and being a decent human being to believe in animal rescue. I think it's a terrible event to have to imagine. I would never leave my dogs behind, no matter what. A pet becomes your child, dependent upon you for survival."

Like many animal-loving people, Molly has given a lot of thought to how animals can be saved from disaster, especially after witnessing the horrors and tragedies of Hurricane Katrina. She says, "I would like to see animal shelters open twenty-four hours for people that have to evacuate in emergencies, so they can drop the animals off beforehand and pick them up when they are able to get back. Volunteers should then be able to go through neighborhoods with the National Guard, as they are enforcing evacuation, and retrieve pets whose owners chose not to think of placing their animals in safe situations. I would also love to see every animal microchipped so in emergencies, when things are crazy and animals get lost in the shuffle, there is a way to connect them back with their families."

We asked Molly why she thinks animal rescue is important, and she responded, "I believe every creature on this planet, animal or person, should have the right to a sense of security in their lives. People have the power to find that for themselves. Animals rely on us to help provide a secure home for them." She added, "It's respect for life and being a decent human being to believe in animal rescue. I think it shows that we have heart, and that we care about everyone in our communities, including our animals. Please get involved, however you can, in helping with animal adoption and rescue. Everyone and everything deserves to know compassion."

## Brigitte Bardot, France's Forever Famous Animal Advocate

Yes, *that* Brigitte Bardot!

Brigitte Bardot leads the Foundation Brigitte Bardot, in Paris, and is an outspoken animal advocate, using her early fame as an actress to fight against practices such as using animals for fur and killing whales and seals.

We wrote her with some questions about animal rescue and to our surprise received a long, handwritten letter from her in French answering all our questions. We had to hurriedly call our French friend, Claudie Courdavault, and ask if she would translate for us. Brigitte also included in the package an open letter that she wrote to President Bush expressing her outrage at the lack of response in saving the lives of animals after Hurricane Katrina.

Brigitte wrote, "Animals are part of the equilibrium of this planet and of nature. Animal life is part of our survival. It is time for the human race to behave as human and respect and protect the animals. I was scandalized when I saw that the rescuers were forbidding people, already traumatized, to take their pets with them. It was a disgrace. It is why I wrote a letter to G. Bush."

Brigitte adds, "I think that racism for animals is as scandalous as racism for people. Life is life, whatever kind of body it takes. And animals, especially pets, like cats and dogs, are members of the family. To separate them from people is cruel, and it would have been out of the question for me. I would have stayed with them till death."

## Tiffani Thiessen, *InStyle* with Animal Rescue

Tiffani Thiessen is a television and film actress with acting credits on series such as *Beverly Hills 90210*. She directed the award-winning short film *Just Pray*, written by author, screenwriter, and producer R. Dean Johnson. Tiffani's wedding to Brady Smith was recently featured on *InStyle Celebrity Weddings*.

We contacted Tiffani and asked why she thinks animal rescue work is such an important aspect of American society today. Tiffani explained in faxed responses that her love for animals is rooted in a childhood with a father who was an animal lover. Her father always brought home abandoned dogs and cats to give them a second chance at a loving home. "Being so young, I was easily influenced. I saw how my father made such a difference by being a kind, gentle, and caring man to animals. To this day my family and I only adopt animals that are in need of homes. I continue to support and give as much time and effort as I can to the many organizations that not only do wonderful work for animal rights but provide rescue, adoption, and placement services. It's something I feel strongly about and will continue to do."

Tiffani has been thinking a lot about the animal rescue efforts following Hurricane Katrina. She says, "A peaceful and secure way of evacuating in emergency situations is necessary. I know it *can* be done. With all of the resources we have as a country, I know we can design a way to evacuate people with their beloved animals. We have the responsibility to take care of our pets, especially in situations of disaster when our animals are unable to take care of themselves. It's about putting *humane* back into *humanity*."

## Lorie Zerweck and *The Pet Gazette*

Lorie Zerweck is the coproducer and unit production manager for the hit television series *Las Vegas*. Lorie told us about contributing to animal rescue as the publisher and editor of *The Pet Gazette*, a bimonthly newspaper that initially focused on pet rescue for the Los Angeles area but has recently gone bicoastal. An animal-loving celebrity always graces the newspaper's front page and provides an interview. Celebrities Lara Flynn Boyle, Nicollette Sheridan, and Tai Babylonia were on the covers of the issues Lorie sent us.

Lorie told us that she has a long history of helping animals, including volunteering with a wildlife rehabilitation organization. She cared for three orphaned baby raccoons in her home last spring. "I had them while they were being weaned, and it was my job to get them off the bottle and to eat dry dog food. After they were about ten to twelve weeks old, they were taken to a ranch where they were integrated with other baby raccoons until their eventual release back into the wild."

Lorie says that as a little kid living in the Santa Cruz Mountains, she used to wake up to the presence of dogs, cats, bunnies, hamsters, and birds, and has always been an animal lover.

Many people on the film crews I worked with have to come to my office, and I would have animal adoption notices up on the wall. I noticed that when people saw a photo of an animal on my wall, they would say, "I want that dog." Just hearing about the animals didn't get a response. So an idea started that the way to rescue animals is to put their pictures in front of people for the rescue groups. I started the newspaper to help get awareness out there about all the homeless animals available for adoption. They need a home and a second chance at life. The *Pet Gazette* promotes animal wellness, awareness, and rescue. I wanted it to be a voice for the animals.

Lorie says that although she had worked in TV and film for twenty years and knew how to produce a movie, she had no idea how to put a newspaper together. Yet she was determined to try. She says, "I was donating money to more than twenty different animal organizaions and I wanted to do more and help them all, to be like an umbrella for every rescue group." Working in her home late into the evening, Lorie wrote and did the layout for the first issue of *The Pet Gazette*. That was the beginning of a successful free local publication that now has paid subscribers nationwide.

I don't charge any rescue organization to put photos of their adoptable animals in the paper. The advertising for rescues are donation based. This is a project of love on my part. We don't have any idea how many animals have been rescued due to the paper, but we do know it has helped. We get incredible comments from people who love the newspaper. Recently three of the cats who had their photos in our paper got adopted. That makes the late nights worthwhile.

I am trying to educate people. I was standing in line at Carson Animal Shelter in Gardena one day, dropping off newspapers. It was really crowded. There was a huge line, and a young kid who plays football started talking to me. His mom came to get a dog because the dog they had was now four years old. He said his mother gets rid of dogs when they become older. She wants only young dogs.

The things people say, like that, are incredible to me. Would you get rid of your kid? How do you get people to see that animals aren't merchandise, not a commodity? With our newspaper we try to get out information that might start to change that kind of behavior. I hope so.

## Tammy Masters and Hollywood Confidential

Lorie Zerweck and Tammy Masters are good friends and avid animal rescuers who work in an underground Hollywood circuit that most of us rarely hear about — the star-studded animal-loving community. Tammy says that while she worked as a set nurse on the shows *Six Feet Under* and *American Dreams*, she made connections from her office with people who wanted to adopt animals. One time her girlfriend, who does animal rescue in downtown Los Angeles, gave Tammy eight little four-week-old puppies she had found, and Alan Poul, the executive producer of *Six Feet Under*, adopted one of them. Between the two television shows Tammy was working for at the time, she managed to get all the puppies adopted.

Tammy worked at Warner Bros. Studio and found it to be a cat-loving place with cat feeding stations all over. An executive producer of major motion pictures who filmed in a studio where Tammy worked absolutely loves cats. She says, "He made the construction crew build the cats a house before starting work on filming his movie. He's awesome. There are a lot of well cared for cats at that studio."

Tammy told us that she and her brother and sister grew up in an orphanage, and this has given her a great deal of empathy for abandoned animals. She is an independent animal rescuer with four rescued dogs of her own. She is also in the U.S. Army Reserve. Watching the little boy in New Orleans lose his dog, Snowball, on the television news, in addition to the images of abandoned animals, took her over the edge. She knew that she had to go save the animals. But first she needed to convince her first sergeant to let her do the physical fitness test that everyone else was required to take that weekend. So she bought her airline ticket, arranged to do her two-mile run, push-ups, and sit-ups at her unit, and drove straight to the airport. Her tour of duty that weekend was at Lamar-Dixon as a search-and-rescue volunteer.

## Animal Rescue in Blogs and Email Newsletters

Eric Rice is chief executive officer of a well known technology company, BulkRegister, in Baltimore, Maryland. During the aftermath of Katrina, Eric went first to Mississippi, then to New Orleans and Lamar-Dixon, where he got credentialed by the HSUS and LA/SPCA and started attending daily morning briefing meetings. Mostly he stayed inside the city, living out of the back of the moving truck he rented and driving to Lamar-Dixon every few days to take a shower and participate in the morning meeting. He had started writing a blog before he left for the Gulf Coast and continued it during his volunteering.

On Eric's blog, Wayne Pacelle, president of the HSUS, took time to answer several questions that Eric had asked of the organization. People were exceptionally active on the blog. Sometimes readers would post as many as 120 comments to a single blog post, which is an amazingly high number. This followed right along with how interested and active people were over rescue of Katrina animals. Eric told us:

> I put my blog on Craigslist on the NOLA.com forums [New Orleans] website. After about the third week I found out that about three to four thousand people were reading it. People wanted good information from the ground. There were "canned stories" coming out, and a lot of rumors and many people had no idea how best to help. They wanted real information, and I gave it to them. Dozens of people called me and said, "I didn't know where to go or how to help but now, after reading specific information on your blog, I am getting on the next plane and will call you when I touch down." They started showing up in droves, and I was able to direct many of them to Lamar-Dixon, Winn-Dixie, or other places to help.
>
> The most amazing experience for me was the fact that hundreds of evacuees found the little group that had joined me through postings on Craigslist. We called our group Rite-Aid Rescue because we were camped in a Rite-Aid parking lot. Volunteers who knew my direct phone line would gather requests for rescues and call me. We dispatched teams of two rescuers to over 200 locations and then reported to the owners what we had found. I was just a point of

communication. All those people who came and worked with me had as much to do with our success as I did. I continue to be in touch with them to this day.

By the time I left Louisiana, we were doing a FEMA-sponsored conference call with forty attendees. I got invited simply because I had compiled a list of contacts over four hundred strong. On the calls someone would ask, "Who can get this?" and I had a name for them to contact 90 percent of the time. I had collected this information so people who needed to communicate with each other could have good resources. We became the go-to group for people outside the area who wanted to rescue animals. This call lasted until well into April 2006, showing the extent and duration of the needs for helping the animals.

Now that Hurricane Katrina animal rescue efforts are mostly in the care of local residents, Eric has broadened his scope with a new email newsletter that reports on the effects of disasters on animals all over the world. He hopes it will become the most informational site on the Web about animals in disasters and focus on where problems exist and which organizations are responding.

## The Pluses and Minuses of Blogs

Stephanie Jehle, a real estate agent working in Los Angeles and Dallas, founded the nonprofit animal rescue group Operation Underdog Rescue, in Dallas. Stephanie traveled to New Orleans on four separate trips for a total of thirty days. Her experience was similar to many other volunteers with whom we spoke. People were motivated to take action after reading one of Eric's accounts or a blog on one of the animal organizations websites.

I wanted to help, but when I sent my volunteer application to LA/SPCA, they said they only wanted animal control officers, vets, and vet techs. Then one evening while I was on the computer, I found Eric's Dog Blog. It stated that they needed people immediately to help out, and it didn't matter if you had experience or not. These were average people who saw a need and responded. I went down there and volunteered for the HSUS, ARNO, and MuttShack.

I have to say that joining together with so many people from so many areas to help this cause was overwhelming and amazing. It made me feel that people still do care. It gave me a sense of gratitude for being able to witness the teamwork.

Bonney Brown, of Alley Cat Allies, says, "I feel that the email letters and blogs are a double-edged sword. There may be a call that goes out for food in an email with the result that enough food comes in after the call. But without knowing the date of the initial request or that the need has been fulfilled, the message will circulate for days, weeks, months, and a glut of food with no place to store it becomes the new problem. A certain amount of hysteria on the email newsletters and blogs after Hurricane Katrina caused part of the frustration, with seasoned groups wanting to label people as rogue rescuers. If there is no phone dialogue, just emails and blogs, people become upset and sometimes hysterical."

Chris Cutter, of IFAW, said, "We had to deal with rumors as an organization. People heard or read stuff and called us. First of all, is it true or not true? False reporting comes out of confusion. People tend to rush to make sense of the events, and they get some of the things wrong. Over time it sorts itself out. I didn't find it a huge impediment to the work we were trying to do, although the rumors were something we had to address. In most cases they turned out to not be true."

## Karen Dawn and Dawnwatch.com

One of the most reliable sources of information we found before, during, and after Hurricane Katrina is an Internet newsletter published by Karen Dawn, animal activist and well-established journalist who has written for the *Washington Post, Los Angeles Times, New York Newsday,* and the *Guardian* (UK). Karen's DawnWatch promotes animal advocacy in the media and connects readers to relevant media outlets. The website also contains additional news alerts and articles.[6]

Karen's worldwide readership helps to alert her to breaking news reports. She sends out an average of one email alert per day, and we've found her alerts to be the best source for learning immediately what is happening in animal rescue.

For an interview about the events that led up to Karen launching DawnWatch, visit the Animals Voice website.

## Radio and Television Aid Animal Rescue

On radio, you can find several animal-themed programs. Karen Dawn hosts *Watchdog Radio*, interviewing animal-loving authors and celebrities and discussing animal issues.

A large radio presence for animals is the Animal Radio Network, which reaches two million animal lovers every week in over eighty American cities. It was founded by animal advocate and major-market radio veteran Hal Abrams. Hal lives and works with his wife and four cats near the Best Friends Animal Sanctuary, in Kanab, Utah. Hal calls his network the most concentrated radio audience of targeted animal lovers anywhere. To see which station near you carries Animal Radio Network's programs, visit the website.

We have to mention *Animal Wise Radio*, one of our favorite shows. It is produced by Mike Fry, the executive director of Animal Ark, in Hastings, Minnesota, and is broadcast locally as well as stored online in MP3 for podcast. The program's website offers more information and archived shows.

Our cat Speedy (along with us) is a big fan of Animal Planet, the cable television network that broadcasts animal-friendly programming twenty-four hours a day. Speedy sits in front of the television and watches the shows with catlike fascination. The network's *Animal Cops* series provides insight into the world of animal sheltering and cruelty investigations, which have become the work of today's animal control officers.

Check out PBS programs such as the *Nature* series, National Geographic specials, and the Discovery Channel. Often these shows provide insights into the world of animals, rescuing, and conservation, not merely skimming the surface but educating the public on the importance of saving animals from disaster.

Look for animal-friendly shows on national and local television that take animal issues seriously and portray pets as family members. Write to the producers to tell them you want more of this type of programming. Karen Dawn says that the media is very attuned to audience response because advertising revenue depends on the numbers of readers or viewers. So if editors or producers get a lot of letters about a certain article or television show, they know people in large numbers are paying attention. They figure that a note by one person represents the opinions of as many as fifty to five hundred other people.[7]

The attention that the media, the Internet, and celebrities have placed on animal rescue is both a boon to the movement and an indication of changing times. Never before have so many articles been written and shows produced that cover the issues affecting animals and the people who love them. We think it's a good thing.

# CHAPTER TWENTY-ONE

# Lessons Learned

This book's message can be summed up in one word: kindness. Kind people are doing the very best they can to help animals. Kind animals are inspiring people to save them.

Can kindness be shaped into a movement? If kindness to animals becomes standard operating procedure, will it lose the spontaneity, the intuitiveness, and the courage that make it so appealing, noteworthy, and effective? Will the spirit of volunteerism at the core of rescuing animals always stay centered in the heart?

We believe that animal rescue endured a rite of passage as organizations and individuals responded in creative and exciting ways after Hurricane Katrina. Volunteers put aside their daily responsibilities and traveled to the Gulf Coast; they transported animals from danger to safety; they adopted and fostered animals; or they spent hours on their computers searching for supplies or clues to the whereabouts of animals and their guardians. They delivered a strong message to the American people: *Animals are important.*

The residents of the disaster zone who stayed behind as deadly storms approached, who hid with pets in their homes, who smuggled small animals in bags onto buses, and who searched or fought for the return of their missing animals delivered yet another message: *Pets are members of the family*.

Love cannot be legislated. Yet these twin aspects of the love — the importance of animals and the place they occupy in America's homes and hearts — became the wake-up calls that penetrated mainstream consciousness. These two messages drove lawmakers, policy makers, and disaster planners to do whatever it takes to ensure that people are never again forced to leave their pets or their farm animals behind and in harm's way.

After Hurricane Katrina hit, five members of the U.S. House of Representatives immediately proposed that pet disaster planning become mandatory for groups that receive federal funds. Already changes in procedures occurred prior to Hurricanes Rita and Wilma. Residents in the paths of those storms were told to bring their pets with them. In Texas officials changed the rules to allow pets into shelters. Other states scrambled to revise their emergency evacuation plans. Emergency planners hastily drafted memorandums of understanding with animal organizations to set up temporary pet shelters located near people shelters.

The January 2, 2006, *Washington Post* included an interview with Lynne Bettinger, a Red Cross–certified instructor of pet first aid. The article reported, "At her [Lynne Bettinger's] class early last month at a Gaithersburg veterinary clinic, many students showed up with Hurricane Katrina fresh on their minds. They learned to take pets' pulses, construct makeshift muzzles, and carry injured animals over long distances."[1]

The media attention to animal rescue after Hurricane Katrina boosted the relevance of pet welfare. People watched televised images that stunned them. As they sat on their couches with their own cats in their laps or their dogs at their feet, they were thinking: This could have been my pet left behind.

Animal organizations that offered training, which before had been attended by only a couple hundred annually, now had thousands of people sign up for courses. Organizations that responded to the disaster by sending staff and volunteers to help, loading supplies to transport, or taking in Katrina animals received more donations than ever in their histories.

Animal organizations were getting together for summits and hashing out their differences in unparalleled levels of cooperation.

In the *Washington Post* article above, Ollie Davidson, senior disaster adviser for the HSUS, is quoted as saying that "people are starting to treat animal advocates less as jokes and more like partners." America is waking up to the fact that the love and devotion between people and pets will not go away or crumble beneath volleys of ridicule. It's here to stay. Everybody, at all levels of society, will have to deal with it.

Months after the dust settled, what had volunteers, animal organizations, and the American people learned from the Katrina response? What stuck with us as a nation?

The lessons below are not meant to be our judgments on how disaster relief was handled or on the current state of affairs in animal shelters and organizations. After all, we represent mainstream American animal lovers who didn't go to the Gulf Coast but rather watched the efforts from a safe distance. These lessons are based on our observations as outsiders, with the benefit of hindsight, looking at a catastrophe and the response to it. Not experiencing the disaster firsthand, we had to search out the stories of others. Our research gave us the opportunity to listen to the experiences of hundreds of others and to assimilate them into messages for readers to consider. We feel honored for this glimpse into what has been the mostly invisible world of animal rescue.

## Lessons History Has Taught

Lumbering giants, saddled with bureaucracy, red tape, and an inability to move fast, get blindsided by guerrilla fighters and entrepreneurs who see a need and fill it with immediacy and, some would say, a certain level of recklessness. No person or agency was prepared for a catastrophe the size of Hurricanes Katrina and Rita. Yet the changes and healthy growth that will occur as fresh energy is assimilated into established procedures will improve responses to the next disasters and will also benefit the daily welfare of animals.

Every social movement in history has gone through the transitions and turmoil that animal rescue and welfare just experienced. George Washington's ragtag army in 1776 faced the highly disciplined British military while roiling with internal strife, deploying soldiers without proper ammunition or uniforms, and dealing with volunteers who had more zeal than discipline. Many of the Revolutionary War militiamen were what Thomas Payne called summer soldiers and sunshine patriots. Somehow General Washington, beset by his own failings and insecurities, managed to pull his troops together for victory.

This is how it often happens. A movement arises out of a change in consciousness that has taken place right under the noses of the old guard. Proponents of change clash with older, more established organizations. Then at some point all have to face a common enemy and figure out that uniting is the only way they will succeed. Hurricane Katrina was the common enemy for this nation's animal lovers.

**Lesson #1:** Hurricane Katrina provided a wake-up call for mainstream Americans to recognize the importance of saving animals from disaster.

In the *Washington Post* article mentioned above, writer William Wan states, "For years, despite an estimated 69 million U.S. households with a pet, animal advocates have been relegated to the fringes of emergency planning. After Katrina, however, and the sight of people in New Orleans refusing to evacuate and in some cases dying with their pets, emergency officials are starting to take animal rescue seriously. By saving the pets, advocates say, owners can be saved as well."

In addition to the unprecedented media and celebrity attention on animal rescue after Hurricane Katrina, another sign suggests that animal rescue has floated to the surface of mainstream awareness: lawyers and politicians are getting more involved.

Barbara J. Gislason's law practice in Minneapolis centers on family law and arts and entertainment law. But her heart is drawn to helping animals. It has been hard to win respect in the legal profession for animal law as a legitimate and important area of practice. After all, who pays for a dog to have an attorney? Even if a dog is intentionally hurt, it's tough to get a judge to consider the value of the animal's injury to the owner, much less to the dog. Most judges will consider only the modest replacement value of an injured or dead animal. How much could a lawyer make on such a case?

In 2003 Barbara formed the Animal Law Committee of the Minnesota State Bar Association and soon began teaching animal law at the Hamline University School of Law. Even though Minnesota is a state with strong ties to farming, hunting, and fishing, it turns out that a lot of lawyers there want to see the interests of animals and companion animal owners protected. Consequently, Barbara's committee gained support from her fellow attorneys and became a section of the Minnesota State Bar, granting it status and respectability.

Buoyed by the state-level response to her efforts, Barbara approached the American Bar Association (ABA), with 400,000 members nationwide, to help her move animal law into the conventional American culture. She forged a place for animal law in the highly respected Tort and Trial Insurance Practice Section (TIPS) of the ABA, which has 44,000 members. The mission of the TIPS ABA Animal Law Committee is to evolve the nation's and the world's thinking on animal issues by attracting the best and brightest lawyers in the country to analyze animal-related problems and issues and find new ways to define, manage, and solve them. Barbara told us, "The TIPS ABA Animal Law Committee will be the instrument of a paradigm shift. It will bring to the table and address legitimate business and economic interests and humane concerns. We are educating lawyers, judges, and the legal world by sharing the expertise of animal law practitioners to address problems of our clients. Our committee is both practical and visionary."

Shortly after Hurricane Katrina hit, the ABA TIPS Animal Law Committee spawned the TIPS Animal Disaster Relief Network (Network) to maintain a national forum for identifying short- and long-term disaster relief needs and to work on developing solutions. Barbara served as the chair of the committee and the director of the Network during and after the hurricane crisis. The committee brought together leaders from forty national and state organizations for biweekly teleconferences in which animal organization leaders talked directly with each other, with the faculty and students of eleven law schools, with the American Veterinary Medical Association, and with various government agencies, like the Department of Agriculture. The list of Network participants reads like a who's who of the animal welfare and protection movement.

Barbara explained, "It's a big step for animal rescue welfare people to talk to governmental officials. I think it's imperative for them to come together for a common purpose. Getting the government working with humane animal rescue organizations is important." She gave the example of Captain Stephanie Ostrowski, a veterinarian from the Centers for Disease Control. (We met her in chapter 14, where she talked about her duties after the hurricanes.) Barbara says, "Everybody listened to and respected Captain Ostrowski as a coalition builder. She made sure problems were addressed, including conflicts among NGO [nongovernmental organization] volunteers and local officials who wanted the out-of-state volunteers and organizations to go home and let the state veterinarians handle the situation with Louisiana's own resources. A lot of people did what they thought was best. Their intentions were good. But they found themselves in difficult situations. They didn't always make the right decisions. Everyone had a steep learning curve."

Kristina Hancock, soon to become chair of the ABA TIPS Animal Law Committee, formed a legislative committee of the Network to work for the passage of the Pets Evacuation and Transportation Standards Act (PETS Act). The House version, H.R. 3858, was sponsored by Representatives Tom Lantos (D-CA) and Christopher Shays (R-CT), who cochair the Congressional Friends of Animals Caucus, and Representative Barney Frank (D-MA). They were joined by Chair Don Young (R-AK) and ranking member James Oberstar (D-MN). A companion bill, S.2548, was introduced into the U.S. Senate on April 15, 2006. Chief sponsors are Senators Ted Stevens (R-AK) and Frank Lautenberg (D-NJ). Other cosponsors are Lincoln Chafee (R-RI) and Maria Cantwell (D-WA).

Jamie Olin, of the University of Michigan Law School and student vice chair of ABA TIPS Animal Law Committee, offered to organize law students from around the country to research answers to the legal questions that arose following Hurricane Katrina. Because of the scope of this project and its connection through student chapters to more than fifty law schools, Dana Campbell, managing senior attorney of the Animal Legal Defense Fund's Criminal Justice Program, spearheaded the Network's effort to research a variety of issues. These are called FAQs (Frequently Asked Questions) that affect Katrina animals. The research is now the foundation for legal research for future disasters.

Some of the many questions being researched are:

- Do Good Samaritan laws grant immunity to rescuers who trespass or break into and enter people's private property to remove abandoned animals?

- Can veterinarians treat, even sterilize, animals without owner consent following a disaster? Will they have liability risks to deal with later?

- What are the local, state, and federal laws, and nongovernmental policies that impact animal disaster relief?

- When more than one person claims to own an animal, how can competing claims be resolved?

- What authority does the military have with regard to local animal rescue operations?

- What are the emergency police powers with regard to rescuing or shooting abandoned or loose animals on sight as possible public health and safety risks?

Frequently asked questions on animal disaster relief issues are available at the website of the Animal Legal Defense Fund. They are eye-openers for all who didn't consider a fraction of these possible legal issues before setting out to rescue animals. The animal organizations that offer training for volunteers are surely keeping an eye on how the legal research defines parameters.

The ABA TIPS Animal Law Committee has been able to influence the setting of priorities within the entire American Bar Association. On February 13, 2006, the ABA passed landmark recommendations for federal laws that will impact state and local governments. The American Bar Association now supports the principle that emergency preparedness plans for people with household pets or service animals should be an essential part of response to any disaster or emergency situation. This means 400,000 lawyers standing behind this recommendation, which acknowledges the importance of planning for animal rescue in disasters. The times, they definitely are a-changin'!

Allie Phillips, senior attorney for the American Prosecutors Research Institute, offered training for the Florida Animal Control Association in November 2005 and told the 250 officers in attendance about her link with the TIPS Animal Disaster Relief Network. The group gave her two standing ovations. They were thrilled that some big hitters were networking with other attorneys, policy makers, and national leaders in the animal welfare community to help with the legalities and logistics of cooperating to save the lives of animals.

Although Barbara J. Gislason is humble about her accomplishments and made a point of letting us know that other people are also forming coalitions of decision makers (Jennifer Fearing at UAN and Marie Belew Wheatley at the AHA come to mind), we believe that Barbara definitely deserves a One Person Makes a Difference for Animals Award.

As further proof that mainstream America is responding to the lessons learned from Hurricane Katrina, other states, including Louisiana, are working on legislation to make pet disaster preparedness and evacuation mandatory.

Legislators and politicians are taking note of their constituents' love for animals. Someday soon they will figure out that six out of ten households in their districts include voters who want disaster protection and consideration for their family pets and would welcome laws that stop abuse and cruelty.

**Lesson #2:** Individuals have to take primary responsibility for their pets. No one can be relied upon to do it for them.

It takes every resource that communities and emergency planners can muster to deal with the volatile actions and reactions of a panicking public. The last thing on their minds in a crisis is thinking about what will happen to people's pets. Every single person we spoke with for this book said the same thing: *Take your pets with you in a disaster evacuation.*

Animals who are left behind for whatever reason are vulnerable beyond your wildest imaginings. They become helpless victims of violence. When communities are in disaster mode, anyone with a gun can shoot an animal. Anyone who is prone to abuse animals can get away with it.

Tammy Masters, our sweet Hollywood connection from chapter 20, had the misfortune (as did others we spoke with) of being one of the rescuers who discovered the animals who had been shot while chained to desks in the St. Bernard Parish High School, one of four schools in the parish where murdered dogs were found. Tammy has never recovered from the horror of what she found in those classrooms. The residents of St. Bernard Parish had evacuated to these schools with their pets. When they were forced to leave without them, rescuers promised that their animals would be in safekeeping. People left heart-wrenching notes scrawled on walls with the names of their pets and instructions for their care. After the humans left, the animals were shot and killed. The Louisiana State attorney general's office is working on the case, and Pasado's Safe Haven has posted a $25,000 reward for information leading to the arrest and conviction of the perpetrators of this vicious crime. So far no one has been arrested.

Hurricane Katrina rescue efforts also resulted in what came to be known as Barkansaw. Tammy Hanson ran a "sanctuary" in Arkansas called Every Dog Needs a Home. She came to several temporary shelters in Louisiana and Mississippi offering to take pit bulls and rottweilers, breeds that the rescuers were having an almost impossible time finding refuge for in animal shelters from other parts of the country. She had the money, she said, to care for them. After Tammy took dogs back to Arkansas, she and her husband, William, were arrested, handcuffed, and charged with twenty-seven counts of animal cruelty in a classic case of animal hoarding. The Baxter County Sheriff's Department had seized about 477 suffering dogs. The Hansons were convicted on all counts.

United Animal Nations spent thirty days in Arkansas and sent one hundred volunteers to care for the dogs after Tammy was forced to relinquish the animals. The HSUS regional coordinator and program coordinator assisted the sheriff's department in building his case against the Hansons, as did Dana Campbell, of the Animal Legal Defense Fund. There was great rejoicing in the animal welfare community when the convictions and sentences were handed down.

## Animal Hoarding

The case of Tammy and William Hanson raises the specter of animal hoarders, people who collect animals and then don't provide basic care for them. Keep this in mind if you ever think you need to relinquish an animal: an animal hoarder may get this pet, who used to be your family member, making him or her suffer terrible cruelty.

Dr. Gary Patronek, at the Center for Animals and Public Policy at the Tufts University Veterinary Medical School, is one of the world's leading experts on animal hoarding. In a presentation for the Hoarding of Animals Research Consortium, in 2004, he identified three characteristics of hoarders. First, they collect a large number of animals. Second, they don't provide for the animals' basic physical and social needs, including food, water, shelter, veterinary care, and sanitary living conditions. Third, they live in denial about the horrible conditions of their animals and, sometimes, of their human children.[2]

The HSUS has studied animal hoarding for more than twenty-five years. Dave Pauli, a regional director with the HSUS, talked with us about what he's learned about stopping hoarders:

I have been on at least twelve cases with over two hundred animals. Each case is individual. From an animal protection perspective, you have to find out the history, how the person got there. Some puppy mills turn into hoarders. Yet each hoarder is in some way an animal person. Something has driven them into wanting to have one hundred to four hundred animals.

I've found that the best tactics are to try to understand the hoarders and explain that what they are doing doesn't meet acceptable standards for the community. In the worst-case scenario, we have to prosecute and distribute all the animals. Most people, when shown that there are alternatives, grasp them.

The best situation is to let hoarders have some animals, spay-neuter their animals, and monitor them closely. If you take away all of the hoarders' animals, they just go out and get more. Hoarders continue to hoard.

It's ineffective if you approach this problem with a command-and-control method. In some cases, that has to be a fallback position. But I've found that you get more accomplished with honey.

Bonney Brown, of Alley Cat Allies, told us that for hoarders, acquiring is important. They gather more animals than they can handle because they can't say no. Hoarders don't adopt animals out or do trap-neuter-return but instead want to bring all the animals into their house. Their emphasis is on saving and rescuing with very little care for animals before they get more. Bonney says, "Typically a hoarder is a lone person with no volunteers or group. No fund-raising. Just one person with a ton of animals they can barely take care of. It's hard to tell sometimes. I've met people with fifty cats who would go hungry before letting their cats be without food or vet care. I've seen people with as few as twenty cats who don't take care of them. One hundred fifty cats is too many for one person. It's impossible to support that many animals by yourself."

Francis Battista writes in the March–April 2006 issue of the *Best Friends* magazine, "People wonder how the animals of New Orleans could have been left on their own with no official plan to save them. But that's the story every day in almost every city in this country. Dogs and cats are picked up off the streets or turned in by their families. Some are adopted or placed with rescues, the rest are killed. And that has been the truth about cats and dogs in this country for over a century."[3]

Whether you are fleeing a disaster or you don't believe you can or want to care for your pet any longer, if you take your animal to a shelter or give the animal over to an unfit home, you leave the animal alone in the world. Violence toward animals is still part of the subculture of America and of the world. This is why the HSUS and other organizations work with legislators like Senator John Ensign to pass laws making puppy mills illegal and stopping the sale of horses for slaughter.

The Animal Legal Defense Fund posts an article on its website titled, "The Five Best States to Be an Animal Abuser." It ranks states according to their laws protecting animals, and it plans to release these rankings annually.[4] Where is your state in the ranking?

**Lesson #3:** Disaster preparedness and planning at every level are the keys to preventing loss of human and animal lives.

You can do everything right. You can have your disaster plans and animal emergency evacuation kits in place. You can believe that you would fight to the death to stay with your pets or not leave them behind. Yet as you have seen from the experiences of evacuees, when rescuers are determined to make you leave, you go. Remember the woman who said she came back to consciousness in a rescue boat after being shot with a Taser (electric shock) gun and forced to leave without her pets? You may think, if it were you, you'd jump out of that boat and swim back to your pet. Would you? Would your animal still be where you left him or her? Would you have the physical stamina to save your pet? None of us can know these things until we are faced with disaster situations.

You will always have to depend on local, state, and federal resources for saving the lives of your pets. And it all starts locally. Look in the Resources section of this book for websites that contain model disaster preparedness plans. Bring them to the attention of emergency preparedness planners in your community. The more animal-loving people who get involved with emergency disaster planning, the better chance animals have of being rescued.

Here are more ideas:

- Find your local chapter of the American Red Cross (ARC). By law, the American Red Cross is supposed to include animals in shelter plans (not necessarily in the shelters themselves). See the website of the National Voluntary Organizations Active in Disaster for the state and national levels of ARC disaster planning in which you could participate. Bear in mind that the ARC is a loose organization with, at this time, some internal management problems and much variation from area to area.[5]

- Find out who is responsible for Mass Care Emergency Support and the Emergency Management Office at your local and state levels. Participate in emergency services planning meetings. Make sure temporary shelters for people and animals will be located in the same vicinity and that animal rescuers will work side by side with human rescuers using a preplanned system for reuniting animals and people. Find out if temporary housing provided by the state or FEMA will allow people to live with their pets again after a disaster.

- Contact your local lawmakers and state government agencies to find out if your state has a State Animal Response Team (SART) or Community Animal Rescue/Response Team. Visit the SART website for information, like the following, on these teams: "State Animal Response Teams are interagency state organizations dedicated to preparing, planning, responding and recovering during animal emergencies in the United States. SART is a public private partnership, joining government agencies with the private concerns around the common goal of animal issues during disasters. SART programs train participants to facilitate a safe, environmentally sound and efficient response to animal emergencies on the local, county, state and federal level."[6] Currently the most highly recommended SARTs are in North Carolina, Colorado, and Florida.

- Find out if the plans for your state and local area include evacuation of farm animals and emergency care for feral cat colonies and wildlife.

- Find out if abandoned animals will be transported more than one hundred miles outside the danger zone. If so, reunions are more complicated and costly.

- Contact your local animal shelters and ask if they have a memorandum of understanding (MOU) or memorandum of agreement (MOA) with another animal shelter out of the area in case there is the need for disaster evacuation. Remember, it might be your pet who is taken to a local animal shelter.

- During an actual emergency, the affected area sets up an Emergency Operations Center (EOC) and a Multiagency Coordination center (MAC). Ask if the agencies that will be in charge of animal rescue (like the LA/SPCA was in New Orleans) will have their head administrators (like Laura Maloney) as part of the EOC and MAC. This puts animal rescue at the decision-making centers during an emergency.

- When you go out of town, whether you regularly board your pets at a boarding facility or veterinary office or a doggy day care center, ask for the facility's animal disaster emergency evacuation plan. If it doesn't have one, tell it to get one, or you'll be taking your business elsewhere.

- Even in nondisaster situations, support pet-friendly hotels and airlines that transport pets safely and economically. Be sure to write and tell them why they are getting your business. Vote pet friendly with your dollars.

We wonder whether it might be advisable for states to appoint a pet czar and put the position into the department of Health and Human

Services. Right now decisions about animals are made in the Department of Agriculture (ESF-11), which is the lead agency for response to animals in emergencies. Is the Department of Agriculture really in touch with the needs and desires of people who have companion animals? Aren't they more in tune with the needs of farmers and rural areas?

The moral of the story is, get involved with local and regional agencies that respond to and plan for disasters, and help take responsibility for the emergency situations that affect animals in your community.

**Lesson #4:** Volunteers for animals need to be recruited, trained, valued, and assimilated into existing organizations.

Animal organizations have to devise more consistent ways of training and credentialing volunteers. We understand that they are working on this project.

By the same token, volunteers need to make a commitment to being seriously trained and credentialed. During the chaos of a disaster, organizations need to be able to distinguish between volunteers and con artists who take advantage of the situation and pass themselves off as being there to help the animals. Volunteers who want to do the extremely rugged and dangerous rescue work need training in conducting swiftwater rescue, handling dangerous and frightened animals, managing ropes and ladders, treating wildlife and rescuing large animals, and protecting themselves and gearing up for the next disaster. Anyone who wants to volunteer has to get used to the Incident Command System (ICS). A disaster is no time to have everybody doing things their own way. It's far too dangerous for both animals and people.

Although some freelance volunteers told us they resented the attitudes of the big organizations, it's time to put differences to rest. From what we can tell, the animal organizations have learned much from their experiences with Hurricane Katrina and from conducting their own internal evaluations and debriefings.

We hope that animal organizations will find ways to assess the skills of spontaneous volunteers, train them on the spot, and put them to good use. It is also our hope that disaster planning finds a way to include the help of volunteers who are not credentialed. Large-scale disasters require all hands on deck. Not everyone will be trained as well as they should be. Yet highly skilled people shouldn't be turned away or put in positions that don't use their expertise.

At the same time, there should be a special place in heaven for volunteers who do the menial jobs of animal rescue and sheltering. From what we can tell, the grunt work is undervalued and the glory jobs are overvalued. Perhaps there could be special incentives and awards for cleaning the most cages and kitty litter pans, reuniting the most people and pets, and placing the highest number of animals in good foster and permanent homes. It seems to us that in the Katrina disaster, not much attention was given to rewarding those vital volunteer tasks.

## Two Missing Elements in Training and Deployment

Two important aspects of animal rescue are overlooked in the training and deployment of volunteers. First, bringing in counselors and individuals who are skilled in trauma stress management has to be put at the top of the priority list. Far too many volunteers came back from Hurricane Katrina dealing with post-traumatic stress disorder. They were sorely neglecting their own emotional needs as were the organizations for which they volunteered.

Mary Pat Boatfield, executive director for the Nashville Humane Society, told us that her team included psychotherapist James E. Doughty. At first Mary Pat was leery of bringing along a counselor and thought he'd try to do a lot of debriefing and therapy. But she said that Jim was, first, a friend to the team and, second, a counselor. Plus, he pitched in with all the work and won the respect of his team. He was available to listen and show concern for their needs. Mary Pat says that when working future disasters, she always wants to have a counselor like Jim on the team.

In addition to counselors, those skilled in crisis intervention are needed. Dr. Mary Lou Randour, of the Doris Day Animal Foundation, says, "There definitely was need for crisis intervention for the people coming to record or find their lost pets. I also participated in two crisis interventions between the civilian and military police and the volunteers, demonstrating an equal need to offer help to responders."

Dr. Becky Rhoades, board member of the Society of Animal Welfare Administrators, recalls having what she calls a meltdown cry. One woman screamed at her when the woman thought Dr. Rhoades had left without cleaning the cage of a dog in an area that housed thirty or forty of what were considered to be dangerous dogs. "I just sat down and cried," says Dr. Rhoades. "I understood. It was all about the animals. We were there for the animals."

The second aspect of volunteer and organizational training that is often overlooked is the establishment of clear and generally accepted guidelines within the animal rescue community for deciding when disaster relief is over and when it's time to go home. In a perfect world, the emergency phase of a response is supposed to last for only about one to two weeks with the ICS structure in use, daily briefing meetings held, and tasks assigned. The emergency response phase is then declared to be finished, and search and rescue ends. Then the disaster becomes a recovery effort. Because animal rescuers were continuing to find stranded animals all over the affected areas for months after Hurricane Katrina, there was disagreement about whether the situation was still an emergency search and rescue effort, requiring the help of people from around the country, or if it had become an animal control issue that could be handled by the LA/SPCA, parish animal control organizations, and local volunteers.

In November 2005 Laura Maloney, of the LA/SPCA, formed a committee of respected organizations to assess whether or not the freelance organizations' urgent calls for volunteers to keep coming to New Orleans to rescue animals was necessary. Local residents were becoming concerned that animal feeding stations would attract rodents. Some volunteers told us that residents would sometimes get rid of the food after volunteers had put it out. Laura's committee concluded that the number of strays needing to be fed had dwindled. The volunteers countered that the committee hadn't assessed the situation at night when all the animals came out looking for food and that the committee had observed only a limited area of the city. The debate still continues.

## Helper's High

We became fascinated by how many volunteers returned three, even four, times for as much as three to six months. Some lost their jobs and suffered financial ruin. We wondered what motivated them.

Studies on altruism have concluded that volunteering brings health benefits. Volunteers often feel rushes of euphoria followed by a sense of calmness and well-being after performing an act of kindness. Dr. Allan Luks, executive director of New York's Big Brothers/Big Sisters, coined the term *helper's high*. Dr. Luks says that helper's high is a physical sensation that reduces stress as the body's natural painkillers, endorphins, are released when a person performs a good deed.[7]

We asked three-time New Orleans volunteer Dr. James Gardner, a clinical psychologist, to share his thoughts on why volunteers made so many sacrifices and returned again and again. He said, "I must confess that while I was down there, all three times, sleeping in deplorable conditions, my sciatic nerve problems were substantially less than normal. I attributed the relief to the effects of added adrenaline."

Ron Silver, an independent filmmaker from Nebraska, went to New Orleans twice to volunteer and planned to return for the Pet Parade prior to Mardi Gras. He told us, "I got chased by a pack of dogs. I jumped a nine-foot fence like an Olympic athlete. There were thirty dogs looking at me like I was food. I saw them all turn on me. I was close to the road and thought if I could jump the fence, I'd make it to my RV. I wish my friend would have caught that on tape."

Dr. Gardner says he suspects each person had their reasons for returning to volunteer in such difficult and dangerous situations. But he identified four factors that he thought contributed to the feel-good feelings that so many volunteers reported to us.

*Camaraderie:* These are "salt of the earth," good people, and it's nice to be around good people. It reaffirms your own goodness. At Lamar-Dixon,

I left my possessions in a tent shared by over three hundred people for a week and never missed an item. Many of these people stay in touch even after they go home.

*Importance:* This was life-and-death. You know what you are doing means that another's life is changed forever. For the people who go, there is no distinction between saving the life of an animal or a person. For most people, the chance to do these kinds of activities is new and very rewarding. It's hard to do such vital work and then go back to your cubicle and answer ludicrous emails.

*Adrenaline rush:* There is too much to do and too few people to do it. You are constantly engaged. The time flies by. You don't know what date it is, what day of the week it is, what's happening in the world. You are in the zone, and all you have is the last moment, what you are doing now, and what you will do next. For people whose lives are filled with drudgery, the zone is like heaven. It relieves migraines, reduces soreness, eliminates loneliness, and revitalizes the spirit.

*Connectedness:* When people asked me why I went down, facetiously I said, "I was on a mission from God." While I said this jokingly, all good jokes have an element of truth. The fact is that this type of work is about more than the work itself. It's the kind of stuff that appeals to our "ego ideal." It's what people *should* do, and it expresses the better side of our nature. This is a powerful motivating force.

Dana Kay Deutsch, a firefighter in the Houston area, told us, "Animals are my passion in life. Animal rescue is one way that I can relate to that passion by enabling me to save lives. I like getting a dog off the street. I love the adrenaline. I love the look in that dog or cat's eyes when they realize I want to help them."

**Lesson #5:** Animal organizations are experiencing growing pains and will have to continue the new era of heightened cooperation and greater accountability.

When we spoke with Barbara Gislason, chair of the ABA TIPS Animal Law Committee, we asked her what she'd like to see happen with the animal organizations in an ideal disaster relief response. Following are some of her ideas:

- I would hope that for each of the six months after Hurricane Katrina, every state has a meeting bringing together all people with expertise in any aspect of disaster relief. The meetings would serve to develop short-term models for preparedness and response.

- Figure out the best paperwork to use, the best phone systems, walkie-talkies, ID systems, even GPS systems.

- Use the same vernacular and common acronyms so if a firefighter and a person from the U.S. Department of Agriculture are speaking to each other, they use the same lingo. Must-know acronyms include NRP, the National Response Plan, and NIMS, the National Incident Management System.

- Use leaders who pull people together and inspire them to use their best qualities. Everybody buys in to the same vision, and respects the different skills people bring.

- Develop a structure to imagine the highest-level solutions.

- Have job descriptions for everybody on the disaster teams. Figure out how many teams are needed for a given situation and where they should be located. Identify what states have teams that would blend with your own team. Have an organization identified that could train new teams before they arrive on-site.

- Have very good advance planning for how to handle the media, and how to control rumors.

- Bring in psychologists and mental health workers to help those dealing with emotionally difficult situations, such as death and euthanasia.

- Have animal behavioral specialists be part of the team. Include people who specialize in disaster relief for wildlife and zoo animals.

- Praise volunteers. Make them feel valuable.

- Have uniform, solid record keeping that generates reports and uses the latest technology.

- Expand and improvise workers' comp and liability insurance so that it covers out-of-state veterinarians, those who transport animals, and volunteers working in the emergency context.

- Have uniform and easy-to-understand owner relinquishment forms.

- Have consistent memorandums of agreement between organizations like the animal groups and the Red Cross. Memorandums of understanding should be clear about who has what responsibility and capabilities, whom can be counted on, and what infrastructure between public and private partners exists.

Barbara also attended the summit that the AHA held for invited leaders of animal organizations and government officials in Florida, in January 2006. She says about the participants, "I have high regard for people in charge. They had to deal with people who are running heavily on emotion and doing the best they could. They were getting bad publicity in the middle of a crisis, unable to deal with both public relations and the horrible disaster situation."

Barbara imagines that many of the people in the room changed as a result of what they experienced during the disaster. "I could see the pain wash over their faces. I didn't feel like judging anybody there. I didn't see one person at that conference who wasn't well intentioned. Whether they had the skills they needed was a different question. But I could see a piece of their hearts." Barbara concludes, "What haunts me is that none of us in that room know what will happen next. The history of the world is disasters. We don't know what time or place. We just know it is inevitable."

## The Work Progresses

More summits are planned. Jennifer Fearing, at United Animal Nations, told us that she created an assessment of individual organizations, naming what each does best, to serve as discussion points for future disaster planning. Julie Morris says that UAN and the ASPCA have teamed up to offer animal disaster relief training and preparedness in fourteen prototype cities with plans for expanding the programs in years to come.

The Animal Legal Defense Fund has been saving animals from disaster for twenty-five years and fighting hard to make sure that animals are protected. We spoke with Dana Campbell, managing senior attorney for criminal justice for the ALDF. She is a former prosecutor who has melded her love of animals (even though she is allergic to them) with her legal expertise. She says that the ALDF is preparing model foster care agreements to help alleviate these court battles over returning pets to their owners. The organization is researching legal issues, such as how states can best work with out-of-state veterinarians. They are considering developing best practices guidelines. The group is supporting federal, state, and local disaster planning.

## Other Issues and Ideas

Now that animal organizations have taken in record amounts of donations, they are being held to higher standards of accountability; the public wants transparency. Organizations are being asked to publicly specify how the money donated for Katrina animal rescue and relief is being or will be spent. An article in the December 2005 issue of *Animal People* says, "Donations to Katrina/Rita relief work cumulatively approached $50 million with about 90 percent of the total going to the Humane Society of the United States, the American SPCA, Noah's Wish, Best Friends, PetSmart Charities, and the Petfinder.com Foundation."[8]

In addition to the suggestions above, other ideas that are being discussed by animal organizations include:

- Implementing the uniform microchipping of animals with standardized microchip readers

- Using implanted GPS tracking devices for animals so lost pets can always be located

- Designating one entity to be a central database for taking in requests for rescue and to generate address lists

- Linking address lists with MapQuest or GPS directional devices

- Using portable wireless computers for immediate record keeping as animals are rescued and transported

- Issuing temporary licenses for out-of-state veterinarians and determining what kinds of emergency services they should provide and for how long

### Experience Matters

Experience is invaluable when planning for disasters. Terri Crisp, founder of Noah's Wish, has written two books on rescuing animals, and Noah's Wish does nothing else but train volunteers for and manage animals during disasters. She told us that certain procedures over time have proven more effective, such as sheltering rescued animals close to the site of disaster:

> We don't send animals to shelters around the country. Because of this, our average reclaim rate is 75 percent. The average for other groups is 20 to 25 percent. Other groups were sending animals all over the country within twenty-four to forty-eight hours of receiving them. We set up our temporary shelters in conjunction with animal control. We keep all animals for at least sixty days. We placed them in foster homes located within an hour, no more than two hours, from the city where the disaster was. We always knew where the owner was and if he was not able to take back the animal. You lose control of the animals if you transport them out of the area.
>
> We have a proven paperwork system for keeping track of animals. We took in 1,974 animals during Hurricane Katrina and didn't lose any

of them. Practice makes perfect. If we were losing animals, we'd better be seriously looking at what we're doing wrong.

Terri Crisp says that Noah's Wish learned through trial and error what works and is always open to sharing the fruits of its hard-earned experience: "We have worked hard to gather information and knowledge and experience that has prepared us well to help animals during disasters. We made all the mistakes through the years. We never will make the same mistake twice though, otherwise it costs animals their lives. The price is too high."

Terri talks about disaster planning that took place after the last major event and put it into historical context:

Hurricane Floyd, which struck North Carolina in 1999, was the last big disaster that caused people to put forth an effort to be better prepared for responding to the needs of animals during disasters. Afterwards, the animal groups all wanted things to be different. There were many meetings which resulted in establishing some memorandums of understanding for the next big one. Interest and enthusiasm eventually disappeared though.

It's aggravating, being involved for as long as I have and watching the same mistakes being made. When disasters happen, a whole new group of inexperienced people responds. If I take the time to share my knowledge and experience, it's almost falling on deaf ears because during the next disaster, none of those people will be there.

We had the impression that Terri would love to be proven wrong. She is hopeful that Hurricane Katrina has a lasting impact on improving methods for saving animals during disasters.

We hope that we are doing our part to help people recall the lessons of the past. When we interviewed Mary Pat Boatfield, of Nashville Humane, she told us something that heartened and motivated us through those long hours, weeks, and months of gathering and digesting information. Mary Pat said, "Without your book, what all of us have learned could be lost."

**Lesson #6:** Millions of animals are dying needlessly due to pet overpopulation.

In a *Best Friends* press release dated November 22, 2005, Paul Berry says,

We are inspired by Mayor Nagin's plan to rebuild a better New Orleans. If funds remain after the rescue efforts are complete, they should be used to build a better New Orleans for companion animals. Once the remaining pets are safe, we can join together to invest in programs that will radically improve the quality of life for animals in the Gulf Coast region. These programs would include: low-cost, high-volume spay-neuter facilities, neighboring no-kill sheltering and adoption capabilities, affordable health care for pets of low-income families, model legislations to end dog fighting and related animal abuse.[9]

You have read in this book about the changing roles of animal shelters and sanctuaries. The spay–neuter–adopt programs that are coming into being through the progressive shelters and organizations, especially those offered through low-cost mobile units, are the wave of the future. We want to mention here one outstanding organization that sets a high standard for using spay–neuter to solve pet overpopulation. Montana Spay Neuter Task Force, in Victor, Montana, is a statewide organization with a worldwide reach due to its success in involving local communities to solve pet overpopulation. Jean Atthowe, a volunteer for the organization, says,

Since November 1996 our Task Force has provided 28,418 spay-neuter surgeries by creating big events that are publicized in local media in twenty-five to thirty communities each year. Since 2003 the Task Force has provided 7,688 of the total surgeries with costs funded by local officials. We were invited to the Crow Nation and achieved great successes by respecting the community's traditions and showing our keen dedication to helping people reawaken their connection to animals and nature. When we go to Native American nations — and we have been to all seven in Montana at least once, as well as to Rosebud Sicangu Sioux in South Dakota — we are honored by their gracious way of thanking us after the spay-neuter event with a community powwow.

Nothing can save more animals' lives than reducing pet overpopulation through humane methods.

**Lesson #7:** Educating children, teens, and young adults about animal welfare, protection, and advocacy will improve the lives of animals and people in future disasters.

We found ourselves asking about animal rescue volunteerism: Where are the twenty-year-old volunteers? Of the people responding to our request for interviews and information, this age group was notably absent. Where are the churches with groups that want to give back to life and offer service to the needy? Where are the colleges that could send students majoring in social work, nonprofit business, veterinary medicine, or any of the helping professions?

Humane education is the wave of the future. See the Resources section for information on how to help children learn the value of animals in their lives. Humane education can decrease violence and increase compassion in children. That's a terrific combination.

**Lesson #8:** The animals will help us all to heal.

Betty Rome's son, Victor, went online to try to find his mother's dog, Missy. Betty was heartbroken at having been separated from her precious companion. She had a photo of Missy with one ear up and one ear down, which Victor uploaded to the Web.

One of those dedicated volunteers who searched through Petfinder.com to help evacuees find their lost pets located Missy. The dog had been rescued and transported to the San Diego Humane Society and SPCA.

Renee Harris, at San Diego Humane, called Betty and offered to bring her to San Diego to reclaim Missy. Betty jumped at the chance. She says, "Thanks to all the people who participated in the rescue of Missy and all the other animals who were left behind. For the rescuers in Louisiana to California, I am grateful."

Betty told us the story of her reunion with Missy:

I arrived on a Friday evening and went to the humane society. They have living rooms where the dogs stay, so you can visit with them. I went into the room where Missy was. She would not look at me. I could tell she was angry with me. Renee said, "That happens with a lot of dogs. She's not sure."

I sat down on the couch. Missy circled the room. Then she walked over to me and put one little paw on my knee. That's how the healing process began. I felt like I had died and gone to heaven. Till death do us part, Missy and me.

*Betty Rome reunited with Missy.*

If an animal is abandoned in a disaster, no matter whether the disaster is caused by nature or humans, trust is broken between that animal and humans. Animals have grown to rely and depend on people for their safety and well-being. People have grown to rely on animals to reconnect them with their hearts and souls.

Each animal who has been betrayed by humans has to learn how to trust again. Missy, by placing a gentle paw on Betty's knee, showed her willingness to heal. No matter what animals have gone through, no matter how alone they must have felt, it is incredible how fast they forgive and love again.

Perhaps these are the greatest lessons of all.

# CHAPTER TWENTY-TWO

# Conclusion

Saving animals from disaster remains low on society's list of priorities. It will be up to animal lovers, the people who read this book, to change those priorities.

We skimmed through a lengthy and supposedly comprehensive White House report on lessons learned from Hurricane Katrina. It made many excellent points. What it didn't have was *one mention* of animals. We just looked at each other and said, "They *still* don't get it!" Not one of the lessons learned contained references to the fact that disaster planning has to include saving animals and keeping people and pets together.

Because this nation had to face and become more sophisticated about animal rescue after Hurricane Katrina, progress has been made. This is a heartening development. More people than ever have recognized that if they must ever evacuate, they should take their pets with them. Are they prepared to do this within five minutes? Probably not. Many people still tell themselves that these things happen only to others. Hopefully those attitudes will change as well.

## To the Volunteers

As for those wonderful human beings, the animal rescuers whom we had the privilege of interviewing, it was as if they had gone to the mountain-top. Some returned with one commandment, others with ten or even twenty. They returned from the battlefield with nuggets of advice: Send small, bite-sized cat food because the cats can't eat the large chunks. Keep pictures of your pets with you in case photos in your home are destroyed. Don't believe them if they say your pets will be safe without you.

Animal rescuers looked into the bulging eyes of starving kittens and puppies who were no more than a layer of skin draped over bones. They shoveled waste, lovingly poured water into bowls, left pounds of dry food and gallons of water on deserted street corners, and spent hours on the Internet searching for lost pets. They returned home from the disaster feeling numb, disheartened — and aching to go back. Because the job wasn't finished. Because thousands of animals were homeless. Because they cared.

The people who volunteered for animal rescue after Katrina and the people who save animals every day at shelters and through rescue groups feel at the same time happy about their work and heartbroken when they see very little progress for their causes. After Hurricane Katrina they were stretched beyond the limits of what they thought they could endure. And they loved it. Had never been happier in their lives. Made friends for life. Felt let down, even dead inside, upon returning home. Couldn't stop thinking about their adventures in altruism. Talked about it till other people asked them to stop. Or couldn't talk about it at all. Needed to bring home a rescued animal to nurture, to remember. They didn't ever want the giving to end.

The good news for Katrina volunteers is that the helper's high can continue through service for animals. Although animal rescue volunteers are still only a fraction of the millions who love *their* dog or *their* cat only, the movement is growing and becoming stronger through enhanced training and communication. Opportunities abound for people to make life better for animals. They can participate in disaster preparation that will save lives and can become more involved in animal sheltering, protection, and welfare in their hometowns.

## To Disaster Survivors and Those Who Didn't Make It

Some of you loved and lost animals. You know the dark hole that will never be filled by an animal who did not return to the safety and comfort of a home that the storms destroyed. We mourn with you.

The Mississippi River, which begins as a trickle in Itasca State Park in our state of Minnesota, builds into the mighty joining of many rivers until it flows through the states of Mississippi and Louisiana into the Gulf of Mexico.

As we sat near the source of the Mississippi during the winter of 2005–6, writing this book, our thoughts and hearts followed the flow of the river to the sea. We are connected by nature to the steamy, humid hurricane zone. We imagined the bowl of New Orleans, where floodwaters drowned out a thriving, colorful city, so different from the solid, built-on-granite environment where we live.

When the Gulf Coast endured winds and floods, it sent shock waves through the entire length of the Mississippi River back to us. We heard the cries of the people, the barking of their dogs, the mewing of their cats, the surreal stillness of their fleeing wildlife.

## To People Who Shared Their Stories and Wisdom

Picture this: Snow glistened as shafts of sunlight bounced off acres of pure white carpets. We sat in an upstairs home office with the blinds open, facing a window where a single crystal hung from a clear strand. Glistening sunbeams transformed the crystal's surface into streams of blue, gold, and red light, which reflected onto the walls of the room. This is the crystal that our tuxedo-marked kitty, Cuddles, loves to swipe at with her white-tipped paw so that it will swing for her amusement. As we talked with the people who poured their hearts out for this book, Cuddles sat serenely on the table where we worked. With her, we gazed out the window and took in images of a frigid Minnesota winter. Cuddles watched falling snowflakes; she was transfixed by their silent dances.

On one side of our worktable, opposite the window, Linda typed at her computer. At the other end of the table, with a side view of the window, Allen took notes on a yellow legal pad. He would lean forward to ask questions, then sit back, scribbling on the notepad while listening to answers. Both Allen and Linda focused on the voice that emanated from the telephone's speaker on the table in front of them.

The voice, on some days, belonged to someone who rescues animals, either as a volunteer or a staff person for an animal welfare organization. Or the voice would be from someone who had lost almost everything in the hurricanes but was (or was not) reunited with the one being who really mattered to him or her — an *animal* family member.

At some point in the interview process, especially for those who were involved in the Gulf Coast crises, the voice would stop. Silence as still as the falling snow would thicken the atmosphere in the room. Then the sound of sniffling or sobbing could be heard.

By this time Cuddles would have forsaken her delight in snowflakes. After the voice from the telephone transformed into a torrent of human words, she tuned in to the emotions. She positioned herself in front of the telephone, hunkering down with all four paws folded beneath her body. And she listened.

As the voice would begin to quiver, we stopped taking notes. We joined together in sacred respect for all that had been lost and for miracles of rescue and reunion. We listened as the voice struggled to tell stories of human-animal bonding that literally make grown men and women cry.

Cuddles would turn her head and gaze at us with emerald eyes that conveyed oceans of wonder and wisdom. With all the curiosity of her cat nature, she looked at us as if to ask, "How could this have happened to the animals?"

The voice, when it was able to speak again, would crack in anguish or with an expression of joy and gratitude. An emotional levee had broken.

Reliving traumatic experiences by talking about them had released a flood. Then the voice would apologize for having wept. We would offer reassurances that most of the people we interviewed for the book had shed tears and that we had cried along with them.

To the voices of the people who teach the world that animals are family.

To the voices of the people and organizations that save animals from disaster.

To the voiceless animals who endure and survive because of their love.

# Notes

## Introduction

1. Antoine de Saint-Exupéry, *The Little Prince*, trans. Katherine Woods (New York: Harcourt, Brace & World, 1971), 88.

## Chapter 1. The Changing Relationship between People and Animals

1. "Spot Reduction: Dogs and Pounds," *AARP: The Magazine*, March–April 2006.
2. Robert K. Anderson, "In the Spotlight: The Changing Status of Animals and Human-Animal Bonds," Center to Study Human-Animal Relationships and Environments, http://www.censhare.umn.edu/spotlight02.html (accessed March 27, 2006).

## Chapter 4. The Doctor, the Actor, the Journalist, and Oprah

1. James Riopelle, MD, quoted in transcript for "Oprah on Location from Mississippi," *The Oprah Winfrey Show* (New Jersey: Burrelle's Information Services, September 7, 2005), 5.
2. Robert Davis, "Hope Turns to Anguish at Intensive-Care Unit," *USA Today*, September 15, 2005, http://www.usatoday.com/news/nation/2005-09-15 -katrina-hospital-cover_x.htm (accessed March 27, 2006).

## Chapter 5. What It's Like to Rescue Animals in Disasters

1. Terri Crisp and Samantha Glen, *Out of Harm's Way: The Extraordinary True Story of One Woman's Lifelong Devotion to Animal Rescue* (New York: Pocket Books, 1996), 198.

## Chapter 6. Over a Century of Making a Difference

1.  Pune Dracker, "Regarding Henry," *ASPCA Animal Watch*, Spring 1996,
    http://www.aspca.org/site/PageServer?pagename=140_history (accessed
    March 27, 2006).

## Chapter 7. Protecting Children and Animals

1.  American Humane Association, "The Real Story of Mary Ellen Wilson,"
    http://www.americanhumane.org/site/PageServer?pagename=wh_mission
    _maryellen (accessed March 27, 2006).

## Chapter 8. New Kid on the Block

1.  Humane Society of the United States, "About the Humane Society of the
    United States," http://www.hsus.org/about_us (accessed March 27, 2006).
2.  Humane Society of the United States, "Animal Care Expo,"
    http://www.animalsheltering.org/expo (accessed March 27, 2006).

## Chapter 10. Why Did People Stay?

1.  Scott Shields, *Bear: Heart of a Hero* (Thornwood, NY: Hero Dog Publications,
    2003); see also the Bear Search and Rescue Foundation, http://www.bear
    searchandrescue.org (accessed April 22, 2006).
2.  Sharon Schlegel, "A Witness to Katrina's Tragedy," *Trenton Times*,
    September 21, 2005.

## Chapter 11. How Were Animals and People Separated?

1.  Anderson Cooper, quoted in *CNN Reports: Katrina, State of Emergency*, ed.
    Michael Reagan (Kansas City: Andrews McMeel, 2005), 144.
2.  Jim Witters, "Rescuer Refuses to Give Up Katrina Cat to Owner," *Dayton
    Beach News Journal*, February 25, 2006.

## Chapter 13. Lamar-Dixon Expo Center:
## Emergency Shelter for Animals after the Storms

1.  Lamar-Dixon Expo Center, "About the Expo Center," http://www.lamar
    dixonexpocenter.com/about2.php (accessed April 9, 2006).
2.  Laura Parker and Anita Manning, "Trapped Pets Still Being Rescued," *USA
    Today*, October 6, 2005.
3.  For a detailed description of Dr. Burge's experiences, including photos, you
    can go to http://burgebirdservices.homestead.com/hurricanekatrina.html
    (accessed April 24, 2006).
4.  Humane Society of the United States, "Reflections on Hurricane Katrina,"
    *Cruelty Can't Stand the Spotlight* (Winter 2005), 1–2.

5. Humane Society of the United States, "From Field to Phone: Even as the Last Dog Was Loaded at Lamar-Dixon, the Lines Continue to Ring about Reunions," October 13, 2005, http://www.hsus.org/hsus_field/hsus_disaster_center/recent_activities_and_information/2005_disaster_response/hurricane_katrina/from_field_to_phone.html (accessed April 9, 2006).

## Chapter 14. Animal Rescue Teams and Emergency Shelters

1. "Katrina's Animal Rescue," *Nature*, produced by Thirteen/WNET New York and National Geographic Television (aired November 2005).
2. American Humane Association, *Animal Emergency Services: A Training Guide 2005*, section 1, "Organization Structure," 6.
3. David Meyer, "The Last Survivors," *Best Friends Magazine*, November/December 2005, 37.
4. "Animal Planet Heroes: Hurricane Rescues," produced by Animal Planet/Discovery Channel (aired September 1, 2005).
5. Animal Rescue New Orleans, "We Cannot Help Them without You," http://www.animalrescueneworleans.com/news/callforhelp.html (accessed May 17, 2006).
6. Code 3 Associates, "Services," http://code3associates.org/services.html (accessed April 10, 2006).

## Chapter 15. More Animal Rescue Teams and Emergency Shelters

1. Rebecca Simmons, "Not-So-Hard Time: Inmates Provide Comfort to (and Get Comfort from) Katrina's Animal Victims," Humane Society of the United States, October 4, 2005, http://www.hsus.org/hsus_field/hsus_disaster_center/recent_activities_and_information/2005_disaster_response/hurricane_katrina/not_so_hard_time.html (accessed April 12, 2006); James Minton, "DCI Inmates Help Care for Animals," *Advocate*, Baton Rouge, Louisiana, September 27, 2005, http://www.2theadvocate.com/stories/092705/sub_dci001.shtml (accessed April 12, 2006).
2. Carrie Allan, " 'So Many Dead Chickens, It Looks Like a Field of Cotton,' " Humane Society of the United States, September 13, 2005, http://www.hsus.org/farm_animals/farm_animals_news/so_many_dead_chickens_it_looks_like_a_field_of_cotton.html (accessed April 12, 2006).

## Chapter 16. Rescuing and Reuniting

1. Martin Savidge, "Pet Reunions Rare after the Storms: Despite Heavy Publicity, Owners Aren't Finding Their Abandoned Pets," December 2, 2005, MSNBC.com, http://msnbc.msn.com/id/10300329/from/ET (accessed April 12, 2006).

2. Susan Thurston, "Continental Notebook: Furry Flights," *Continental*, November 2005, 21.

3. Lisa Carter, "Operation Just Paws," *Animal Guardian*, Spring 2006, 10–13.

4. North Shore Animal League of America, "Hurricane Katrina Animal Rescue: Sadie Mae Reunited with Her Family," http://www.nsalamerica.org/feature/katrina/sadie_mae.html (accessed May 17, 2006); Sandy Bauers, "Pets Given Shelter from the Storm, Dogs Stranded by Katrina Are Airlifted to Pa.," *Philadelphia Inquirer*, October 19, 2005.

5. Petfinder.com, "Animal Emergency Response Network FAQ: What Is Petfinder.com and the Petfinder.com Foundation?" http://disaster.petfinder.com/emergency/faq/aboutpetfinder.html (accessed April 14, 2006).

6. Petfinder.com, "Animal Emergency Response Network FAQ: How Did AERN Begin?" http://disaster.petfinder.com/emergency/faq/index.html#howaernbegin (accessed April 14, 2006).

## Chapter 17. Today's Sanctuaries, Breed and Horse Rescues, and Animal Shelters

1. "Numbers," *Time*, March 27, 2006, 22.

2. The Association of Sanctuaries, "Code of Ethics," http://www.taosanctuaries.org/accredit/ethics.htm (accessed May 13, 2006).

3. People for the Ethical Treatment of Animals, "Animal Shelters: Hope for the Homeless," http://www.peta.org/mc/factsheet_display.asp?ID=40 (accessed April 16, 2006).

4. Animal Humane Society, "Red Cross Disaster Assistance," http://www.animal humanesociety.org/gen_red_cross.asp and http://www.animalhumanesociety.org/gen_facts.asp (accessed May 14, 2006).

5 "The Disturbing Facts about No-Kill Shelters," http://www.peta.org/Living/AT-Fall2005/nokill.asp (accessed March 30, 2006).

6. Karin Bruilliard, "Euthanasia a Strain for Animal Care Workers: Loudoun, Other Shelters Try to Help Staffs Cope," *Washington Post*, September 26, 2005.

## Chapter 18. Training and Careers in Animal Rescue

1. Joy Powell, "Hurricane Helpers Get Some Relief from the IRS," *Minneapolis Star Tribune*, February 23, 2006.

2. The White House, *The Federal Response to Hurricane Katrina: Lessons Learned*, "Chapter Two: National Preparedness — A Primer," http://www.whitehouse.gov/reports/katrina-lessons-learned/chapter2.html (accessed April 17, 2006).

3. Green Cross Foundation, *Green Cross Assistance Deployment Protocol Manual*, http://www.deploy.gcprojects.org (accessed April 17, 2006).

4. Claire Davis, "Planning for the Next Disaster in Louisiana," Best Friends

Network, April 30, 2006, http://network.bestfriends.org/News/PostDetail
.aspx?np=3397&g=3e44461c0-52d8-4523-a058-0c744df72a60 (accessed
May 4, 2006).

5. Debra Bennetts, "Firefighters across the U.S. Now Equipped with Pet Oxygen
Masks," PRWEB, June 29, 2005, http://press.arrivenet.com/business/article
.php/661989.html (accessed April 17, 2006).

## Chapter 19. Preparing Animals for Disaster and Evacuation

1. Karen Nelson, "Staying with Animals in Katrina Was a Deadly Choice for
Some, and the Hurricane Left Other Owners Seeking Shelter from the
Storm," *Biloxi Sun Herald*, April 30, 2006.

2. Claire Davis, "Planning for the Next Disaster in Louisiana," Best Friends
Network, April 30, 2006, http://network.bestfriends.org/News/PostDetail
.aspx?np=3397&g=3e44461c0-52d8-4523-a058-0c744df72a60 (accessed
May 4, 2006).

3. Humane Society of the United States, "Disaster Preparedness for Horses,"
http://www.hsus.org/hsus_field/hsus_disaster_center/disaster_preparedness
_for_horses.html (accessed April 17, 2006).

4. Dana N. Zimmel, DVM, "Disaster Planning for Horse Farms," American
Association of Equine Practitioners, http://www.xcodesign.com/aaep/
displayArticles.cfm?Id=263 (accessed April 17, 2006).

5. Humane Society of the United States, "Disaster Preparedness for Livestock,"
http://www.hsus.org/hsus_field/hsus_disaster_center/disaster_preparedness
_for_livestock.html (accessed April 17, 2006).

## Chapter 20. Celebrities, the Internet, and Media Bring Attention to Animal Rescue

1. Michael Reagan, ed., *CNN Reports: Katrina, State of Emergency* (Kansas City:
Andrews McMeel, 2005), 35.

2. *Anderson Cooper 360⁰*, CNN, September 19, 2005, http://transcripts.cnn.com/
TRANSCRIPTS/0509/16/acd.01.html (accessed April 17, 2006).

3. Andrew Adam Newman, "Another Hurricane Side Effect: Some Soul-Searching
about the Pet Coverage," *New York Times*, November 28, 2005.

4. Humane Society of the United States, "Star Power: Hollywood's Response to
Help Pets Hurt by Katrina," http://www.hsus.org/about_us/celebrity
_support/celebrities_support_disaster_response_efforts_to_katrina.html
(accessed April 19, 2006).

5. "Current News," Linda Blair WorldHeart Foundation, http://www.linda
blairworldheart.com (accessed February 1, 2006).

6. Karen Dawn, "About DawnWatch," http://www.dawnwatch.com (accessed
April 19, 2006).

7. Ibid.

## Chapter 21. Lessons Learned

1.  Lynne Bettinger, quoted in William Wan, "A Lesson from Katrina: Pets Matter," *Washington Post*, January 2, 2006.

2.  Gary Patronek, VMD, PhD, quoted in "Animal Hoarders: The Illness and the Crime," People for the Ethical Treatment of Animals, http://www.helping animals.com/factsheet/files/factsheetdisplay.asp?ID=27 (accessed March 23, 2006).

3.  Francis Battista, "It Takes a Hurricane: How a Katrina Is Happening Near You," *Best Friends*, March–April 2006, 38.

4.  "The Five Best States to Be an Animal Abuser," Animal Legal Defense Fund, http://www.aldf.org/article.asp?cid=547 (accessed May 13, 2006).

5.  Stephanie Strom, "Red Cross Sifting Internal Charges over Katrina Aid," *New York Times*, March 24, 2006.

6.  "State Animal Response Teams," North Carolina State Animal Response Team, http://www.ncsart.org (accessed May 10, 2006).

7.  Allan Luks, quoted in "Kindness: How Good Deeds Can Be Good for You!" Random Acts of Kindness Foundation, http://www.actsofkindness.org/ inspiration/health/detail.asp?id=1 (accessed March 20, 2006).

8.  Merritt Clifton, "Hurricane Katrina and Rita Rescuers Shift Gears from Rescue & Reunion to Rehoming," *Animal People*, December 2005, 6.

9.  Paul Berry, quoted in "Hurricane Katrina: Campaign Urges National Animal Organizations to Spend the Millions Raised to Help Family Pets, as Intended," Best Friends Animal Society press release, November 22, 2005, http://network.bestfriends.org/hurricane/news/108.html (accessed May 18, 2006).

# Resources

## Disaster Preparedness Websites

*Alert Chicago* • www.webapps.cityofchicago.org/ChicagoAlertWeb

*Alley Cat Allies* • www.alleycat.org

*American Humane Association* • www.americanhumane.org •

*American Red Cross* •
www.redcross.org (Disaster Services>Be Prepared>Animal Safety) •

*American Veterinary Medical Association (AVMA)* • Disaster Preparedness:
www.avma.org/disaster

*Best Friends Animal Society* • www.bestfriends.org

*Code 3 Associates* • Disaster Planning, Emergency Release Form: •
www.code3associates.org/planning.html

*Emergency Animal Rescue Service (EARS)* • www.uan.org/ears/index.html •

*Farm Sanctuary* • www.farmsanctuary.org

*FDA, Center for Veterinary Medicine* • Protecting Pets in a Disaster:
www.fda.gov/cvm/disaster.htm

*Federal Emergency Management Agency* • FEMA Independent Study •
Program: IS-10 Animals in Disaster, Module A: Awareness and Preparedness:
www.training.fema.gov/EMIweb/IS/is10.asp

*Figley Institute* • www.figleyinstitute.com

*Florida Disaster* • www.floridadisaster.org/documents/CEMP/floridaCEMP.htm

*Florida State Agricultural Response Team (SART)* • www.flsart.org/PPT/
PET-pers-plan.ppt

*Hillsborough County, Florida* • www.hillsboroughcounty.org/animalservices/
information/disaster.cfm

➤ *Humane Society of the United States* • www.hsus.org

*MuttShack Animal Rescue* • www.muttshack.org

*My Horse Matters (American Association of Equine Practitioners)* •
www.myhorsematters.com

*National Voluntary Organizations Active in Disasters (VOAD)* •
www.nvoad.org

*Noah's Wish* • www.noahswish.org

*North Carolina State Animal Response Teams (SART)* • www.ncsart.org

*Oregon Humane Society* • www.oregonhumane.org/petcare/Disaster
preparedness.htm

*People for the Ethical Treatment of Animals (PETA)* • www.peta.org

*Pets and Animal World* • www.petsandanimals.org/pet_disaster_tips.asp

*PETS 911 (search for local animal shelters to ask about disaster plans)* •
www.pets911.com/organizations/organizations.php

*Stolen Horse International (Horse Theft and Disaster Recovery)* •
www.netposse.com

*United Animal Nations* • www.uan.org

*Veterinary Medical Assistance Teams (VMAT)* • www.vmat.org

## Animal Shelters, Sanctuaries, and Rescue/Reunion Organizations
### (Including Those Mentioned in This Book)

*1-800-Save-A-Pet.com* • www.1-800-save-a-pet.com

*911 Parrot Alert* • www.911parrotalert.com

*Alley Cat Allies* • www.alleycat.org; (202) 667-3630

*American Bar Association TIPS Animal Relief Network* • www.abanet.org/tips/animal

*American Humane Association* • www.americanhumane.org

*American Sanctuary Association* • www.asaanimalsanctuaries.org

*Animal Ark* • www.animalark.org

*Animal Humane Society* • www.animalhumanesociety.org

*Animal Rescue League of Boston* • www.arlboston.org

*Animal Rescue New Orleans (ARNO)* • www.animalrescueneworleans.com

*Animal Shelter Directory* • www.adoptapet.com/states/state-index.html

*Arizona Humane Society* • www.azhumane.org

*Asilomar Accords* • www.asilomaraccords.org

*Association of Sanctuaries* • www.taosanctuaries.org

*Bat Rescue/West End Animal Clinic* • www.westendanimal.com

*Bear Search and Rescue Foundation* • www.bearsearchandrescue.org

*Best Friends Animal Society* • www.bestfriends.org

*Chimps Inc.* • www.chimps-inc.com

*Col. Potter Cairn Rescue Network* • www.cairnrescue.com

*Cruelty-free Circuses* • www.circuses.com

*Denver Dumb Friends League* • www.ddfl.org

*Disaster Response Animal Rescue (DRAR)* •
   groups.msn.com/disasterresponseanimalrescue

*Dog Detective* • www.dogdetective.com

*Dogs Deserve Better (DDB)* • www.dogsdeservebetter.com

*Donkey Sanctuary* • www.thedonkeysanctuary.org.uk

*Elayne Boosler's Tails of Joy* • www.tailsofjoy.net

*Elephant Sanctuary* • www.elephants.com

*Feral Cat Coalition* • www.feralcat.com

*Ferret Rescue* • www.texasferret.org

*Foundation Brigitte Bardot* • www.fondationbrigittebardot.fr

*Front Range Equine Rescue* • www.frontrangeequinerescue.org

*Fund for Animals/Cleveland Amory's Black Beauty Ranch* •
   www.fundforanimals.org/ranch

*Grassroots Emergency Animal Rescue* • www.grassrootsrescue.org

*Greyhound Pets of America* • www.greyhoundpets.com

*Hacienda de los Milagros Inc.* • www.haciendadelosmilagros.org

*Heart of the Redwoods Horse Rescue* • www.redwoodrescue.com

*Hedgehog Rescue* • www.milehighhedgehogs.com

*Helen Woodward Animal Center* • www.animalcenter.org

*Helping Animals* • www.helpinganimals.com

*Home for Life* • www.homeforlife.org

*Hopeful Haven Equine Rescue* • www.hopefulhaven.com

*Houston SPCA* • www.spcahouston.org

*Humane Farming Association* • www.hfa.org

*Humane Society of Southern Louisiana* • www.humanela.org

*Humane Society of South Mississippi* • www.hssm.org

*Humane Society of the United States* • www.hsus.org

*Illinois Doberman Rescue Plus* • www.ildoberescue.com

*Karen O'Toole* • www.karenotoole.org

*Liberty Humane Society* • www.libertyhumane.org

*Linda Blair WorldHeart Foundation* • www.lindablairworldheart.com

*Los Angeles Animal Services (LAAS)* • www.laanimalservices.com

*Louisiana SPCA* • www.la-spca.org

*Louisiana State University School of Veterinary Medicine* •
    www.vetmed.lsu.edu

*Maddie's Fund* • www.maddiesfund.org

*Marin Humane Society* • www.marinhumanesociety.org

*Montana Spay Neuter Task Force* • www.mtspayneutertaskforce.org

*MuttShack Animal Rescue Foundation* • www.muttshack.org

*Nashville Humane Association* • www.nashvillehumane.org

*National Disaster Animal Relief and Supply* • www.ndars.org

*New Leash on Life* • www.newleash.org

*No Animal Left Behind* • www.noanimalleftbehind.blogspot.com

*No Kill Solutions (Nathan Winograd)* • www.nokillsolutions.com

*Noah's Wish* • www.noahswish.org

*North Carolina Iguana Rescue Association* • www.iguana-rescue.com

*North Shore Animal League (NSAL)* • www.nsalamerica.org

*Oregon Humane Society* • www.oregonhumane.org

*Parrot Education and Adoption Center* • www.peac.org

*Pasado's Safe Haven* • www.pasadosafehaven.org

*PAWS/LA* • www.pawsla.org

*People for the Ethical Treatment of Animals (PETA)* • www.peta.org

*Petfinder* • www.petfinder.com

*Pet Savers Foundation* • www.petsavers.org

*PETS 911* • www.pets911.com

*Rescue Ranch* • www.rescueranch.net

*San Francisco SPCA* • www.sfspca.org

*Shambala* • www.shambala.org; (661) 268-0380

*Siamese Cat Rescue* • www.siameserescue.org

*Snake Rescue* • www.snakegetters.com

*Society of Animal Welfare Administrators (SAWA)* • www.sawanetwork.org

*Southern Animal Foundation* • www.southernanimalfoundation.org

*SPAY/USA* • www.spayusa.org; (800) 248-SPAY (7729)

*Stealth Volunteers* • marilyn@marilynlitt.com

*St. Francis Animal Sanctuary* • www.stfrancisanimalsanctuary.com

*United Animal Nation* • www.uan.org

*United Poultry Concerns/Chicken Rescue* • www.upc-online.org

*Vermillion Animal Aid* • 105 Lincoln St., Abbeville LA 70510; (318) 893-7388

*Wylie Animal Rescue Foundation* • www.tahoewarf.com

## Pet Insurance Providers

*Pet Care Insurance* • www.PetCareInsurance.com

*Pet Health Insurance* • www.petshealthplan.com

*Shelter Care Insurance* • www.sheltercare.com

## Animal Poison-control Hotlines

*Angell Poison Control Hotline* • (877) 2ANGELL; www.mspca.org/poisonhotline

*Illinois/ASPCA National Animal Poison Control Center* • (888) 426-4435; www.napcc.aspca.org

*PetPlace.com* • (800) 365-8951; www.petplace.com/ppch/default.asp

## Pet Safety Products

*24PetWatch* • www.24petwatch.com

*Animal Rescue Car Kit* • www.petacatalog.org/prodinfo.asp?number=CA150

*Avid* • www.avidmicrochip.com

*Best Friends Pet Care* • www.bestfriendspetcare.com

*Dog-e-Tag* • www.Dog-e-Tag.com

*First Aid Videos for Pets* • www.apogeevideo.com

*HomeAgain* • www.homeagainpets.com

*Pet First Aid Kits* • www.medipet.com/first-aid-kit-products.htm

*Pet Rescue Sticker, ASPCA* • www.aspca.org

*Rescue Alert Sticker* • www.oregonhumane.org/news/GetRescueSticker.htm

*Vestergaard Frandsen Group* • The LifeStraw: www.lifestraw.com

*Vet-Link.com Microchip* • (800) 838-8563

## Websites for Jobs, Careers, and Volunteer Opportunities in Animal Rescue

*Alley Cat Allies* • www.alleycat.org/jobs.html

*American Humane Association* • www.americanhumane.org

*American Humane Association and Regis University* •
www.americanhumane.org, www.regis.edu

*Animal Concerns* • www.animalconcerns.org

*College View* • www.collegeview.com

*Humane Society of the United States* • www.animalsheltering.org

*Humane Society University* • www.humanesocietyu.org

*Idealist* • www.idealist.org

*In Defense of Animals* • www.idausa.org

*National Animal Control Association* • www.nacanet.org

*National Animal Control Association and Animal Care and Control Professionals* • www.nacanet.org/careeropps.htm

*PETS 911* • www.pets911.com

*Princeton Review* • www.princetonreview.com

*Society of Animal Welfare Administrators (SAWA)* • www.sawanetwork.org

*Volunteer Abroad* • www.volunteerabroad.com

*Volunteer Match* • www.volunteermatch.com

## Animal Rescue Training Websites

*American Humane Association* • www.americanhumane.org

*American Red Cross* • www.redcross.org

*American Society for the Prevention of Cruelty to Animals* • www.aspca.org

*American Veterinary Medical Association* • www.avma.org

*Animal Welfare Federation of New Jersey (AWFNJ)* • www.awfnj.org

*Association of Avian Vets* • www.aav.org

*Code 3 Associates* • www.code3associates.org

*Federal Emergency Management Agency (FEMA)* •
www.usfa.fema.gov/training/nfa/independent/

*Felton Fire Department* • www.largeanimalrescue.com

*Green Cross (protocols for deployment)* • www.deploy.gcprojects.org

*Humane Society of the United States* • www.hsus.org

*Marin Humane Society* • www.marinehumanesociety.org

*Minnesota Veterinary Medical Association (Dr. Janet Olson's training for firefighters and EMTs)* • www.mvma.org; (651) 645-7533

*Noah's Wish* • www.noahswish.org

*Oregon Humane Society Technical Animal Rescue* • www.oregonhumane.org

*United Animal Nations* • www.uan.org

## Corporations That Support Animal Rescue

*PETCO Foundation* • www.petco.com (go to PETCO community then to PETCO Foundation)

*PetSmart Charities* • www.petsmartcharities.org

*Whole Foods* • www.animalcompassionfoundation.org

## Corporations That Supported Animal Rescue During Hurricane Katrina Disaster

*MapQuest* • www.mapquest.com

*PetSmart Charities* • www.petsmartcharities.org

*UPS* • www.ups.com

*Wal-Mart* • www.walmartstores.com; www.walmartfoundation.org

*Winn-Dixie* • www.winndixie.com

## Pet-friendly Hotels and Airlines

*Continental Airlines PetSafe Program* • www.continental.com/travel/
policies/animals/default.asp; (800) 575-3335

*Delta Airlines* • www.delta.com; (800) 352-2746

*DogFriendly.com* • www.dogfriendly.com

*Loews Hotels (charges nothing extra for pets)* • www.loewshotels.com

*Pets on the Go* • www.petsonthego.com

*PetsWelcome* • www.petswelcome.com

*Pet Travel Inc.* • www.pettravel.com

*TravelPets.com* • www.travelpets.com

## Publications for Keeping Informed about Animal Rescue and Welfare

*All-Creatures.org* • www.all-creatures.org

*Animal Guardian (Doris Day Animal League)* • www.ddal.org

*Animal Legal Defense Fund* • www.aldf.org

*Animal People* • www.animalpeoplenews.org

*Animal Sentience Newsletter* • www.animalsentience.com

*Animals' Agenda Magazine* • www.animalsagenda.org/default.asp

*Animal Sheltering Magazine* • www.animalsheltering.org/publications/magazine

*Animals in Disaster News (Eric Rice)* • www.animaldisasternews.com

*Animals in Print* • www.all-creatures.org/aip

*Animal Welfare Institute Quarterly* • www.awionline.org

*Best Friends Network* • www.network.bestfriends.org

*BUAV: Exposing Animal Experiments* • www.buav.org

*CENSHARE* • www.censhare.umn.edu

*Compassion in World Farming Animal Sentience* • www.animalsentience.com

*Compassion: The Official Journal of Beauty Without Cruelty* • www.bwcsa.co.za

*Dawn Animal World News Watch* • www.dawnwatch.com

*Farm Sanctuary* • www.farmsanctuary.org

*Firepaw Newsletter* • www.firepaw.org

*Good Medicine: From the Physicians Committee for Responsible Medicine* • www.pcrm.org

*HumaneLines* • www.hsus.org

*Justice for Animals* • www.justiceforanimals.org

*Kinship Circle* • www.kinshipcircle.org

*National Welfare Institute* • www.awionline.org

*Paws to Think* • www.petsavers.org

*Pet Gazette, The* • www.thepetgazette.org

*TAOS: The Association of Sanctuaries* • www.taosanctuaries.org

*United Animal Nations Journal* • www.uan.org

*United Poultry Concerns* • www.upc-online.org

## Radio for Animals

*All Pets Radio* • www.wpr.org/pets

*Animal Radio Network* • www.animalradio.com

*Animals Voice* • www.animalsvoice.com

*Animal Wise Radio* • www.animalwiseradio.com

*Dog and Cat Radio* • www.dogcatradio.com

*Watchdog Radio* • www.watchdogradio.com

## Television for Animals

*Animal Planet* • www.animal.discovery.com

*Discovery Channel* • www.discovery.com

*National Geographic* • www.nationalgeographic.com/channel

*PBS* • Nature: www.pbs.org/wnet/nature

## Educating Children about Animal Rescue

*American Humane Association* • www.americanhumane.org

*Animal Guardian* • Doris Day Animal League: www.ddal.org

*ASPCA Humane Education Tools* • www.aspca.org/education

*Association of Professional Humane Educators* • www.aphe.org

*Best Friends Network* •
   www.bestfriends.org/atthesanctuary/humaneeducation/classroomresources.cfm

*Family Paws* • www.familypaws.com

*Humane Education Network* • www.hennet.org/home.php

*Humane Teen* • www.HumaneTeen.org

*IFAW* • www.ifaw.org; The Ultimate Pet Rescue Game: www.ifaw.org/ifaw/
   general/default.aspx?oid=139665; Video and Education Pack for Teachers:
   www.ifaw.org/ifaw/general/default.aspx?oid=137608

*National Association for Humane and Environmental Education (NAHEE)* •
   www.kindnews.org; www.nahee.org

*National Humane Education Society* • www.nhes.org

*PETA AnimalActivist.com* • www.animalactivist.com/education.asp

*PETA Kids* • www.petacatalog.org/products.asp?dept=10

*Share the World* • www.sharetheworld.com

## Wildlife and Marine Animal Rescue

*African Wildlife Foundation* • www.awf.org

*Austin Wildlife Rescue* • www.austinwildliferescue.org

*Compassion in World Farming Animal Sentience* • www.animalsentience.com

*International Fund for Animal Welfare* • www.ifaw.org

*International Primate Protection League* • www.ippl.org

*Jane Goodall Institute for Wildlife Research, Education, and Conservation* •
   www.janegoodall.org

*Marine Mammal Care Center* • www.mar3ine.org

*Marine Mammal Center* • www.tmmc.org

*Mediterranean Association to Save the Sea Turtles* • www.medasset.org/medas.htm

*Raptor Center at the University of Minnesota* • www.raptor.cvm.umn.edu/

*Southwest Wildlife Rehabilitation and Educational Foundation* • www.southwestwildlife.org

*Wild at Heart Inc.* • www.mirror-pole.com/wild_at_heart/intro/wah_intro_fs.html

*Wild Foundation, Wild Network* • www.wild.org/network/wlt.html

*Wildlife Waystation* • www.wildlifewaystation.org/

*World Wildlife Fund* • www.wwf.org

## International Animal Rescue Organizations

*Animal Welfare Institute* • www.awionline.org

*Compassion Over Killing* • www.cok.net

*Concern for Helping Animals in Israel and Hakoi Chai (Everything Lives)* • www.chai-online.org

*EarthSave International* • www.earthsave.org

*In Defense of Animals–Africa* • www.ida-africa.org

*International Fund for Animal Welfare* • www.ifaw.org

*International Primate Protection League* • www.ippl.org

*World Society for the Protection of Animals* • www.wspa-usa.org

## Donation Organizations

*Animal Charities of America* • www.animalcharitiesofamerica.org

*Charity Navigators* • www.charitynavigators.org

*Guidestar* • www.guidestar.org

# Recommended Animal Rescue Reading

Brown, D. M. *Hurricane Katrina: The First Seven Days of America's Worst Natural Disaster*. New York: Lulu Press, 2005.

Crisp, Terri. *Emergency Animal Rescue Stories: True Stories about People Dedicated to Saving Animals from Disasters*. New York: Prima, 2000.

Goodman, Susan. *Animal Rescue: The Best Job There Is*. New York: Aladdin, 2001.

Heath, Sebastian E. *Animal Management in Disasters*. St. Louis: Mosby, 1999.

Hedren, Tippi. *Cats of Shambala*. Rev. ed. Acton, CA: Tiger Island Press, 1991.

Knauer, Kelly, ed. *Hurricane Katrina: The Storm That Changed America*. New York: Time, 2005.

Marino, Susan, and Denise Flaim. *Getting Lucky: How One Special Dog Found Love and a Second Chance at Angel's Gate*. New York: Stewart, Tabori & Chang, 2005.

Masson, Jeffrey Moussaieff. *The Pig Who Sang to the Moon: The Emotional World of Farm Animals*. New York: Ballantine Books, 2003.

Moyer, Susan. *Hurricane Katrina: Stories of Rescue, Recovery, and Rebuilding in the Eye of the Storm*. New York: Spotlight Press, 2005.

Patterson, Charles. *Eternal Treblinka: Our Treatment of Animals and the Holocaust*. New York: Lantern Books, 2002.

Reagan, Michael, ed. *CNN Reports: Katrina, State of Emergency*. Kansas City: Andrews McMeel, 2005.

Roth, Melinda. *The Man Who Talks to Dogs: The Story of Randy Grim and His Fight to Save America's Abandoned Dogs*. New York: St. Martin's Press, 2004.

# Photo Credits

The credits for the color photographs appearing between pages 172 and 173 can be found in the captions to those photographs.

Introduction: p. xvi: Major Mike Pagano; p. xix: courtesy of Dave Pauli, Humane Society of the United States.

Part 1: p. 1, left to right: Chris Robinson; courtesy of Richard Crook; courtesy of Jane Garrison; p. 4: Jane Garrison; p. 33: Matthew Huber, *Danville Commercial-News* (Illinois); p. 67: courtesy of Dave Pauli, Humane Society of the United States.

Part 2: p. 69, left to right: Candice King-Palgut; Terry Paik, San Diego HS and SPCA; Lisa Schoppa; p. 76: courtesy of Captain Scott Shields; p. 77: courtesy of Captain Scott Shields; p. 104: Belinda Thibodaux.

Part 3: p. 109, left to right: Terry Paik, San Diego HS and SPCA; Luana Maria Rathman; Karen Ducey, courtesy of Pasado's Safe Haven; p. 117: courtesy of Ron Silver; p. 122: Julie Burge, DVM; p. 125: courtesy of Lt. Randy Covey; p. 128: courtesy of Kerri Burns; p. 133: courtesy of Richard Crook; p. 137: courtesy of Major Mike Pagano; p. 140: Amanda St. John; p. 144: Terry Paik, San Diego HS and SPCA; p. 146: courtesy of Jane Garrison; p. 155: Troy Snow, Best Friends Animal Society; p. 158: Anne

Chadwick Williams, courtesy of United Animal Shelters; p. 161: courtesy of Terri Crisp, Noah's Wish; p. 165: courtesy of June Towler; p. 166: Karen Ducey, courtesy of Pasado's Safe Haven; p. 169: Matt Green, Farm Sanctuary; p. 180: Lisa Schoppa; p. 182: courtesy of Marin Humane Society; p. 184: courtesy of Barb Peterson.

Part 4: p. 195, left to right: courtesy of American Humane Association; Simran K. Zilaro, San Diego HS and SPCA; Troy Snow, Best Friends Animal Society; p. 198: © © 2006 by Bill Dow, Shambala; p. 200: © 2006 by Bill Dow, Shambala; p. 211: courtesy of Rory Goree; p. 250: courtesy of Melissa McGehee Smith; p. 252: courtesy of Stephanie Jehle; p. 297: courtesy of Betty Rome.

Author photograph p. 345: Daniel Tardent.

# Index

# About the Authors

A llen and Linda Anderson are inspirational speakers and the authors of a series of books about the spiritual relationships between people and animals. In 1998 they cofounded the Angel Animals Network, which is dedicated to increasing love and respect for all life through the power of story. In 2004 Minnesota Governor Tim Pawlenty presented Allen and Linda a Certificate of Commendation for their contributions as authors to the economy and welfare of the state of Minnesota.

*Allen and Linda Anderson.*

Allen Anderson is a writer and photographer. He was profiled in Jackie Waldman's book *The Courage to Give*. Linda Anderson is an award-winning playwright as well as a screenwriter and fiction writer. She is the author of *35 Golden Keys to Who You Are & Why You're Here*. They teach writing at the Loft Literary Center in Minneapolis, where Linda was awarded the Anderson Residency for Outstanding Loft Teachers. The Andersons share their home with a dog, two cats, and a cockatiel. They donate a portion of the revenue from their projects to animal shelters and animal-welfare organizations.

You are welcome to visit www.angelanimals.net, Allen and Linda's website, and to send them stories and letters about your experiences with animals for possible future publication. At the website, you may also request a subscription to the free online publication *Angel Animals Story of the Week*, and each week you'll receive by email an inspiring story.

Contact Allen and Linda Anderson at:
Angel Animals Network
P.O. Box 26354
Minneapolis, MN 55426
www.angelanimals.net
or
www.rescuedsavinganimals.net